SADCC

The Political Economy of Development In Southern Africa

Margaret C. Lee

Winston-Derek Publishers, Inc.
Pennywell Drive—P.O. Box 90883
Nashville, TN 37209

Copyright 1989 by Margaret C. Lee

All rights reserved, including the right to reproduce this book or portions thereof in any form without written permission from the publisher, except by a reviewer who may quote brief passages in a review to be printed in a magazine or newspaper.

PUBLISHED BY WINSTON-DEREK PUBLISHERS, INC.
Nashville, Tennessee 37205

Library of Congress Cataloging in Publication Data

Lee, Margaret C.
    SADCC—The Political Economy of Development in Southern Africa

    1. Southern African Development Coordination Conference.
2. Africa, Southern—Economic conditions.
3. Africa, Southern—Economic integration.　　I. Title.
HC900.L44 1989   338.968   88-50765
    ISBN: 1-55523-156-X

First Edition

Printed in the United States of America
10   9   8   7   6   5   4   3   2   1

ISBN: 1-55523-156-X

DEDICATION

This book is dedicated to my mother, Carol Carruthers Lee; to my friend, Evan Gregory Moore, M.D.; and to all my Southern African sisters and brothers.

TABLE OF CONTENTS

Page

List of Tables vii

List of Figures ix

List of Charts ix

SADCC Member States—Currencies xi

Preface xiii

Acknowledgments xv

Chapter 1
Introduction 1
From Political to Economic Liberation 4
Apartheid and Destabilization 5
Regional Cooperation and Development 6
Objective of Study 13
Approach to Study 14
Theoretical Framework 15

Chapter 2
The Political Economy of Southern Africa: Colonial Period 25
South Africa Within the Capitalist World-Economy 25
The SADCC Member States' Incorporation into the
    Capitalist World-Economy 33

Chapter 3
The Political Economy of Southern Africa: Post-independence 65
External Dependency 66
Internal Distortions 95
1987/88 Update 110

Chapter 4
SADCC's Strategy for Regional Cooperation and Development 127
Transport and Communications 133
Food, Agriculture, and Natural Resources 140

v

TABLE OF CONTENTS (Cont'd.)

Page

    Industry and Trade 146
    Energy 151
    Manpower 156

Chapter 5
SADCC's Institutional Framework 163
    SADCC Organizational Structure 163
    SADCC Project Cycle 166
    Annual Consultative Conference 168
    Implementation of the SADCC Program of Action 170

Chapter 6
SADCC and South Africa 183
    Structural Transformation of South Africa's
        Regional Hegemony 183
    SADCC's Program of Action 187

Chapter 7
SADCC and the West 241
    Western Hegemony Over Southern Africa 241
    SADCC: 1980-1986 245
    SADCC: 1987 256
    SADCC: 1988 and Beyond 260

Chapter 8
Conclusion 271

Appendix A
SADCC Organizational Documents 275
    Southern Africa: Toward Economic Liberation 276
    Memorandum of Understanding of the
        Institutions of the Southern African
        Development Coordination Conference 283

Appendix B
Regional Transport and Communications Sector 291
    Port Transport Systems Projects 292
    Intra-Regional Surface Transport Systems Projects ... 293
    Regional Surface Transport Networks and Airports 294
    Telecommunications System Projects 295

LIST OF TABLES

SADCC Member States

1. Foreign Trade Balance 71
2. Gross Official Development Assistance (ODA), 1982–1985 80
3. Official Development Assistance (ODA), by Largest OECD-Country Donors, 1982–1985 83
4. Foreign Debt 89
5. Balance of Payments and Reserves 92
6. Level of General Welfare 107

❦ ❦ ❦

7. SADCC Project Financing Status by Sector, 1988 130
8. Transport and Communications Financing by Subsector, 1988 135
9. SADCC Cereal Imports from South Africa, 1984–1985 145
10. Industry and Trade Financing by Subsector, 1988 149
11. Energy Financing by Subsector, 1988 153
12. SADCC Energy Imports from South Africa 156
13. Percent Distribution of Zimbabwe's External Trade by Route, 1981–1987 190
14. Percent Distribution of Malawi's External Trade by Route, 1981–1987 203
15. Distribution of Zambia's External Trade by Route, 1981–1984 206
16. Customs Union Revenue as Percentage of Total Government Revenue, 1981–1987 216
17. Beira Corridor Project Funding by Donors, Phase II 250

LIST OF FIGURES

1. Contemporary Political Economy 16
2. Political Economy Model of Southern Africa 18
3. Allocation of Coordination Within the SADCC Program of Action 132
4. SADCC Organizational Structure 164
5. Office of the Executive Secretary 169
6. Railroads and Ports of Southern Africa 196
7. Port Transport Systems Projects 292
8. Intra-Regional Surface Transport Systems Projects 293
9. Regional Surface Transport Networks and Airports 294
10. Telecommunications System Projects 295

❦ ❦ ❦

LIST OF CHARTS

1. Destabilization of the Transport and Communications Sector 192
2. Destabilization of the Energy Sector 225

SADCC MEMBER STATES — CURRENCIES

The reader should refer to the following when attempting to translate SADCC member states' currencies into U.S. dollars.

ANGOLA
Kwanza (KZ) = 1 wei. Nonconvertible, linked to dollar, at KZ 29.916 = $1 (1986).

BOTSWANA
Pula (P) = 100 thebe. Average exchange rate, P 1.868 = $1 (1986).

LESOTHO
Loti (plural, maloti) (M) = 100 lisente. On par with South African rand. Average exchange rate, M 2.269 = $1 (1986).

MALAWI
Malawi Kwacha (MK) = 100 tambala. Average exchange rate, MK 1.86 = $1 (1986).

MOZAMBIQUE
Metical (MT). Average exchange rate, MT 43.18 = $1 (1985); MT 200 = $1 (January 31, 1987); MT 580 = $1 (July 1988).

SWAZILAND
Lilangeni (plural, emalangeni) (E) = 100 cents. Formally delinked from the rand on July 1, 1986, but as of mid-1987 still at par with it. Average exchange rate, E 2.269 = $1.

TANZANIA
Tanzanian shilling (TSh) = 100 cents. Average exchange rate, TSh 32.70 = $1 (1986); TSh 63 = $1 (1987); TSh 94.99 = $1 (May 1988).

ZAMBIA
Zambian Kwacha (K) = 100 ngwee. Average exchange rate, ZK 7.305 = $1 (1986); ZK 8 = $1 (1988).

ZIMBABWE
Zimbabwe dollar (Z$) = 100 cents. Average exchange rate, Z $1.665 = $1 (1986).

PREFACE

This book culminates 14 years as a student of Southern African politics. I first became intrigued with the region, especially South Africa, in 1974, as a sophomore at Spelman College. There were many seeming similarities between the African-American struggle for civil rights and the struggle being waged by the African majority in South Africa. Being naive, I initially thought that the African majority's struggle for civil rights was at the same stage as the African-American struggle during the civil rights movement of the 1950s and 1960s. However, I was mistaken. I came to appreciate that the struggle being waged by the African majority was comparable to the period of slavery in the U.S. Currently, the non-white population of South Africa continues to fight against the white-minority regime for liberation from the shackles of slavery.

As Angola and Mozambique gained their independence in 1975, my interest in the entire Southern African region intensified. It quickly became obvious that in order to really understand the dynamics of the apartheid regime, it was necessary to understand Southern Africa. Specifically, I came to appreciate that the very foundation of apartheid South Africa was built upon the ability of the white minority to gain regional hegemony over Southern Africa. Therefore, the survival of apartheid is predicated upon its continued regional hegemony.

Although the people of Southern Africa anticipated that as independence from white-minority-ruled regimes spread throughout the region, peace would follow, Pretoria has waged a violent war against its regional neighbors, with a view toward preserving regional hegemony. The genocide that is taking place among the African population, both in South Africa and in the region, can only be compared to the Holocaust. As the executive secretary of the Organization of African Unity (OAU) and its ambassador to the United Nations, Oumarou G. Youssoufou, noted in the foreword to my recent publication, *Resource Guide to Information on Southern Africa,* "The U.S.S.R., the U.S.A., and Western Europe joined forces to fight the fascist Hitler. The Fourth Reich is now installed by the Boers in South Africa. Africans died in Europe fighting the Third Reich as members of the European Armed Forces. Today, Africa is not given the same assistance in fighting the Fourth Reich. Is this fair?"

It is indeed unfortunate that the "great" powers of the world not only have refused to join forces and destroy the apartheid regime, but that many have encouraged and supported the regime's internal as well as its regional war. And as I lecture throughout the U.S. on the Southern African region, many individuals complain that there has been a virtual blackout of U.S. coverage of South Africa's two wars.

Despite the refusal by the "great" powers to confront the apartheid regime, the real menace to development in Southern Africa, the independent nations of the region, through the Southern African Development Coordination Conference (SADCC), continue to struggle for economic and political liberation from South Africa's stranglehold. As this book will show, however, economic and political liberation in Southern Africa will be possible only after the apartheid regime is destroyed. Although the demise of the regime is inevitable, how much more death and destruction must be suffered before its eradication?

I hope this book will make a small contribution toward helping the people of the world—particularly Americans—come to terms with their responsibility to promote freedom and democracy in Southern Africa, so that the genocide taking place in the region will be stopped.

MCL
March, 1989

ACKNOWLEDGMENTS

This book would not have been possible without the assistance of many people, from both the U.S. and Southern Africa. As I was preparing to return to graduate school in 1981 to work on my doctorate, Gay McDougal, Director of the Southern Africa Project of the Lawyers' Committee for Civil Rights Under Law, in anticipating that SADCC would become a major regional organization, suggested that I write my dissertation on SADCC. This book is in fact an outgrowth of my dissertation.

The person who gave me the support and encouragement to write on SADCC is my mentor and friend, Dr. Ladun Anise, associate professor of Political Science at the University of Pittsburgh. He deserves a great deal of credit for my success in the area of Southern African politics, and it was he who reminded me when I wanted to take the easy way out that as an African-American female political scientist I would always have to strive for excellence in order to be competitive in a white-male-dominated profession. For his insistence that I do my best, I am most appreciative. I am also grateful that he provided me with feedback on each draft of this book.

I would like to thank Dr. Paul Stephenson, Chairperson of the Department of Political Science at Tennessee Technological University, for the support he gave me during the 2 1/2 years I spent working on this manuscript. Although I am the junior faculty member in the department, Dr. Stephenson always gave me a flexible schedule so that I could concentrate on my writing. Fortunately my colleagues in the department were cooperative and never complained about the obvious special privileges accorded me. I would also like to thank the departmental secretary, Janet Rogers, for typing the entire first draft of the manuscript and various sections of subsequent drafts. The Dean of the College of Arts and Sciences, Dr. Joseph Lerner, and the Interim Vice President for Academic Affairs, Dr. Leo McGee, were both very supportive of my research. Finally, the two trips I made to Southern Africa during the Summers of 1987 and 1988 were made possible as a result of two Faculty Research Grants.

While undertaking field research in Southern Africa, I had the opportunity to converse with many individuals about SADCC. The SADCC Secretariat in Gaborone, Botswana, welcomed me with open arms, and I would like to thank the following individuals from the Secretariat for providing me with interviews and/or SADCC materials: Nkwabi Ng'wanakilala, SADCC Information Officer; Emang Motlhabane Maphanyane, SADCC Economist; Candido A. Sitoie, SADCC Administrative Assistant; and Charles J.G. Hove, SADCC Economist/Project Officer.

My trip to Mozambique during the summer of 1988 was perhaps the most exhilarating experience of my two trips into the region. It coincided with the 1988 Annual SADCC Summit. During the summit I benefited tremendously from conversations with the following SADCC officials: Nthabiseng Letsie, SADCC Tourism Sector Coordinator; Mathato A.M. Matlanyane, Senior Marketing Officer, SADCC Tourism Co-Ordination Unit; Dr. S.R. Magembe, SADCC Livestock Production and Animal Disease Control Sector Coordinator; Dr. Martin L. Kyomo, Director, Southern African Center for Cooperation in Agriculture Research (SACCAR); and E.P.A. Simwela, Senior Economist, SADCC Industry and Trade Co-Ordination Division.

While in Maputo, Mozambique, I had an opportunity to have lengthy discussions with Mugama M. Matolo, Director of the Southern African Transportation Communication Commission (SATCC), and Pedro Figueiredo, Director, Caminhos de Ferrode Mozambique Sul (CFM Sul), the regional railway system servicing the southern area of Mozambique. Sidik Juma Abdula, Public Relations Director for Maputo Port provided me with a tour of Maputo Port.

Goncalo Antonio Ferrao Junior, Economist for the Beira Corridor Authority (BCA), invited me to Beira, Mozambique. While there I had an opportunity to visit Beira Port and have extensive conversations about SADCC with Ferrao as well as with Rui Fonseca, Executive Director of the BCA, and Mads H. Tiemroth, an Economist with the BCA.

I would like to thank Antonio Matonse, Press Attache for the Embassy of the People's Republic of Mozambique in Washington, D.C., for arranging my trip to Mozambique. Upon arriving in the country, I met some of the most beautiful people I have ever come in contact with. While it would be impossible to thank them all, I would like to acknowledge several: Abel Jonaze; Felix Mambule, Filipe Mata; Bantchi Panguene; and Joel Chizione, a photographer with the Mozambique Information Agency (AIM).

While in Zimbabwe, I had numerous invaluable conversations about SADCC with Tadius Chifamba in the Ministry of Finance, Economic Planning and Development, and K.J.M. Dhliwayo, SADCC Food Security Sector Coordinator. I would also like to thank M. Charles Chitambo, Undersecretary in the Ministry of Trade and Commerce, and Mrs. E. Kono, Assistant Secretary in the Ministry of Trade and Commerce, for granting me an interview. Others in Zimbabwe I interviewed in connection with this study include: Eddie Cross, Director, Beira Corridor Group (BCG); Hasu Patel, Professor of Political and Administrative Studies, University of Zimbabwe; and Nelson Moyo, Chairperson, Department of Economics, University of Zimbabwe. Professor Moyo also served as a reviewer of the manuscript. I am truly appreciative of his thorough review and the constructive criticism he provided with a view toward enhancing the quality of the book. Molesti Mbeki, Senior Reporter for the *Herald* (Zim.), and a dear friend, also served as a reviewer of the manuscript. Our numerous discussions about SADCC and Southern Africa allowed me to gain a greater understanding of the dynamics of the forces at play in the region.

I would like to thank the Zimbabwe Institute of Development Studies (ZIDS) for allowing me to share my research about SADCC at one of their seminars during the Summer of 1988. Dr. Donald Chimanikire in the Department of Southern African Studies and International Relations at ZIDS was an invaluable resource person for me during my visits to Zimbabwe, and also served as a reviewer of the manuscript.

The library research for this study was undertaken at the Melville J. Herskovits Library of African Studies at Northwestern University. I would like to extend a special thanks to all the staff members who have been most gracious to me for over a decade.

Since it would be impossible to recognize individually all my family members and friends throughout the country who have been supportive during this research endeavor, I just want you to know that I appreciate your love and patience.

Finally, I want to thank Dr. James Peebles, the owner of Winston-Derek Publishers, for allowing his company to serve as a conduit for my research.

CHAPTER 1

Introduction

The independent nations of Southern Africa (Angola, Botswana, Lesotho, Malawi, Mozambique, Swaziland, Tanzania, Zambia, and Zimbabwe), along with the black majority in Namibia and South Africa, are currently struggling to survive a war that is wreaking havoc over the entire region of Southern Africa. This war is being waged by the white-minority government of South Africa for the survival of apartheid.

The war to maintain apartheid in the region is not a new phenomenon. However, what is new is the strategy that has been used by the white-minority government since 1980 to convince the independent nations and the black majority in Namibia and South Africa to work cooperatively with the apartheid regime. In this regard, the white-minority government continues its attempt to dissuade the anti-apartheid forces from challenging its hegemonic regional control.

Needless to say, this advice has not been heeded, and the anti-apartheid forces in the region continue their commitment to the liberation of Southern Africa from apartheid's war machine. The problem, however, is that all these forces collectively cannot begin to match the apartheid regime's military might. Consequently, the war is extremely one-sided, and "despite years of aggression, the military or security forces of the neighboring states have never crossed into South Africa." [1]

The independent nations continue to pay dearly for their commitment to the eradication of apartheid. Between 1980 and 1984, South African military aggression cost those nations $10 billion, more than all the bilateral and multilateral aid they received during that period. By the end of 1985 it was estimated that regional destabilization was costing $4 billion per year. The human cost of destabilization includes more than 700,000 dead, approximately 8 million internally displaced, and 1.5 million who have fled to neighboring countries for refuge.[2]

In 1986, as a result of South Africa's destabilization, 140,000 children died in Angola and Mozambique, and these two nations currently have the highest infant and child mortality rates in the world.[3] During August 1987, according to first-hand accounts, South African-backed Mozambique National Resistance (MNR) terrorists (also known as Renamo) had eaten Mozambique children like chicken, after chopping them up and roasting them over a fire.[4] On July 18, MNR terrorists massacred 424 Mozambique civilians in the small town of Homoine in Inhambane Province, and a similar massacre of at least 278 Mozambicans occurred on October 31 in the town of Taninga, 50 miles north of the capital, Maputo. Similar atrocities were reported throughout 1988.[5]

Insurgents of the South African and United States-backed National Union for the Total Independence of Angola (UNITA) currently operate in almost all provinces of Angola. And until August 1988, South African military forces continued to occupy parts of southern Angola. Invasions were daily events. In September 1987, the South African government admitted that "South African security forces were 'definitely involved' in heavy fighting between government troops and UNITA rebels." [6]

This continued until a cease-fire was agreed between South Africa, Angola, and Cuba in August 1988. According to the agreement, the more than two thousand South African troops would withdraw from southern Angola into Namibia by September 1, and plans would be made to begin implementing United Nations Security Council Resolution 435 on November 1. This UN resolution outlines the plan for Namibian independence. The actual implementation of Resolution 435, however, seemingly rested upon an agreement among Angola, Cuba, and South Africa to a timetable for the withdrawal of Cuban forces from Angola.[7] By November 1, however, Resolution 435 had not been implemented since an agreement had not been reached on the timetable for withdrawal of Cuban troops from Angola. It was announced that the new date for the implementation of the Resolution would be January 1, 1989, although this deadline was not met either.

Then, on December 22, a Peace Accord for Namibia was signed between Angola, Cuba, and South Africa following an agreement on the phased withdrawal of Cuban forces from Angola. According to the Accord, the forces will be withdrawn over a 27 month period. By July 1, 1991, all Cuban forces are scheduled to be out of Angola. The Accord also identifies April 1989 as the date for the beginning of the implementation of UN Resolution 435.[8]

If Resolution 435 is finally implemented in Namibia, which South Africa has occupied illegally for more than twenty years, the long war between the races will finally come to an end. There is reason to be optimistic as well as cautious about the Accord, since the apartheid regime has failed to implement previous regional peace agreements (e.g., the 1984 Nkomati Accord with Mozambique and the 1984 Lusaka Accord with Angola).

In South Africa it is being projected that, as a result of the nature of torture currently being administered to the children of apartheid, an entire generation will be destroyed. In fact, scholars and activists compare the practice of apartheid to Naziism, and it is speculated that if present trends continue, the atrocities committed against the black majority may be comparable to those of the Holocaust—or even worse, the massacre of an estimated 49 million African slaves.

In response to apartheid, the independent nations in Southern Africa joined together in 1980 to form the Southern African Development Coordination Conference (SADCC). Their major objective was to decrease regional economic dependence on South Africa. Although SADCC was officially established following the independence of Zimbabwe, the idea of development coordination in Southern Africa dates back to 1974, when Kenneth Kaunda, president of Zambia, "spoke of the day when the independent states of southern Africa 'could meet to discuss liberation—not liberation from political oppression but liberation from poverty.'" [9]

Formal efforts to begin development coordination were begun by the Frontline States (Angola, Botswana, Mozambique, Tanzania, and Zambia) during 1977 to 1978 when the initial plans of action were outlined. In May 1979, in Gaborone, Botswana, the foreign ministers of the Frontline States met. It was decided to convene a conference of economic ministers and representatives of bilateral and multilateral external cooperating agencies and institutions to discuss the ministers' ideas for development coordination. The subsequent conference was held in

Arusha, Tanzania, in July 1979, where the economic ministers of the Frontline States drafted the broad lines of the declaration and the program of action. The Frontline States recognized the need for all the independent nations in the region to become active participants in regional development and coordination.[10]

The Arusha Conference, SADCC 1, was followed by a meeting in Lusaka, Zambia, in April 1980, where SADCC was officially established. The organizational document, the Lusaka Declaration, *Southern Africa: Toward Economic Liberation*, was signed by all nine heads of government. In addition to decreasing dependence on South Africa, other objectives of the organization were outlined in the declaration: the reduction of economic dependence in general; the forging of links to create a genuine and equitable regional integration; the mobilization of resources to promote the implementation of national, interstate and regional policies; and concerted action to secure international cooperation within the framework of the strategy outlined for economic liberation.[11]

FROM POLITICAL TO ECONOMIC LIBERATION

In 1975, when Angola and Mozambique became independent nations, a major watershed occurred in the history of Southern Africa—the beginning of the demise of the "white hinterland." Prior to 1975, Southern Africa was called a white hinterland because South Africa and Rhodesia (Zimbabwe) were under the control of white-settler regimes; both Angola and Mozambique were under the control of the Portuguese, and South Africa illegally occupied Namibia. In 1975, however, when Angola and Mozambique became independent, the very survival of the white hinterland was in question. And in 1980, when Zimbabwe became independent, the white hinterland was eradicated, and apartheid South Africa was left alone to maintain regional hegemony.

As political liberation from colonial rule spread throughout Southern Africa after the early 1960s, the nations found that economic liberation was not also forthcoming, for various reasons: (1) limited economic development during colonial rule; (2) small

Introduction

export markets; (3) fluctuations in the international price of commodity goods; (4) internal constraints to development; (5) external economic dependency, especially on South Africa; and (6) South Africa's regional destabilization. These newly independent nations realized that as long as economic liberation did not also occur, the true capability of the region could not be realized.

In fact, the combined SADCC member states do have the resources necessary for an industrial revolution. They have oil, coal, uranium, and hydroelectric power potential, as well as infinite reserves of solar energy, when it can be harnessed. In addition, they collectively have vast supplies of copper, cobalt, nickel, iron, chrome, lead, zinc, gold, and diamonds.[12]

Although the assets of these nations are tremendous, South Africa remains the major hindrance to development. This point was emphasized at the SADCC Annual Consultative Conference in January 1986, when the participants were reminded that "the single largest threat to economic development in Southern Africa is apartheid and South Africa's destabilization."[13]

South Africa is not only a regional military power; it is also an economic power. In fact, the combined gross domestic product (GDP) of the SADCC member states is only one-third that of South Africa's. In addition, South Africa is a major trading partner, a significant employer of labor, a major supplier of power and fuel, an important source of foreign investment, and a crucial transport conduit.[14]

Decreasing economic dependency on South Africa was identified as the major objective of SADCC because such dependency has forced many SADCC countries to make not only economic compromises with the apartheid regime, but also political compromises. Ironically, since SADCC was formed, several nations have *increased*, rather than decreased, their economic dependence. Indeed, regional development has been difficult amidst regional destabilization. The SADCC countries, however, continue to be committed to the idea of economic liberation.

APARTHEID AND DESTABILIZATION

Throughout the SADCC region, a unique sense of unity exists. In fact, the organization's name, SADCC, is a household word, though its organizational structure may not be easily understood by the lay person. It is understood, however, that SADCC aims to enhance both regional development and the ability of member states to withstand South Africa's destabilization. Clearly, there is no mystery to SADCC's unifying power. All member states have defined South Africa as a common enemy and thus have used SADCC as a strong anti-apartheid forum domestically, regionally, and internationally. Without apartheid and destabilization, SADCC probably would not have been established, since fundamentally, the organization symbolizes the desire of the member states to liberate themselves from South Africa's stranglehold. It was therefore within the context of their unique problems that the member states decided to pursue a strategy that never before had been attempted.

REGIONAL COOPERATION AND DEVELOPMENT

The strategy adopted by SADCC involves regional cooperation, designed to enhance the economies of member States through the development of the major regional sectors: transport and communications; food, agriculture, and natural resources; industry and trade; energy; manpower; mining; and tourism. The member states have determined that, given the present economic and political situation, their interests can best be served by collectively working toward mobilizing the resources of the region.

Regional Integration? Or Regional Cooperation?

SADCC currently is not pursuing a strategy of regional integration, although the SADCC secretariat admits that in the future, it is hoped that regional integration will be possible. However, the member states determined that before integration could occur, with the objective of increasing trade though the establishment of a free trade area and later a customs union, the region must first be developed so that member states would have products to trade. Therefore, regional integration models based on the concept of free trade areas (where tariffs and quantitative restrictions are abolished between participating countries, but each country retains its own tariffs against nonmembers)[15] and customs unions (the suppression of discrimination in the field of commodity movement and the equalization of tariffs in trade with nonmember countries)[16] were rejected. As the former president of Botswana Sir Seretse Khama noted:

> Our states believe that it is vitally important that we trade more among ourselves within the Southern African region. We must diversify domestic production as well as outside import sources . . . Intra-regional trade can increase without the creation of a free trade area or a common market. Each of our states in SADCC has experience with those models of trade to enrich externally based firms and interests and to hamper national planning. The words of Mozambique's Finance Minister, Rui Baltazar, at Arusha are very relevant: 'We must look squarely at our mistakes lest we fall into repeating them.'[17]

What lessons have been learned from the Third World experience with regional integration strategies, and is SADCC really different?

Regional Integration in the Third World

The regional integration strategies first attempted by Third World nations were based upon traditional integration theory and constructed on the European Economic Community (EEC) pattern of free trade areas. According to the traditional theory of economic integration, the benefits are static and dynamic—the former being "welfare gains arising from a marginal reallocation of production and consumption patterns as a result of freeing trade" and the latter "being effects of integration on the rate of economic growth."[18] The theory recognizes, however, that certain conditions must prevail in order for free trade to produce benefits that lead to increased welfare. The theory assumes the existence of a highly industrialized region, where intra-regional trade will be increased substantially. It also assumes that the economies of scale will operate and that "preexisting patterns of trade accurately reflect the comparative advantage of countries in traded commodities."[19]

In developing regions, the above conditions do not exist, which makes the traditional regional integration theory irrelevant. The developing regions are not highly industrialized, their markets are limited, and "trade is directed overwhelmingly toward production and consumption patterns with the industrialized countries." Fundamentally, "the benefits from economic integration which are developed from the traditional theory are not at all likely to be produced within integration schemes of underdeveloped countries." [20]

For industrialized nations, regional integration is envisaged as a strategy to foster trade-creation. For Third World nations, regional integration means development-creation,[21] usually equated with industrialization. Specifically, Third World nations conceive of regional integration as a means to improve the economic and social conditions within their countries, as an avenue to alter the unequal relationship that exists between themselves and industrialized countries.[22]

When the Latin American Free Trade Association (LAFTA) and the Central American Common Market (CACM) implemented regional integration schemes in 1960, they were based on traditional integration theory. Unfortunately, neither organization realized its objectives. While intra-regional trade increased under LAFTA, it was concentrated mostly among the three more developed countries of the region—Argentina, Brazil, and Mexico—the major beneficiaries of this regional trade liberalization. In fact, when the organization was established, these three countries produced 64 percent of the total manufactured exports of the region.[23] The asymmetrical trading patterns resulted in equity problems, which occur when benefits from integration are not distributed among all member countries. As a result of this problem, six of the less developed members later formed a subregional organization of LAFTA—the ANDEAN Pact.

While CACM also experienced some success with respect to increased intra-regional trade, it was short-lived. The lesson to be learned from the experiences of LAFTA and CACM was explicit: Traditional integration theory applied to developing countries is not an appropriate strategy for increasing intra-regional trade or for enhancing regional development.

One response to the failure of the traditional regional integration strategy was the adoption of a planning strategy—a strategy that not only would increase intra-regional trade, but also would include measures designed to ensure a more equitable distribution of the gains. Specifically, it includes "redistributive measures of a compensatory and corrective nature through which the problems of unequal gains and polarization can be solved collectively." Such measures include development planning on a regional level, the formation of regional development banks, and the allocation of industry among member countries.[24] Examples of this approach include the East African Community (EAC), the Caribbean Community and Common Market (CARICOM), and the Economic Community of West African States (ECOWAS).

But this planning strategy failed to increase regional trade, neither prevented the unequal distribution of benefits, nor enhanced regional development. Evans Young concludes:

> It was thought that planning could regulate or compensate for the unbalanced effects of trade liberalization. New industries to diversify the developing economies could be promoted on an equitable basis . . . But planned means to regional cooperation also encountered conflicts of interest. Sovereign states were unwilling to relinquish control over their national economies in order to coordinate regional development planning . . . planning was just as objectionable to local and foreign business interest as trade liberalization . . . When not obstructed by such means, the implementation of planned industrial growth also turned out to be unequally beneficial to the members of regional groups.[25]

A third strategy of regional cooperation was pursued by the ANDEAN Pact, the subregional organization of LAFTA. Upon formation, there was an automatic elimination of intra-regional trade barriers and the establishment of a common external tariff.[26]

The countries of the ANDEAN Pact, influenced by the *dependencia* school of thought, realized that any strategy for regional cooperation aimed at development must address the crucial question of economic dependence on the most advanced nations within the global political economy. The counter-dependency strategy of the ANDEAN Pact thus adopted policy measures aimed at "reducing dependence on metropolitan countries resulting from the existing international division of labour and activities of the TNEs" (transnational enterprises).[27] Specific policies adopted were controls on foreign direct investment; the creation of sectoral industrial development programs; and preferential allocation of new industries to the poorer members, in order to ensure that the richer countries and foreign transnational corporations did not benefit disproportionately.[28]

This strategy, like the previous ones, ran into many difficulties. For example, agreement on a common foreign investment policy was narrowed because of disagreements between member states and the opposition of foreign corporations. In addition, Bolivia and Ecuador proved to be unattractive to potential investors; polarized development continued, and governments, local businesses, and foreign corporations continued to have conflicts of interests; the transnationals dominated the sectoral development programs because the industries developed required large-scale, high-technology, capital-intensive operations; and the economic and social conditions of the region's workers and peasants were not improved.[29]

The Association of Southeast Asian Nations (ASEAN) pursued a fourth strategy of regional integration, a middle ground between free trade and planned measures for regional development. With respect to intra-regional trade cooperation, selective trade liberalization was adopted in order to control the movement of trade in a step-by-step, product fashion.

In addition to fostering planned trade liberalization, ASEAN adopted means for regional development by instituting policies for production cooperation. This particular strategy of intra-regional trade cooperation, production cooperation, and infrastructure development has two major objectives: the reduction of barriers to regional and global trade and investment; and the increase of regional resources by pooling capital, knowledge, and bargaining power to better exploit the ASEAN economies' comparative advantage in the world economy without imposing severe restrictions on national or sub-national actors in the course of planning.[30]

While the economies of the member countries have grown significantly as a consequence of the increase in external regional trade, the patterns of growth have affected the internal structures of the countries, exacerbating the problem of unequal distribution of wealth and limited employment opportunities.[31] With respect to increasing intra-regional trade (the major objective of the organization), the Preferential Trade Arrangement has done little to increase such trade.[32]

SADCC: Toward Structural Transformation

While SADCC represented the first attempt by the Third World to

Introduction 11

pursue a strategy of regional cooperation and development without creating a free trade area or a customs union, it was not the first organization to incorporate development planning in its strategy. SADCC's strategy was unique, however, because such planning was undertaken with the major objective not of increasing intra-regional trade, but regional development leading to regional structural transformation.

SADCC's strategy reflected the need among developing countries to establish regional strategies that grew out of the concept of collective self-reliance: "cooperation among developing countries on a South-South basis in order to attain a fundamental redistribution of world production and allocation of surplus in developing countries, and the power of these countries to make their own decisions on matters affecting their own societies." [33]

In order for collective self-reliance to be realized, structural transformation is required. This entails an alteration in the present asymmetrical structural relationships that exist between industrialized and developing countries, as well as an alteration in the political, economic, and social structures that perpetuate underdevelopment within developing countries. With structural transformation as the major objective, developing countries must set as their primary goal the transformation of the structure of production, rather than concentrating on trade-creation or import substitution.[34] Indeed, the overall objective of SADCC is to transform the structure of production. As Ed Brown notes:

> The difference between SADCC and other regional organizations is SADCC's attempt to integrate its economies at the level of production. By extending the concept of cooperation beyond the economic function of exchange and trade, relations between members are reinforced in a permanent manner.[35]

When the SADCC countries developed their strategy, they also considered the question of unequal distribution of benefits, which had been a major problem for many regional integration organizations among Third World nations. Historically, the regional giant benefited most from the creation of free trade areas or customs unions, since it produced most of the manufactured goods. Such is the case in Southern Africa, for example, with the South African

Customs Union (SACU). South Africa, as the economic giant, accrues far more benefits from SACU than do the other members—Botswana, Lesotho, and Swaziland.

In an effort to guarantee that this issue would not be divisive, the SADCC countries first accepted the fact that all their economies were in varying stages of development, with different resource potential. For example, while Mozambique's greatest potential is in the development of regional transport systems leading to its three ports, Lesotho's greatest potential is in the continued development of its hydroelectric power as a result of its large water supply. Therefore, it was understood that though some nations may seemingly benefit more than others, such development would be for the collective good of all SADCC members. For example, six of the nine SADCC countries are landlocked, and most have been forced to increase their use of South Africa's transport network to export their goods out of Southern Africa because of regional destabilization. All these nations will, therefore, benefit from the development of Mozambique's transport network. In addition to decreasing dependency on the apartheid regime, the shorter Mozambique route is significantly less expensive.

Notwithstanding the fact that all nations cannot possibly benefit equally, the member states determined that in order for all nations to feel that some benefits would be forthcoming, each nation was assigned the responsibility for coordinating the development of an entire regional sector or subsector (see chapter 4 for country responsibility). In addition, such development was directly related to the national development plans of each SADCC country, in that projects presented for funding at SADCC sector meetings originated from the national development plans of each respective government. The objective behind this strategy was to ensure that member states did not feel pressured to make a choice between national development and regional development. Instead, regional development was to be seen as part of national development.

Finally, the organizational structure of SADCC was unique in that it was a highly decentralized and participatory system of functional delegation, specifically designed to avoid bureaucratic and technocratic delegation. This was done in an effort to secure the maximum involvement of all member States.[36] All nations shared equally in the decision-making process, and the SADCC Secretariat had the major responsibility of coordinating events (see chapter 5).

Eight years after its establishment, SADCC supporters, as well as critics, abound. One of the major contradictions of SADCC is that in the process of attempting to decrease dependence on South Africa, SADCC member states have increased their dependency on the advanced capitalist nations of the West. In fact, SADCC project development is dependent mainly on economic assistance from governments and international organizations. The majority of such funding is secured at the SADCC Annual Consultative Conference. Can this strategy, critics and supporters alike ask, enhance regional economic liberation? Critics also ask whether SADCC is able to determine development priorities, or are such priorities determined by SADCC's international cooperating partners, as a result of increased dependency on the West?

Others wonder who really is supposed to benefit from SADCC development: the masses, the elite, or both? Critics argue that the development strategy is not designed to benefit the masses, but to address the political and economic aspirations of the elite. SADCC supporters argue, however, that project development is designed to benefit everyone in the region.

While SADCC, eight years later, is a controversial regional entity, the SADCC Secretariat reminds its critics that the organization is new. It takes time to implement a plan for development among nations as diverse as those in Southern Africa, and amidst South African regional destabilization. In fact, when SADCC was established in 1980, the South African government announced its intentions of ensuring the failure of the organization. And South Africa has effectively begun to undermine SADCC strategy through increased destabilization.

OBJECTIVE OF STUDY

Through its successes and failures, SADCC has become a major regional institution in Southern Africa, and if allowed to flower and develop, it could make a significant contribution toward regional self-reliant development. This study is about SADCC's successes, failures, and problems, as well as its prospects for the future. It is designed to provide a macro overview of SADCC and Southern Africa, to fill a major gap in the literature on that area. This study, like most, has its limitations, and two in particular need to be brought to the reader's attention.

The first relates to class analysis. Since the unit of analysis in this study is the entire Southern Africa region, it is not possible to undertake an in-depth analysis of class structures within each country and their relationship to SADCC's strategy. Such an investigation must be reserved for a later study.

A second limitation relates to the issue of SADCC and transnational corporations in Southern Africa. While this is a relevant and important subject, it too requires a separate in-depth study.[37]

APPROACH TO STUDY

This study adopts a political economy framework. Special emphasis is placed on analysis of the extent to which regional structural transformation (decreased dependency and increased development) is possible under the SADCC program of action, given the external and internal constraints to development among the SADCC member states.

The major constraints are reviewed in chapters 2 and 3, since those chapters provide a historical overview of the political economy of Southern Africa: chapter 2, the colonial period; chapter 3, the post-independence period. Those two chapters provide the reader with an understanding of many of the problems that confront SADCC in its effort to foster regional structural transformation.

Chapters 4 through 8 focus on SADCC. Chapter 4 contains an in-depth look at SADCC's strategy for regional cooperation and development; chapter 5 examines SADCC's institutional framework. In chapter 6, the SADCC strategy is analyzed at the regional level—namely, the problems the organization has experienced in its attempt to decrease economic dependence on South Africa and develop the region. Chapter 7 analyzes the SADCC strategy at the international level—specifically, the dynamics of the relationship that exists between the SADCC member states and the West (the advanced capitalist nations). Particular attention is given to the contradiction inherent in the fact that in the attempt to decrease economic dependence on South Africa, the SADCC region is increasing its dependence on the advanced capitalist nations of the West.

Conclusions are reached in chapter 8.

THEORETICAL FRAMEWORK

The political economy approach adopted for this study includes world-system theory,[38] underdevelopment theory,[39] unequal development theory,[40] dependency theory,[41] and theories of imperialism.[42] According to theorists such as Samir Amin, Giovanni Arrighi, Andre Gunder Frank, and Immanuel Wallerstein, "there is a social whole that may be called a capitalist world-economy," whose genesis dates back to around the sixteenth century. By the late nineteenth century, it had expanded historically from its European origins to cover the globe. The world economy is considered to be capitalist, in that accumulation is its motor force and that "appropriation by the world bourgeoisie of the surplus value created by the world producers have involved not merely direct appropriation at the marketplace, but also unequal exchange, transferring surplus from peripheral to core zones."[43]

The global center, or core zones (see Figure 1), of the capitalist world-economy consists of the advanced capitalist nations that have developed market economies; the global periphery (see Figure 1) of the capitalist world-economy consists of Third World, or developing nations, with weak and dependent economic structures. In fact, while development was occurring in the global center, a historic process of underdevelopment and/or dependent development was taking place in the global periphery, resulting in structural linkages of dependence between the global periphery and the global center. The outcome of this process was the development of unequal economic relations between the global center and the periphery. The development of these historic patterns and structural linkages took place during colonial rule, and very few Third World nations have been able to alter their peripheral status. In this study, Southern Africa is considered the global periphery; the advanced capitalist nations (i.e., United States, Britain, France, West Germany, Canada, the Nordic countries, Japan), the global center.

In addition to a global center and a global periphery, the capitalist world economy also has a global semiperiphery (see Figure 1). In fact, global semiperipheries are central to the normal functioning of

FIGURE 1
CONTEMPORARY POLITICAL ECONOMY

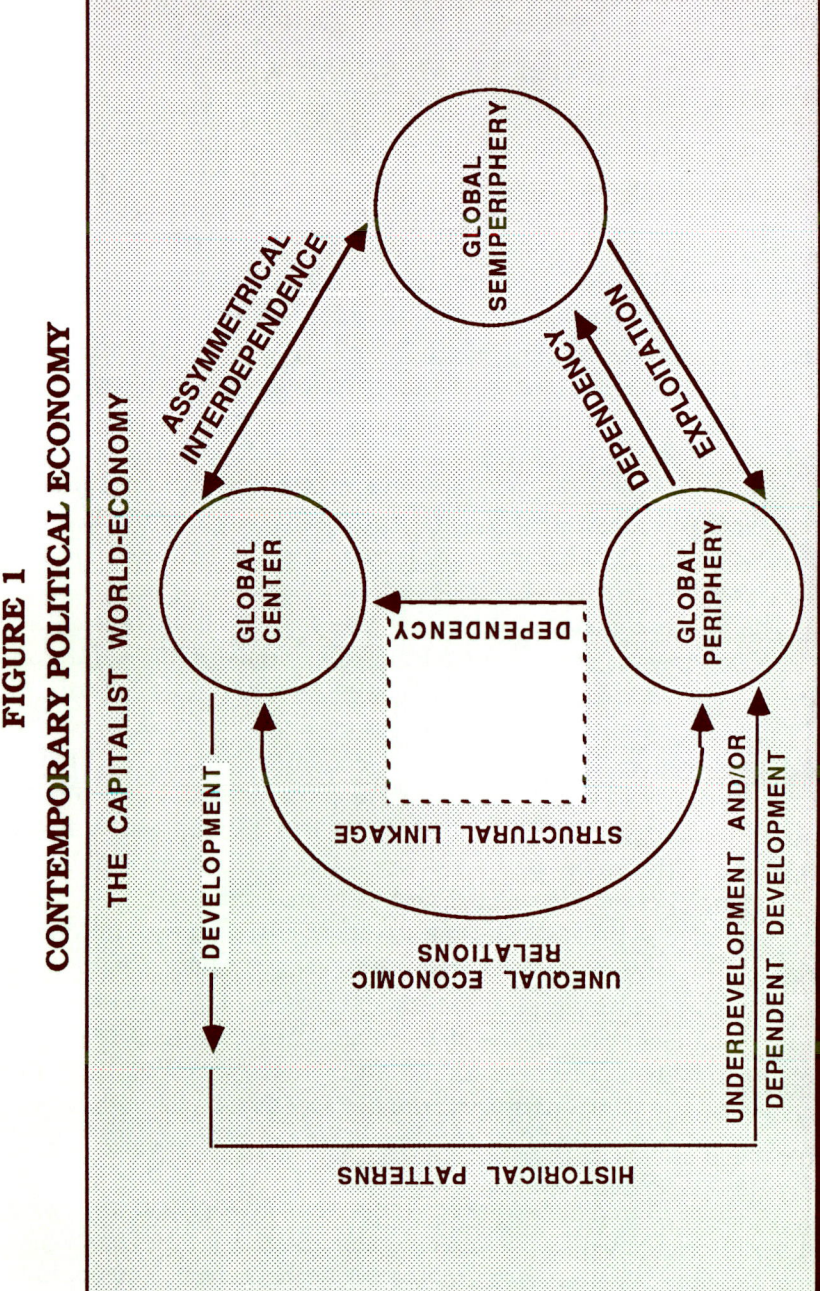

Introduction

the capitalist world-economy. Economically, semiperipheral areas are used by the global center for redistributing surplus products with the aim of increasing profit. Politically, they serve as buffers between the high-status, high-income sector (the global center) and the relatively homogeneous low-status and low-income sector (the global periphery), to prevent the oppressed elements (the overwhelming majority of individuals in the system) from rebelling. Thus, the major political means by which crises are averted in the system is through the creation of "middle" sectors, which primarily tend to think of themselves as better off than the lower sectors, rather than as worse off than the upper sectors.[44] The economic relationship between the global center and the global semiperiphery is one of asymmetrical interdependence. While the global periphery is economically dependent upon the global semiperiphery, it also is exploited by the semiperiphery. In this study, South Africa is the semiperipheral nation of concern.

The political economy model for this study (see Figure 2) is used to describe and analyze: (1) the position of Southern Africa within the capitalist world-economy; (2) the present level of dependency that exists between South Africa and SADCC member states and between advanced capitalist nations and SADCC member states; (3) the general level of regional underdevelopment among SADCC member states; and (4) the prospects for structural transformation in the region.

In the political economy model of Southern Africa, there exist two orders of dependency within the capitalist world-economy—the international and the subsystem. The dynamics of the relationship between South Africa and the SADCC member states (subsystem) has been classified as the first order of dependency, since the SADCC member states have identified as their major objective the decreasing of regional economic dependence on South Africa. In the second order of dependency, the focus of analysis is the dynamics of the relationship between the advanced capitalist nations and the SADCC member states (international). For the SADCC members at this stage of their planned development, structural transformation of regional dependence on the global center in general is of secondary consideration. In fact, they have determined that increased financial assistance from the global center is crucial if decreased dependence on South Africa is to be realized.

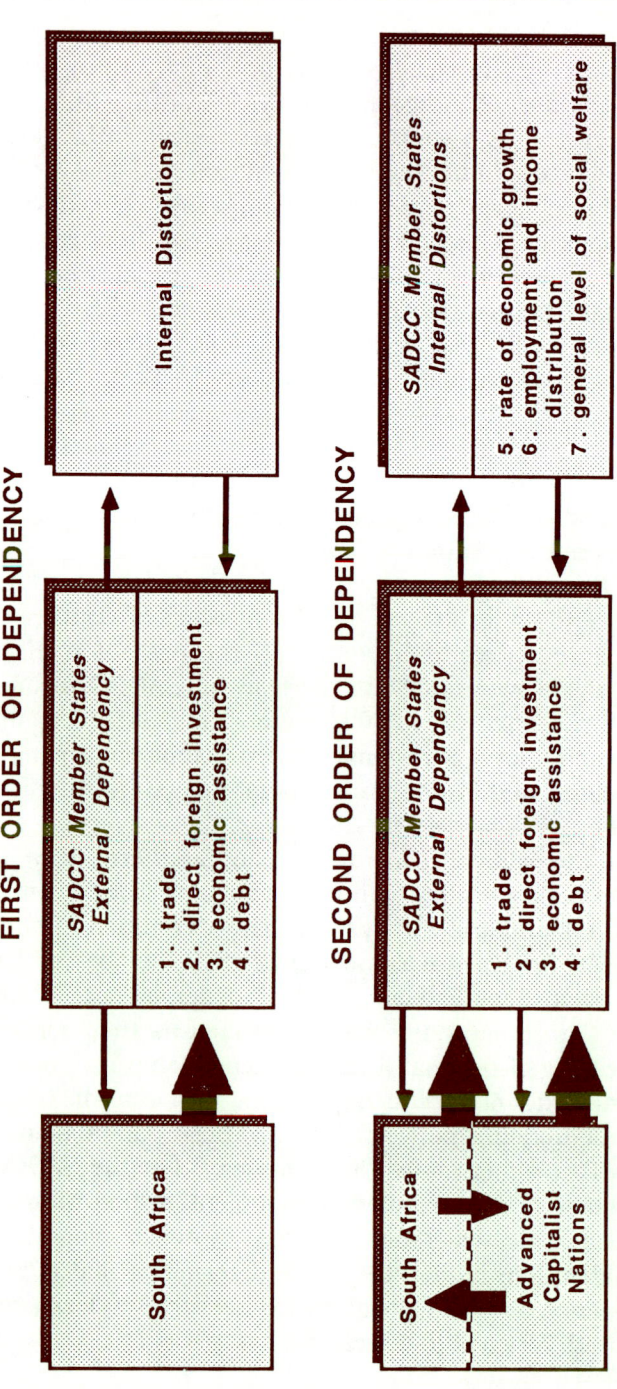

FIGURE 2
POLITICAL ECONOMY MODEL OF SOUTHERN AFRICA

NOTE: The different size arrows indicate the asymmetrical economic relationships that exist between the various nations.

It is reasonable that the SADCC member states would identify as their major objective the structural transformation of their first order of dependency, since they are chronically dependent on the apartheid regime; what perhaps is not reasonable is the extent to which they have increased their dependence on the global center. In fact, even if these nations are successful in decreasing their dependence on the apartheid regime, they will have created an even greater problem by becoming locked more chronically into the global capitalist market—the precise market that developed South Africa as a global semiperiphery, with the capacity to control the economic structures of the SADCC countries. Herein lies the major contradiction of SADCC: By increasing their dependence on the global center, the SADCC states are coming no closer to realizing their objective of economic liberation.

In addition, another major problem exists. Since South Africa is a preferred member of the global center, how much help can the SADCC states really expect from the advanced capitalist nations? Can they expect enough assistance to contribute to the economic demise of the apartheid regime, so that the economic liberation of the SADCC states can be realized? Certainly this type of assistance will not be forthcoming, since South Africa is the West's "baby." Clearly, its survival as a global semiperiphery has proved to be more important than the political and economic liberation of the independent regional nations from apartheid's stranglehold. These issues, and many more, will be explored further in subsequent chapters.

NOTES

1. Joseph Hanlon, *Apartheid's Second Front: South Africa's War Against Its Neighbours* (London: Penguin Books, 1986), p. 1.

2. Carol Thompson, "SADCC's Struggle for Economic Liberation," *Africa Report*, July–August 1986, p. 62; Joseph Hanlon, "South Africa's Destabilization Policies," summary of a paper presented at a Third World Foundation Conference on Southern Africa, *Third World Quarterly*, Vol.9, No. 4, 1987, pp. 1455-6; Paul Fauvet, "To Fight, and to Count the Cost," *Guardian* (Britain), March 3, 1988. Abel Jonaze, from the Ministry of External

Affairs in Mozambique, informed me in July 1988 that Mozambique had 6 million internally displaced persons.

3. UNICEF, *Children on the Frontline: The Impact of Apartheid, Destabilization and Warfare on Children in Southern Africa and South Africa*, report prepared for UNICEF by Reginald Herbold Green, Dereji Asrat, Marta Mauras, and Richard Morgan (New York: UNICEF, 1987).

4. These accounts were televised on Zimbabwe Broadcasting Corporation (ZBC) News, August 1987; "Reports of MNR Eating Human Flesh Increase," *Herald* (Zim.), August 24, 1987.

5. "Survivors Recount the Horror of Homoine Massacre," *Herald* (Zim), July 23, 1987; "Victims of MNR Massacre Buried," *Herald* (Zim), July 24, 1987; "Massacre Toll," *Herald* (Zim), August 13, 1987; "Mozambique Rebels Leave Trail of Death," *Independent* (Britain), November 2, 1987. For atrocities committed by the MNR throughout 1988 the reader is referred to *Facts and Reports*, International Press Cuttings on Southern Africa, published by the Holland Committee on Southern Africa, Amsterdam, Holland.

6. *Guardian* (Britain), September 30, 1987.

7. "Text of Angola Ceasefire Statement," *Independent* (Britain), August 8, 1988.

8. See "Peace Accord for Namibia," *The Washington Post*, December 23, 1988.

9. Sir Seretse Khama, "Introduction," *Southern Africa: Toward Economic Liberation*, ed. Amon J. Nsekela (London: Rex Collins, 1981), p. xi.

10. *Ibid.*

11. *Southern Africa: Toward Economic Liberation: A Declaration by the Governments of Independent States of Southern Africa* Made

at Lusaka on the 1st of April, 1980.

12. Aloysuis Kgarebe, ed., *SADCC 2—Maputo* (London: SADCC Liaison Committee, 1981), p. 11.

13. Simbarashe Makoni, "Interview," *Africa Report*, July–August 1986, p. 41.

14. Overseas Development Institute, "Sanctions and South Africa's Neighbours," May 1987, p. 1.

15. Bela Balassa, *The Theory of Economic Integration* (Homewood, Ill.: Richard D. Irvin, 1961), p. 2.

16. *Ibid.*

17. Khama, "Introduction," p. xii.

18. W. Andrew Axline, *Caribbean Integration: The Politics of Regionalism* (New York: Nichols Publications, 1979), p. 4.

19. See Vasant Kumar Bawa, *Latin American Integration* (Atlantic Highlands, NJ: Humanities Press, 1980), p. 3; Evans Young, "Development Coordination in ASEAN: Balancing Free Trade and Regional Planning" (Ph.D. diss. University of Michigan, 1981), p. 43.

20. Axline, *Caribbean Integration*, p. 6.

21. Young, "Development Coordination," p. 5.

22. Axline, *Caribbean Integration*, p. 6.

23. Alicia Puyana, "Latin America: Lessons of the Strength and Weakness of Regional Cooperation," *Regionalism and the New International Economic Order*, ed. Davidson Nicol and Luis Echeverria (New York: Pergamon Press, 1981), p. 51.

24. W. Andrew Axline, "Underdevelopment, Dependence, and

Integration: The Politics of Regionalism in the Third World," *International Organization*, Vol. 31, No. 1, 1977, p. 87.

25. Young, "Development Coordination," pp. 7-8.

26. David E. Hojam, "The Andean Pact: Failure of a Model of Economic Integration?" *Journal of Common Market Studies*, Vol. 2, No. 2, 1981, p. 13.

27. Axline, *Caribbean Integration*, p. 47.

28. Young, "Development Coordination," p. 8.

29. *Ibid.*, pp. 8-9, 15; D.V. Vaitos, "Crisis in Regional Economic Cooperation/Integration Among Developing Countries: A Survey," *World Development*, Vol. 6, No. 6, 1978, p. 725.

30. Young, "Development Coordination," pp. 11, 16.

31. Marta Gonzalez and Gemma Cruz Guerrero, "ASEAN—A Case Study of Regionalism in Southeast Asia," *Regionalism and the New International Economic Order*, ed. Davidson Nicol and Luis Echeverria (New York: Pergamon Press, 1981), p. 75.

32. *Ibid.*, p. 76; Stuart Drummond, "Fifteen Years of ASEAN," *Journal of Common Market Studies*, Vol. 20, No. 4, 1982, p. 306.

33. Axline, *Caribbean Integration*, p. xvi. The concept of South-South refers to cooperation among Third World nations. The North consists of the advanced capitalist nations of the West; the South, the developing, or Third World, countries.

34. John P. Renninger, "The Future of Economic Cooperation Schemes in Africa with Special Reference to ECOWAS," *Alternative Futures for Africa*, ed. Timothy M. Shaw (Boulder, Colo.: Westview Press, 1982), p. 157.

35. Ed Brown, "Foreign Aid to SADCC: An Analysis of the Reagan Administration's Foreign Policy," *Issue*, Vol. 12, No. 3/4, 1982,

p. 29.

36. SADCC, "SADCC Lusaka—Overview," paper presented at the SADCC conference at Lusaka, 2/3 February, 1984, p. 15.

37. For an initial introduction, readers are referred to Ann Seidman, Robert Seidman, Daniel B. Ndlela, and Kempton Makamure, eds., *Transnationals in Southern Africa* (Harare, Zimbabwe: Harare Publishing House, 1986).

38. See Immanuel Wallerstein, *The Modern World-System* (New York: Academic Press, 1974) and *The Capitalist World-Economy* (Cambridge: Cambridge University Press, 1979).

39. See Samir Amin, *Accumulation on a World Scale: A Critique of the Theory of Underdevelopment* (New York: Monthly Review Press, 1974).

40. See Ronald Chilcote, *Theories of Comparative Politics: The Search for a Paradigm* (Boulder, Colo.: Westview Press, 1981); Colin Leys, *Underdevelopment in Kenya: The Political Economy of Neo-Colonialism, 1964–1971* (Berkeley: University of California Press, 1974).

41. See Theotonio Dos Santos, "The Structure of Dependence," *American Economic Review*, Vol. LX, 1970; Fernado Henrique Cardoso and Enzo Faletto, *Dependency and Development in Latin America* (Berkeley: University of California Press, 1979); James A. Caporaso, "Dependency Theory: Continuities and Discontinuities in Development Studies," *International Organization*, Vol. 34, No. 4, 1980.

42. See Johan Galtung, "A Structural Theory of Imperialism," *Journal of Peace Research*, Vol.8, No. 2, 1971.

43. Samir Amin, Giovanni Arrighi, Andre Gunder Frank, and Immanuel Wallerstein, *Dynamics of Global Crisis* (New York: Monthly Review Press, 1982), pp. 9-10.

44. Immanuel Wallerstein, "Dependence in an Interdependent World: The Limited Possibilities of Transformation Within the Capitalist World Economy," *African Studies Review*, Vol. 17, 1974, p. 4.

CHAPTER 2

The Political Economy of Southern Africa: Colonial Period

The current structural linkages of dependency and underdevelopment that exist between the SADCC member states and South Africa, and the SADCC member states and the advanced capitalist nations, were established during colonial rule. It is precisely these structural linkages that the SADCC nations are desirous of altering through SADCC. In order to understand the challenge the SADCC states face in their effort to decrease dependency and foster development, it is necessary to examine the history of colonial rule in Southern Africa.

The first part of this chapter contains a historical overview of South Africa's incorporation into the capitalist world-economy. In the second part, the history of the incorporation of the SADCC countries into the capitalist world-economy is reviewed.

SOUTH AFRICA WITHIN THE CAPITALIST WORLD-ECONOMY

Comprehensive and thorough analyses of South Africa's incorporation into the capitalist world-economy have been previously undertaken.[1] The objective of this section is not to replicate such studies, but to place in historical perspective the structural links that exist today between South Africa and the major advanced capitalist nations, and between South Africa and the SADCC nations. Three time periods have been identified for this undertaking.

1652 – 1867
The Conflict Between Traditional and Colonial-Settler Modes of Production

The Dutch occupation of the Cape of Good Hope in 1652 began a process that continued even after the takeover of the Cape Colony by Britain in 1806. Whereas Africans occupied their land in accordance with precapitalist traditions, the European settlers were determined to occupy the same land in accordance with the laws of capitalist property. The struggle for control of the land and labor determined the political and economic status of the African in the settlers' scheme of things.[2]

In 1652 three traditional modes of production had existed in South Africa among the San, the Khoikhoi, the Nguni-speaking groups, and the Sotho. The San and Khoikhoi inhabited the Cape of Good Hope when the Dutch arrived.[3] The mode of production of the San was hunting and gathering; for the Khoikhoi, herding.[4]

The Nguni-speaking groups (Xhosa and Zulu) had well-organized and highly developed states, with a mixed mode of production that consisted of cattle herding, agriculture, and hunting. Similarly, the Sotho's mode of production was cattle herding and agriculture. In addition, the Sotho mined and smelted iron, copper, and tin.[5] Within a short time, the colonial-settlers stripped the indigenous African population of their land and traditional modes of production, forcing them to participate in new modes of production compatible with the mercantile interests of the Dutch and, later, the British.

Although the initial occupation of South Africa took place under the leadership of the mercantile monopoly of the Dutch East India Company (DEIC), its power was later weakened by the emergence of a local mercantile-commercial bourgeoisie. The wealth and power of this group was based on surplus accumulated from the indigenous population (resulting in the underdevelopment of areas owned by Africans) and through the creation of new modes of production.[6]

Martin Legassick identifies five modes of production in existence during the conflict between traditional and colonial-settler methods of producing. The initial mode was slavery; labor was imported from the East and other parts of Africa. Following the abolition of slavery in the early nineteenth century, a second mode grew out from a rural proletariat of ex-slaves and other Africans whose land had been expropriated. These individuals, who participated in agriculture conducted on the basis of capitalist relations, were subjected to various forms of extraeconomic coercion. The third mode was feudalism, in areas that were not "deeply" colonized. The fourth mode of production was identified among an indigenous land-owning peasantry; and the final mode consisted of seasonally or temporarily migrating peasants, who offered themselves to supplement the labor force.[7]

During this period in South Africa's history, no one mode of production was dominant. Although the mercantile-commercial group had become powerful, it remained under metropolitan control. After 150 years of control by the Netherlands, the British gained control over the Cape Colony, and under British governance, there emerged a "class of import-export merchants acting on behalf of metropolitan capital, who were the inheritors of political authority in the Cape Colony as Britain delegated formal power to it in the form of self-government in 1854." [8]

Those two centuries laid the foundation for transformation from a precapitalist to a capitalist mode of production in South Africa. This transformation was enhanced through the adoption by the white settlers of policies of racial discrimination. These settlers had already determined that the indigenous African population would remain in a subjugated position.

1867 – 1945
South Africa's Incorporation into the Capitalist World-Economy.

With the discovery of diamonds in 1867 and gold in 1884 at Kimberley and the Transvaal ridges of Witwatersrand, economic changes were brought about that were "tantamount to a full-fledged revolution." [9] No part of the country or of the Southern African region was left untouched by the changes that were to occur. For the international capitalist world, the discovery, particularly of gold, meant the identification of large deposits of the world monetary commodity. This discovery sparked international concern in the development of a country which heretofore had been of no major interest.

Following the discovery, the predominance of direct imperial capital over local capital was greatly accelerated. Specifically, the local bourgeoisie did not have the type of capital necessary for mining both diamonds and gold. Britain and other countries in western Europe provided the needed capital, mainly because of the "urgent needs of the international economy for gold currency."[10] Thus between 1887 and 1913, total British and European investment in gold mining was sizable. However, in an effort to retain mining capital within South Africa, the South African Reserve Bank was established, denying mine owners the right to sell gold. In addition, local control over monetary policy was gradually established, and by the 1930s local share ownership had been increased from 15 to 40 percent.[11]

The continued need to acquire foreign capital for the further development of the mining industry was most evident when American capital was invited to penetrate the South African economy during World War I. According to Bernard Magubane:

> The war inaugurated a phase of monetary instability. The international gold standard, which had provided an unlimited market at fixed prices for the output of the gold mines, was no longer working well. The problem for the mining industry was to acquire sufficient capital to open up new mines despite the unwillingness of investors to risk capital.[12]

In 1917 Ernest Oppenheimer of South Africa was able to secure capital from Morgan Guaranty & Trust Company in the United States. The merging of financial capital from Oppenheimer and Morgan Guaranty resulted in the formation of the Anglo-American Corporation (AAC). As Magubane notes, "The AAC has developed into the backbone of mining life in both South Africa and the former British dependencies."[13]

The development of the mining industry did not occur without great cost to the colonial-settlers. In fact, a series of wars erupted between the British and Boers as a consequence of conflict of interest over the mining industry, dating back to the British occupation of the Cape Colony in 1806. When the British arrived, they had introduced an economic system alien to the Boers. According to Magubane:

> While the Boers stood for outdated slavery on a petty scale, the foundation of their patriarchal peasant economy, the British colonist represented large-scale capitalist exploitation of the land and Africans. The abolition of slav-

ery and the trend it represented were seen as a threat by the Boers, whose pure peasant economy had been dependent on slave labor.[14]

Land and cheap African labor were plentiful in the interior of Africa, so in an effort to escape British rule and establish "free and independent states" of their own, the Boers set out to expand further into South Africa. The exodus of the Boers from the Cape Colony is know as the Great Trek.[15] By the mid-1850s two Boer republics—the Orange Free State and the Transvaal, and two British republics—the Cape Colony and Natal, had been established. The discovery of gold in the Transvaal, however, served to heightened the British/Boer conflict once again.

According to Legassick, the conflict existed between the "nouveau riche and foreign-controlled mining houses" and a feudal, rather than a capitalist, "land-owning ruling class."[16] This conflict spread throughout South Africa, eventually resulting in the Anglo-Boer War. As Bethuel Setai notes, "The Boer War was a capitalist war. The British waged it so that they could gain effective control of the mining industry."[17]

The British victory ensured "the establishment of a dominant capitalist mode of production throughout South Africa."[18] The uniting of the British and the Boer (Afrikaner) culminated in the May 31, 1910, inauguration of the Union of South Africa. The British maintained economic control over the country while the Afrikaners established political control.

Another conflict, however, came to the forefront among the colonial-settlers at this juncture—the desire by some to diversify the mining economy. Specifically, one group insisted that taxes derived from the profits of the gold mines be used to industrialize the country; a second group wanted to maintain a primarily mining economy. Those who favored industrialization won out, largely as a consequence of the reduction in mining caused by the post-World War I recession.[19] Thus an iron and steel corporation (ISCOR) established by the government was the first in a series of state industries which served as a catalyst for private industry and secondary industrial growth in South Africa.[20]

South Africa's incorporation into the capitalist world-economy had serious implications for the political, social and economic status of the indigenous African population. The mining, agricultural, and secondary industrial growth rested on cheap African labor. As Magubane notes:

> If the capitalist mode of production was to develop, it was necessary to do more that deprive the immediate producers of the means of production and make them "free" paupers; wealth also had to be concentrated in the hands of the conquering settlers. The process of "imperialization" involved the restructuring of the African subsistence economy in such a way that peasants in the areas set aside for them after conquest could never again become economically self-sufficient.[21]

For colonial-settlers, permanent racial segregation was the solution. Thus, the 1913 Land Act identified 7.3 percent of the land in the country as "scheduled African areas." The act also prohibited farming on-the-half, a system which allowed Africans to "cultivate, graze stock, and live on a white landowner's property in return for giving him half the harvest." Thousands of Africans were uprooted as a consequence of the abolition of this policy. "After the passage of the 1913 Land Act, even more than before it, the areas set aside for Africans became reservoirs of labor for the mines, towns, and white farms." [22]

Dispossessed of land, political power, and means of economic power as a consequence of the 1913 Land Act and a series of subsequent acts, the African became a major source of cheap labor. From the African reserves, Africans migrated into the industrial areas to work in the mines for secondary industry. Once their contracts had expired or they were no longer capable of rigorous work, they were exported back to the economically poor reserves, which by the 1920s and 1930s "had been reduced from production of a surplus to subsistence" (i.e., were not able to meet their bare subsistence needs).[23]

The indigenous African population, however, did not provide totally for the labor needs. Consequently, arrangements were made between the South African government and colonial governments in surrounding countries to supplement South Africa's labor needs with Africans from those countries. Thousands of migrant laborers poured into South Africa to work for bare subsistence wages. This was the first in a series of events that contributed to the underdevelopment of the South African periphery.

Post-World War II Deepening Incorporation into the Capitalist World-Economy

South Africa's deepening incorporation into the capitalist world-economy after World War II was facilitated by an economic crisis that occurred among major corporations in the advanced capitalist nations. Specifically, economic and political factors were limiting their growth at home. Consequently, they began to search for "safe investment havens abroad." For many transnationals, South Africa was among the few desirable countries.[24] According to Ann Siedman and Neva Makgetla, in South Africa, transnationals found:

> authoritarian regimes, backed by powerful military machines capable of holding in check the aspirations of the masses of their people. These welcomed their capital and, above all, the sophisticated new techniques needed to build their military-industrial might. The transnationals poured roughly half of all the capital they invested in Africa in the 1960s and 1970s into South Africa.[25]

Transnationals from Great Britain, the United States, West Germany, France, and Japan became the major investors in the country. Their penetration took the form of direct investment, mobilization of international credits, provision of technology and managerial assistance, and played "a complex role in transforming South Africa's mineral-based economy into a modern, industrial, increasingly militarized state."[26]

As an advanced capitalist semiperipheral nation, South Africa presently produces 80 percent of the capitalist world's gold and is one of the major producers of uranium, platinum, antimony and other important minerals. In addition, the country is strategically important for facilitating Western control of the petroleum transport route from the Middle East to Europe and America.[27] These links (and others), have not been established only between South Africa and the advanced capitalist nations. As Magubane notes:

Between Southern Africa, Britain, the United States, West Germany, France, and Japan there exists a complex network of horizontal and vertical economic, political, diplomatic, and military relations of considerable and enduring importance.[28]

South Africa's deepening incorporation into the capitalist world-economy was enhanced by the further consolidation of white power. In 1948 the National Party (Afrikaner) institutionalized the concept of racial separation with the introduction of apartheid. With the promotion of the Bantu Self-government Act of 1959, the South African Bantustans were "legally" created. The act designated eight small areas, or Bantustans, for "mandatory" African occupation. These Bantustans (presently there are ten) are scattered throughout South Africa on the most mountainous, driest, least cultivable land in the country.[29] The poverty and deprivation in the Bantustans forces able-bodied men to leave their families and migrate to the urban areas to work for subsistent wages. These Africans, along with "temporary" inhabitants in African urban areas and migrant laborers from surrounding countries, form the backbone of South Africa's economy. In fact, "the African migrants who are recruited to the gold mines are subjected to a kind of exploitation tantamount to slavery." [30]

The historical development of South Africa's incorporation into the capitalist world-economy as an advanced semiperipheral capitalist nation has resulted in the creation of a white elite whose structural links to advanced capitalist nations have allowed them to develop and maintain one of the most ruthless industrial-military societies presently in existence. Simultaneously, South Africa's incorporation into the capitalist world-economy resulted in the underdevelopment of the indigenous African population. Specifically, African land was expropriated and traditional modes of production were disrupted, forcing Africans to provide cheap labor for colonial-settlers and, later, for transnationals. The subjugation of Africans was accomplished through the institutionalization of the worst system of racism that presently exists in the world.

Southern Africa's incorporation into the capitalist world-economy was part of a similar process of exploitation and domination by white settlers and advanced capitalist nations.

THE SADCC MEMBER STATES' INCORPORATION INTO THE CAPITALIST WORLD-ECONOMY

This review of the historical incorporation of Southern Africa into the capitalist world-economy is divided into four parts: the former High Commission territories; the former Portuguese colonies; the former Central African Federation; and former British Tanganyika.

The Former High Commission Territories — Bechuanaland, Basutoland, Swaziland

The incorporation of Bechuanaland (Botswana), Basutoland (Lesotho), and Swaziland into the capitalist world-economy occurred simultaneously with South African settler-colonial expansion into the interior of Southern Africa, and with British colonial control over these three territories. In fact, Boer (or Afrikaner) expansion beyond the borders of South Africa posed a serious threat to British continental interests. At the request of tribal chiefs from Bechuanaland, Basutoland, and Swaziland, the British provided protection for these countries from further Afrikaner expansion by declaring them British protectorates. They were placed "under the administrative control of the high commissioner acting through local resident commissioners until 1963, when the post of high commissioner was abolished." [31] Thus for at least a century, the British were able to secure their interests in this part of Southern Africa.

Afrikaner expansion and British colonial rule over these territories began the process of their incorporation into the capitalist world-economy as underdeveloped peripheral colonies. Traditional precapitalist modes of production were challenged and, in many instances, replaced by capitalist modes of production. Once self-sufficient independent countries, by 1907 these colonies had become "almost totally dependent on the adjacent South African colonies for their markets and employment." [32]

Frank Baffoe identifies two basic types of relationships that emanated from capitalist penetration of Bechuanaland, Basutoland, and Swaziland. The first relationship was that of the integration of these colonies into the capitalist world-economy "in a dependent and a peripheral status in relation to the colonial power Britain." This relationship was further complicated by the assumption on the part of Britain and South Africa that these High Commission territories eventually would be absorbed into the Union of South Africa. This assumption continued until 1963.[33]

The second relationship identified by Baffoe was that established between South Africa and the three territories. As a consequence of their geographical and economic position, the three colonies were propelled into joining the South African Customs Union in 1910; sending large numbers of their laborers to work in the industrial and agricultural sectors of the South African economy; establishing a high level of dependence on trade with and through South Africa; and becoming involved in significant investment by South African capital and skilled manpower. South Africa's major intention was the "ultimate integration of the Territories into the Union of South Africa." [34] While the territories were never integrated into South Africa, prior to independence, all three territories were dependent on South Africa for over 80 percent of their domestic economic needs.

The Bechuanaland Protectorate

Prior to settler-colonial expansion and precolonial rule, Bechuanaland (Botswana) was a relatively self-sufficient country. "European penetration and the introduction of colonial economic structures brought profound changes to the traditional economy." [35] A series of attempts by the Afrikaner trekkers from the Transvaal to expand their territorial conquest into the Bechuana region resulted in requests by Cape Colony representatives and Bechuana chiefs for British protection. It was not, however, until Germany showed an interest in South West Africa that Britain became involved in the Afrikaner-Bechuana conflict. British interest was sparked by fear that a link would be established between German territory on the Atlantic and Afrikaner settlement in the interior.[36] In 1885, an area south of latitude 22, part of what is now Botswana, was declared a British protectorate (Bechuanaland Protectorate), while the area south of the Molopo and north of the Cape Colony was declared a British colony (British Bechuanaland). "The Bechuanaland Protectorate was thus established by the British, after much hesitation and reluctance, in order to guarantee the route to the north." By 1895, on the other hand, British Bechuanaland was incorporated into the Cape Colony.[37]

The Bechuanaland Protectorate was administered through indirect rule, and the British, who had declared in 1885 that they did not intend to invest much capital in the colony, informed the Tswana (the indigenous population) that they must incur the cost of British protection themselves. A series of taxes were imposed on the Tswana between 1899 and 1965. "The introduction of taxation had profound implications for the evolution of socio-economic structures and relationships in Botswana." Two institutions in particular were affected—the system of migrant labor and the distribution of cattle ownership.[38]

In order to pay the high taxes, many Bechuana men were forced to migrate to South Africa to work in the mines and on the farms. While initially the majority of workers came from the southern area of the country, by 1934, mining employers from South Africa, in collusion with the Bechuanaland and tribal authorities, began to recruit and coerce workers from the northern area. This policy was perpetuated in spite of the high death rate of miners from the southern region. "The Resident Commissioner at the time justified his position as follows: 'it will help the natives to get a little more money which they badly need, and will enable the Administration to get in a certain amount of additional hut tax, which they need no less badly.'" While at the turn of the century only a few hundred Batswana migrated to South Africa for employment, by the 1960s this number had increased to 50,000, representing a significant increase in the dependence of Bechuanaland on South Africa.[39]

The introduction of taxation also had an effect on the distribution of cattle ownership in Bechuanaland. Specifically, it served to increase the unequal distribution of ownership of the major source of wealth.[40] As Christopher Colclough and Stephen McCarthy note:

> The main economic change that occurred as a result of the years of British rule was that self-sufficiency of the Batswana was undermined . . . The Batswana received few of the benefits of 'modernizing' forces that can be

pointed to in other territories. Investment in Bechuanaland was minimal throughout the colonial period . . . the administration was not very active in improving the welfare of the African population.[41]

The Basutoland Protectorate

Basutoland (Lesotho) was declared a British territory in 1868 and placed under the control of the British high commissioner in 1884. As far back as 1843, however, Chief Moshoeshoe, the father of the Basuto nation, had requested British protection from Afrikaner domination.[42] By the time the British declared Basutoland a British territory, the Afrikaners had "systematically destroyed Basotho cultivation east of the Caledon. By a treaty of 1869 Lesotho finally lost the 'conquered territory' west of the Caledon to the Orange Free State, a loss which has remained a touchstone of political grievance ever since." [43]

In the 1870s, shortly after the British gained control, there was a brief economic "golden age." During this period there was rapid technical change, and the "Basotho flourished economically as peasant farmers and teamsters, exporting grain and other agricultural products, especially to the growing mining population at Kimberley." Numerous trading stores were in existence, and the economy became highly motivated and commercialized.[44] In fact, according to Neil Parsons and Robin Palmer:

> By the 1880s it appears that Lesotho needed to maximize the export of agricultural produce and of labour in order to finance the importation of subsistence and luxury items . . . upon which the Lesotho economy had become dependent . . . It was therefore in this period of prosperity up to 1900 that the seeds of later underdevelopment were sown. The rising market led to overcultivation, overgrazing, and habitual labour migration.[45]

Eventually, "the Basotho rapidly lost their effective comparative advantage in marketed agricultural products as a result of the action of white governments and the development of transport networks that largely by-passed them." By 1892, 30,000 Basotho were employed to work in the mines of South Africa and on Cape Colony railway construction.[46] During this early period the seeds were sown for Basutoland's dependency on South Africa for employment. Between 1921 and 1936 the proportion of Basotho migrating to South Africa increased from 8.7 to 15.3 percent of the population. Many of these workers never returned home, depleting the country of much needed brainpower and manpower. By 1960 an estimated 23.2 percent of Basutoland's working population was employed in South Africa.[47]

By the time Basutoland received her independence from the British, she had been incorporated into the capitalist world-economy as an underdeveloped peripheral country, economically dependent on South Africa. Peasant agricultural production had declined, and the country had become a labor reserve for South Africa.

The Swaziland Protectorate

By the time Swaziland was placed under the control of the British high commissioner during the early twentieth century, the British had expropriated two-thirds of the Swazi land on behalf of settler interests.[48] Like the indigenous populations of Bechuanaland and Basutoland, the Swazis had fought against Afrikaner encroachment, only to be defeated and placed under the control of a provisional government which consisted of representatives from Swaziland, Britain, and the Transvaal. Then in 1894 and until the Anglo-Boer War in 1899, Swaziland was under the control of the Transvaal. During the war, authority of the territory was given to the Swazi queen regent; following the war and until late 1906, it was administered by "a special commissioner under the British governor of the Transvaal . . . After that time Swaziland came under the British high commissioner at the Cape." [49]

Prior to European penetration, the economy of Swaziland was "traditional, subsistent, local and self-sufficient." [50] Swaziland's incorporation into the capitalist world-economy commenced in the nineteenth century with the gradual introduction of a money economy, characterized (in addition to land expropriation) by "the concomitant substitution of capitalist agricultural production over large areas of the country, the introduction of a rigorous taxation system, and the demands for cheap labor by settlers and South African mining interests." [51] The British, who reluctantly took control of Swaziland, had no interest in its development.

While Swaziland may have been self-sufficient in food production prior to the European invasions, following the 1896-1897 disasters of rinderpest, drought, and famine, the territory became a major importer of food. Although the 1920s "witnessed a resurgence in Swazi peasant production," [52] by 1934 the Swazis were producing only "20 percent of their basic food requirements." [53] In order to secure the necessary cash to buy food during this period, an average of 10,000 Swazis migrated to South Africa for employment each year.[54]

Swaziland's further incorporation into the capitalist world-economy is explicated by Jonathan Crush:

> The absorption of Swaziland into the capitalist orbit was made complete in the post War II period by the influx of foreign capital to exploit mineral and agricultural resources, and supplies of cheap Swazi labor. This was the direct result of the penetration of South African and British multi-national corporations . . . It is estimated that private investment alone in the period of post War II investment was of South African origin. The incipient enclave economy came to rely heavily upon South Africa for marketing, transport facilities, supplies of machinery, and technical expertise.[55]

These colonial links were to have serious implications for post-independence development in Swaziland.

The Former Portuguese Colonies — Angola, Mozambique

> Portugal's role in Africa is a study in contradiction. A small and underdeveloped country, Portugal maintains possession of African territories which dwarf it in size and natural resources, some ten years after the wave of independence that swept over British, French, and Belgian colonies . . . Portuguese propaganda proclaims a policy of non-racialism and even exalts miscegenation. But the oppression suffered by Africans in Portuguese Africa is comparable to that under South Africa's rigid and explicitly racist apartheid. The uniqueness of Portuguese capacities for colonization is trumpeted to the world. But the

economies of the "overseas provinces," and even of Portugal itself, depend heavily on foreign capital and enterprise. Perry Anderson sums up Portugal's rule with the term "ultracolonialism": at once the most primitive and the most extreme form of colonialism.[56]

Although the Portuguese first arrived in Angola and Mozambique during the fifteenth century, it was not until the nineteenth century that they penetrated into the interior of these countries, defeating the indigenous population and placing them under colonial rule. During the time the Portuguese remained along the coastline, they participated in the trading of material goods as well as slaves. It has been estimated that during the centuries of slave trading, the Congo-Angolan states alone lost more than seven million people, and in Mozambique the experience of the slave trade was only marginally less horrifying.[57]

Portugal's power over Angola and Mozambique was consolidated in the two decades preceding World War I, following its victory over armed African resistance.[58] This consolidation of power was deemed ironic in light of Portugal's status within the capitalist world-economy. With respect to this, William Minter notes: "On the one hand Portugal has not entered the modern world but remains economically dependent and politically rigid; on the other, it enlarged its empire in Africa at the same time as the more developed European powers." [59]

In fact, the "ultracolonialism" imposed on the indigenous populations of both Angola and Mozambique was a reflection of Portugal's insecure position within the capitalist world-economy. As an underdeveloped country itself, it had been in many respects a colony, mainly of Britain. According to John Saul, "from a very early point in the modern era, Portugal had developed a relationship with the rest of Europe whereby it supplied raw materials to advanced countries and imported manufactured goods." [60]

Portuguese colonial rule in Angola and Mozambique is most noted for its racial prejudice, its system of forced labor, its refusal to relinquish colonial control, its underdevelopment of the agricultural sector, and its close economic and military alliance with advanced capitalist nations.

While the Portuguese maintained that they practiced a policy of "multiracialism" within their colonies, this in fact was not the case. As far as the Portuguese were concerned, "multiracialism" meant the assimilation of the African into the Portuguese nation (i.e., the adoption of Portuguese culture and language).[61] By "1950, only half of one percent of the African population had become assimilados (about 30,000), while over 99 percent remained indigenous, or unassimilated, 'uncivilized' persons without political or civil rights."[62] Mozambique, for example, contained fewer than 5,000 assimilados.[63]

In addition to pursuing a policy of racial discrimination to maintain control, the Portuguese implemented a system of forced labor so extreme that it is said to be the major factor that distinguished Portuguese colonialism from all others. Even after the abolition of slavery, laws were introduced to maintain the master-slave relationship.[64] For example, a decree of 1899 declared that "all natives of Portuguese overseas provinces are subject to the obligation, moral and legal, of attempting to obtain through work the means that they lack to subsist and to better their social condition." [65]

Dispossessed of their land, Africans were forced to work on European plantations and in the mines. As far as the Portuguese were concerned, subsistence farming was not considered work, and because those who did engage in it were considered idle, they were committing a crime.[66]

In Angola, Africans were forced to work on the coffee, sisal, and cotton plantations and in the diamond mines, under a system of "contract labor." Workers who did not meet the expectations of their employers were punished with a wooden mallet.[67]

Even though the forced-labor system of Angola attracted more attention, in Mozambique, the system was more diversified.[68] African indentured and contract laborers worked "on road making, ports, and sanitation, and the agricultural estates in producing crops for the metropole." In addition, they worked in the mines of South Africa.[69]

Following the discovery of gold and diamonds, Africans from Mozambique became a major source of needed labor for the South African mines. A large percentage were recruited from southern Mozambique, robbing that area of males and thus encouraging Portuguese reliance on female and child labor.[70]

In 1901 the colonial government signed an agreement with the Witwatersrand Native Labor Association (WNLA) to recruit African labor. According to the agreement, the colonial government was to receive 13 shillings per worker, in addition to an extra sixpence for each month's service beyond the initial one-year contract period. The agreement also stipulated that half the workers' salaries would be paid directly to the colonial government in gold, at a fixed rate of exchange. Since the rate of exchange was appreciably below the market price, the Portuguese government resold the gold on the world market at a substantial profit.[71] "Throughout the colonial period, the recruitment tax, together with the sale of gold, was a major source of income and ensured Mozambique's continued economic dependence on South Africa." [72]

In return for supplying laborers for its mines, the South African government guaranteed that "47.5 percent of the seaborne import traffic to the Johannesburg area," would pass through Mozambique's Lourenço Marques port.[73]

With respect to the overall impact of the forced-labor system on Mozambique, James Mittleman notes:

> The system of forced labor set back the development of modern farming among Africans while productivity declined. In order to provide cheap materials for the textile mills in Portugal, the imperial authority assigned land to "native" farmers requiring them to plant cotton. Although Mozambique's soil and climate are not well suited for cotton growing, Africans had no choice other than to raise such cash crops. Meanwhile producers received officially fixed extraordinarily low prices.[74]

As a consequence of its colonial policies in Angola and Mozambique, Portugal was able to partially rectify her problem of trade deficits with advanced capitalist countries with the surplus balance of trade in these two territories. In addition to the capital accrued from the migrant labor system and the transportation agreements between Portugal and South Africa, the trade surplus was made possible as a result of forced agricultural specialization and foreign investment.

With respect to forced agricultural specialization, two phenomena were occurring. Dispossessed of their land, Africans were forced to produce agricultural crops suited to the needs of Portugal. The export of primary products was crucial. Angola thus became a major exporter of coffee to the world market, while Mozambique exported cashew nuts, sugar, tea, and sisal. In addition, both Angola and Mozambique grew cotton for Portugal's textile industry. The cotton was exported to Portugal, and the finished products were sold back to the colonies,[75] thus making the indigenous population a major purchaser of Portuguese goods.

Foreign investments were important to the development of the mineral sector. Diamonds, iron ore, and oil in Angola were made possible, for example, by international capital. "Even in the initial stages of Portuguese colonization, major enterprises were under foreign control. In Angola, the Benguela Railway and the Angola Diamond Company are under the control of British, South African, and Belgian financial interests . . . In Mozambique, Sena Sugar Estates, the largest producer of sugar in the country, is British owned." [76] As Saul notes:

> In agriculture, in mineral extraction, and in the light industrialization of the colonies, one soon saw busily at work a full range of corporations from Western countries, from Japan, and of course from Rhodesia and South Africa . . . Most ominous of all, perhaps, was the growing economic involvement of the United States, dramatically exemplified in the absolutely crucial role played by the Gulf Oil Company . . . Moreover, as Minter demonstrated, the involvement of American corporations stretched beyond Gulf to companies such as Bethlehem Steel, which was, at one point, developing concession rights within the battle areas of Mozambique.[77]

The Mozambique-South African connection that developed during this period was to be of particular significance in postindependence development. In addition to migrant labor and transportation agreements, South African capital was largely represented in the building of the Cahora Bassa Dam, the largest dam in Africa and the fourth largest in the world. Eventually, South Africa replaced Portugal as the major exporter to Mozambique, and on the African continent, Mozambique traded more with South Africa than with any other country.[78]

The resistance against Portuguese colonial rule that began during the fifteenth century never ceased. In 1961 in Angola, and in 1962 in Mozambique, the resistance assumed a new level that could not be stopped even with Portuguese military support from both NATO and the United States.[79] On June 25, 1975, Mozambique, under the leadership of the Front for the Liberation of Mozambique (FRELIMO), became an independent nation; and on November 11, 1975, under the leadership of the Movement for the Popular Liberation of Angola (MPLA), Angola became an independent nation.

The fight the indigenous populations of Angola and Mozambique waged against Portugal had been long and hard. It has been suggested that Portugal's refusal to grant independence to these countries earlier was related to her status as an underdeveloped country. Specifically, she feared that as a result of her position "in the imperial hierarchy," she was "a mere 'middleman' with respect to Angola and Mozambique;" a status that would not allow her to continue to dominate the countries after colonial rule in a neo-colonial manner.[80]

Prior to 1975, Angola and Mozambique had been incorporated into the capitalist world-economy under one of the worst forms of colonial rule. Portugal, as an underdeveloped country, maintained her control over her colonies through established links with advanced capitalist nations, and these links eventually became more important than Portugal's. Consequently, she began to play a marginal role in the economic structures of these countries. The new Mozambique government inherited an underdeveloped country heavily dependent upon South Africa economically; the new Angolan government inherited an underdeveloped country economically dependent upon several advanced capitalist nations. These dependent links were to have serious implications for post-independence development.

The Former Central African Federation
Southern Rhodesia, Northern Rhodesia, Nyasaland

European and white-settler control over the Southern African region was further consolidated in 1953 with the establishment of the Central African Federation (CAF), consisting of the British-ruled territories of Southern Rhodesia (Zimbabwe), Northern Rhodesia (Zambia), and Nyasaland (Malawi). While the CAF was not established until 1953, the idea of a federation was first proposed by Britain in the 1920s. The initial attempt to unite the three territories, however, never reached fruition because of opposition both from Africans and from Southern Rhodesia settlers. Opposition from the latter grew out of the concern that federation would decrease their power through an enlargement of British control; also, it would not be of benefit economically, since the resource base of the other two countries was desperately poor.[81]

As a result of the discovery of vast deposits of copper in Northern Rhodesia in the 1930s, however, the white settlers altered their position. Almost overnight, the economic potential of Northern Rhodesia was transformed, and the Southern Rhodesian settlers became eager to unite the territories. Simultaneously, the Northern Rhodesian settlers began to look at federation as a way to curtail colonial office control and prevent the British from preparing the protectorate for African rule.[82]

African opposition to the formation of a federation (the major opposition came from Northern Rhodesia and Nyasaland) grew out of fear of further "political, economic, and spatial expansion of the Southern Rhodesia settler colonial system." [83]

African opposition played a major role in the ultimate demise of CAF in 1963, and following its demise, rapid changes occurred. In 1964 Nyasaland became Malawi, an independent African-ruled nation, and Northern Rhodesia became Zambia, an independent African-ruled nation. And in 1965, Southern Rhodesia became an independent white-ruled settler colony. Another fourteen years would elapse before Rhodesia would become an independent African-ruled nation, for as Patrick O'Meara notes, "The demise of the federation ushered in the new era of white extremism in Rhodesia." [84]

Southern Rhodesia

The first plans to begin expansion into Southern Rhodesia were made by Cecil Rhodes in 1878.[85] However, it was not until 1890 that whites moved into Cecil Rhodes' "Pioneer Column." [86] This decision to move into the territory followed the Rudd mineral concession granted to Rhodes in 1888 by Lobengula, king of the Ndebele, one of the major ethnic groups in the area. This concession gave Rhodes a monopoly on mineral rights in Lobengula's kingdom. The presence of the settlers in Southern Rhodesia sparked great resistance from the indigenous African population, and there were major uprisings in 1893 and 1896-1897. But the Africans were defeated and left demoralized.[87]

Under the leadership of Rhodes, Southern Rhodesia was administered by the British South Africa Company (BSA) until 1923. The BSA had hoped to find large deposits of gold in Southern Rhodesia, similar to those recently discovered in South Africa. Disappointed, "the company tried to recoup its investment in the railways and other infrastructure by promoting white farming and other forms of mining." [88] In 1923 the power of the BSA was surrendered to a settler government, and Southern Rhodesia was formally annexed to the British Crown as a white-minority-ruled self-governing colony.[89]

Under BSA domination, patterns of land expropriation had begun in 1890. Specifically, African land was seized by the BSA and other white settlers, resulting in the removal of large numbers of Africans from their ancestral lands to less productive regions. Eventually a landless class of Africans was created, dependent upon selling their labor to white farms, mines, and ultimately industrial entrepreneurs, for their livelihood. The process of land expropriation reached its climax with the 1930 enactment by the Legislative Assembly of the Land Apportionment Act.[90]

Munhamu Utete identifies two distinguishable phases in the process of land expropriation up to 1930. The first phase (1890 to the eve of WWI) was that of conquest and expropriation, while the second phase was that of consolidation. With the Land Apportionment Act of 1930, 30.1 percent of the land was set aside for African use (Native Reserves and Native Purchase Areas); and 69.0 percent was set aside for white settler use.[91] The settlers in Southern Rhodesia (many of whom were from South Africa) thus commenced policies of land expropriation similar to those in South Africa. Southern Rhodesia's incorporation into the capitalist world-economy, as the second most advanced territory in the Southern African region, was facilitated through policies of racial separation that guaranteed the settlers a large supply of land and cheap African labor.

The issue of land expropriation was part of another phenomenon—the desire of the white settler to destroy the traditional system of peasant production. This was accomplished directly by eliminating peasant producers as competitors in the capitalist market, and indirectly by inducing Africans to work for the settlers. With respect to the first approach, policies were adopted that prevented peasants from obtaining a fair market value for their produce; decreased the amount of land available for African use; and identified African reserves in areas of limited agricultural potential, and distant from potential markets. Eventually, a government agricultural marketing monopoly was introduced, along with regulations that declared African agricultural production inferior to that of the settler farmers.[92]

The second approach that resulted in underdevelopment of peasant production concerned the introduction of certain measures to guarantee cheap African labor. Utete identifies four such methods of inducing Africans to work for the white settlers. The first method was the introduction of taxation policies. Such policies were first introduced by the British South Africa Company in 1884. Dispossessed of their land and a competitive position in the agricultural market, Africans were forced to become involved in cash employment in order to obtain money to pay the mandatory taxes.[93]

The second method was forced labor, whereby African chiefs and village headmen were compelled to contribute a specified number of able-bodied men to the local farming and mining enterprises of the settlers. The third method employed to induce Africans to work for settlers was the squatter system. The squatters were Africans whose land had been expropriated, but who were given the option to remain on the land as hands of the settler farmers. This policy was very similar to serfdom.[94]

The final method employed was migrant labor. As a consequence of the inability of the indigenous African population to fulfill all the labor needs of the settlers, workers were recruited from Nyasaland (Malawi) and Mozambique. In fact, in 1923, 65 percent of the African labor force in wage employment was made up of migrant laborers, and as late as 1962, such workers composed 42 percent of the total wage employment.[95] With respect to the effect of colonial policies, Utete notes:

> It seems clear that the overall effect of settler colonial policies and practices in the economic field was the creation of a structure contributing inevitably to the progressive impoverishment of the bulk of the African people. At the same time, as the obverse of this, the structure provided the foundation for a steadily and surely growing affluence for the white settler minority.[96]

The affluence of the white settler minority was further enhanced by foreign investors who "aimed primarily to develop a source of cheap raw materials." As Ann Seidman and Neva Makgetla note:

> Three major export sectors emerged by the 1920s—the foreign-owned, relatively large mines, and the mainly settler-controlled agriculture and small-scale mining. The settler producers depended on the British and South African companies that ran wholesale trade and finance. Much of the profit they reaped from Southern Rhodesia went to build up the South African economy.[97]

During WWII, economic expansion occurred in Southern Rhodesia largely as a result of the increase in the demand for raw materials.[98]

Separation of the races had become the established practice by 1965, when the Unilateral Declaration of Independence (UDI) was declared following the failure of the British and settlers to agree on the future direction of the territory. The British had announced that independence would only be granted to the settlers based on the NIBMAR principles—No Independence Before Majority African Rule.[99] Rejecting the British principles, the settlers declared Southern Rhodesia an independent nation. Although Britain immediately imposed sanctions on Rhodesia, the relationship between the two countries was not ruptured. The imposition of sanctions, did, however, further consolidate white settler control over the Southern African region as a consequence of the deepening South Africa-Southern Rhodesia connection, with South Africa becoming Southern Rhodesia's major trading partner.

While economic, political, and social ties had been developing between South Africa and Southern Rhodesia from the beginning of settler colonialism in Southern Rhodesia,[100] UDI and the imposition of sanctions by Britain and other nations resulted in a closer alliance between both South Africa and Portugal. According to Sam Nolutshungu:

> International sanctions imposed at the instance of the United Kingdom government made Rhodesia utterly dependent on South Africa and Portugal for goods and services that could be supplied within that colony. South African and Portuguese policies on Rhodesia converged, and the two powers found themselves in the common international position of providing Rhodesia with the means of evading – in the event, successful—the sanctions that were imposed upon it.[101]

Prior to UDI, Southern Rhodesia had been incorporated into the capitalist world-economy, with at least 80 percent of all capital investment of international origin, most of it from Britain. Capital from the United States and South Africa were also present in smaller amounts. The bulk of the capital was invested in mining, manufacturing, banking, insurance, and commercial agriculture.[102]

Post-UDI witnessed a deepening incorporation of Southern Rhodesia into the capitalist world-economy. British, American, and South African corporations increased their dominance over the mining sector,[103] and transnationals from the Federal Republic of Germany invested in Southern Rhodesia via their subsidiaries in South Africa.[104] Transnationals from other Western countries also adopted the strategy of investing via their South African subsidiaries.

Between 1965 and 1974, in spite of international sanctions, Southern Rhodesia's economy grew tremendously. The GDP rose by 36 percent, manufacturing as a percentage of the gross domestic product (GDP) increased from one-fifth to one-quarter, and the mining and agriculture sectors also made up one-quarter of the GDP.[105] Seidman and Makgetla identify three major contributing factors to the economic boom:

First, having declared UDI, the tiny white minority exercised its control of state power to duplicate the attractive climate for private investment found in its larger neighbor to the South. It systematized and expanded the exploitative, racist labor system. Simultaneously, it intervened directly to encourage domestic and transnational corporate investors, particularly to build up manufacturing.[106]

While UDI resulted in Southern Rhodesia's further development as an industrialized state, it also resulted in the further subjugation of the indigenous African population. In 1969 a new constitution was accepted which reinforced the concept of a segregated society and all but eliminated the possibility of majority rule. On March 1, 1970, the settlers declared Southern Rhodesia a republic, "claiming to end its '80-year link with the British Crown.'" "The Land Tenure Act of 1969 redivided Rhodesia into two parts: 45 million acres for Africans and 45 million for whites. By the end of 1966, tribal trust lands were 40,020,000 acres of a total Rhodesian area of 96,600,000 acres."[107]

Events in the Southern African region following the 1974 Portuguese Coup had an effect on the economic and political prosperity of the white settlers in Southern Rhodesia. Specifically, the independence of Angola and Mozambique in 1975 marked a major turning point in the history of Southern Africa, symbolizing the beginning of the end of white-minority-ruled governance. In Southern Rhodesia, the protracted war against settler colonial rule by the indigenous African population heightened. The war began to have a serious impact on the country: the GDP dropped; the unemployment level of Africans increased, forcing thousands to migrate to South Africa for employment; transnational corporations began to transfer their business to South Africa or remove invested capital overseas; and many whites began to flee the country.[108]

The imminent demise of the white settler regime became so evident that even South Africa participated in convincing the settlers to relinquish control over the territory. Eventually, the military-economic crisis confronted by the settlers resulted in independence, and in 1980, Zimbabwe became an independent nation. The leadership of the country was placed in the hands of the Zimbabwe African National Union (ZANU), with Robert

Mugabe as prime minister.

Northern Rhodesia

The consolidation of British control over Northern Rhodesia occurred in 1899 under the leadership of the British South Africa Company. In 1899 the company divided the territory into North-Eastern Rhodesia and North-Western Rhodesia, but by 1911 it had been united again as one territory. During this period, the territory became economically important as a source of labor for the mines of Katanga and Southern Africa. The status of the territory as a major source of labor for the surrounding areas was not altered until the 1920s, when large deposits of copper were discovered, intensifying Northern Rhodesia's interdependence with the rest of the world.[109]

Under company rule, taxation policies were introduced to guarantee the continued supply of labor for the mines. At the same time, however, the taxation policies were designed to maintain a stable rural base in African "native" life. While the company wanted African males to become involved in the cash economy in order to satisfy the demand for labor, they also wanted their involvement restricted to such a level that the rural economy would not be disrupted nor permanent urbanization encouraged.[110]

For the majority of Africans, the engagement in wage-labor outside Northern Rhodesia was the only way to obtain cash to pay taxes, since there were few opportunities to accrue cash within the territory. For example, where there did exist a demand for marketed foodstuffs, "the produce of white farmers was given preference." In addition, the local craft market was underdeveloped as a consequence of competition from mass-produced wares that became available with the development of the railway; and finally, there was a limited demand for African labor within Northern Rhodesia.[111]

In 1924 the administration of Northern Rhodesia was transferred from company control to Colonial Office control. Under the Colonial Office, efforts were made to make the territory a "white man's country." Blocks of the best land were subsequently set aside and made available for exclusive European use. A distinction was thus drawn between "Crown land" and "African reserves," the former being available for purchase and the latter unavailable for purchase.[112] This new land policy eventually resulted in underdevelopment of the subsistence farming sector.

The discovery of copper in the 1920s changed the position of the territory within the international division of labor. Instead of a major exporter of labor, the territory became a major exporter of copper. Major mining financiers, especially in South Africa and the United States, took a new interest in the territory, particularly given the fact that "the expansion of electrical and automobile industries during and after the First World War had greatly increased world demand for copper."[113]

In addition to transforming Northern Rhodesia's foreign trade, the discovery of vast deposits of copper served to increase employment opportunities, providing a new market for migrant labor. While overall the territory benefited economically from the development of the Copperbelt, the benefits to the inhabitants was spread unevenly, resulting in "vast differences between the material living standards of Europeans and Africans." As Andrew Roberts notes, "If the Copperbelt in general is contrasted with the rest of Northern Rhodesia, it appears throughout its history to have been an island of comparative plenty in a vast sea of rural poverty. Indeed, in some ways, this poverty was actually increased by the growth of the mining industry."[114]

The decision by the white settlers of Northern Rhodesia to join the white settlers of Southern Rhodesia, in an effort to safeguard their position in the region through federation, sparked the African population to become involved in a movement dedicated to overthrowing colonial rule.[115] On October 24, 1964, following the demise of the Central African Federation, Northern Rhodesia became an independent nation—Zambia. Kenneth Kaunda became head of state as well as chief executive, and the United National Independence Party (UNIP) became the ruling party. Zambia opted to become a republic within the British Commonwealth.[116] The new government of Zambia inherited from the British a country that was underdeveloped and dependent upon copper exports. It had an agricultural output dominated by white commercial farmers and infrastructural links and investments from South Africa and Southern Rhodesia. In addition, the country was characterized by racial, ethnic, regional, and class inequalities.[117]

The Nyasaland Protectorate

Even though the colonization of Nyasaland (Malawi) by European missionaries commenced in the 1870s, Nyasaland did not become a British protectorate until 1891. In 1894, prior to Nyasaland's incorporation into the capitalist world-economy as a major supplier of labor to South Africa and Southern Rhodesia, the indigenous African population was peaceful and industrious, and excellent at agriculture and metalworks. The transformation of the territory into a labor reservoir, however, was one of the major factors that contributed to the underdevelopment of the territory.[118] As in other British territories, this was accomplished through land expropriation and the introduction of taxation policies. In fact, taxation policies were imposed upon the indigenous population almost immediately after conquest.[119] These colonial policies resulted in the underdevelopment of the agricultural sector and the creation of a large migrant labor population.

The roots of the underdevelopment of agriculture date as far back as the 1880s, when the Europeans acquired African land, forcing the indigenous inhabitants to become labor tenants. In addition, the tenants could trade only with the new overlords. "Since the labor was demanded during the very season when Africans had to tend their fields, the self-sufficiency of the peasant economy was constantly eroded."[120] As Gus Liebenow notes:

> The coercive nature of taxation as well as the direct involvement of government in recruitment facilitated the flow of cheap labor for the European estates. One of the worst manifestations was the legal sanctioning of the thangata system, under which resident Malawians supplied virtually free labor to the estate owners in return for the "privilege" of cultivating what had once been their ancestral land. Not only were the tobacco, tea, and other crops produced on the European estates of little relevance to the food and other needs of Malawians, but Malawians were legally barred from cultivating coffee, flue-cured tobacco, and other crops which might put them in competition with Europeans.[121]

Compared to Southern and Northern Rhodesia, production for

export in Nyasaland was very limited.

Nyasaland, like most countries in the Southern African region that lacked the potential for industrial development, became a major source of labor for the surrounding countries. In 1903 the colonial government and the Witwatersrand Native Labor Association (WNLA) established an agreement that guaranteed the exportation of labor to the South African gold mines. Thus Nyasaland was deprived of much of its able-bodied manpower, both through exportation and death from mining accidents. According to H. M. Tapela, the major reason for stunted economic growth in Nyasaland was the territory's role as a labor reservoir.[122]

Colonial policies resulted in Nyasaland being incorporated into the capitalist world-economy as an underdeveloped territory and a labor reservoir for the South African mines. It was under these conditions that Nyasaland (Malawi) became an independent nation on July 6, 1964, under the leadership of Kamuzu Banda.

Former British Tanganyika

From 1888 until approximately 1917, Tanganyika was under German colonial rule. Following WWI, however, the Germans lost control of this territory, and in 1920 it was placed under British administrative control as a League of Nations mandated territory. And so it remained until 1946, when it became a "trusteeship territory" of the United Nations. In 1961, Tanganyika was granted independence as a sovereign nation. During the entire British colonial period, it was administered indirectly.[123]

By 1914, under German rule, a "balance had been achieved between plantation agriculture, white settlers, and small-scale African farmers." The main plantation crop had been sisal, which grew along the railways and depended on migrant labor for production. Most Africans were dependent on their wages as migrant laborers as well as returns from small-scale farming. Their involvement in the cash economy largely grew out of the demands imposed by taxation policies. As in other territories, migration had an adverse effect on the environment.[124]

Under British colonial control, many of the administrative policies adopted by the Germans remained unaltered. Perhaps most ironic was the fact that the British encouraged the retention of traditional small-scale farming by the indigenous population and discouraged large-scale white settler farming. In fact, policies adopted by the British were hostile to land alienation. Specifically, in 1921, the colonial government declared Tanganyika "'primarily a black man's country' and a law was soon introduced to protect African customary tenure."[125]

According to Susanne Mueller, the colonial policies adopted by the British:

> acted to retard capitalist development by discouraging primitive accumulation, promoting small-holder agriculture, and by embarking on a series of decisions which made the emergence of an industrial capitalist state after independence unlikely.[126]

The status of Tanganyika as a League of Nations mandated territory was a problem for Britain. In fact, during WWII, the British feared that Germany would regain control over the territory. Notwithstanding this concern, as administrators of a mandated territory, not only did the British not have full control, but they were required to implement policies that would "protect the local population by prohibiting the separation of land and labour." Also, the mandate inhibited private investment. Thus capital accumulation and European settlement were discouraged.[127]

Industrial development was eliminated, largely as a consequence of the proximity and greater attractiveness of Kenya. In fact, Kenya's industrial base was already established by the late 1930s, and it was protected by the East African Common Market. During the mid-1920s Tanganyika had become a member of the common market, whose "common customs and transport policies operated as protectionist devices, which turned Tanganyika into a dumping ground for Kenyan goods. Most of Tanganyika's trade went through Kenya's ports and by the nineteen thirties she had an unfavorable balance of trade within the common market that continued after independence."[128]

During the colonial period, in addition to becoming a major exporter of sisal, other primary products such as cotton, coffee, and rubber were exported. According to Andrew Coulson, following WWII, the British continued to implement the policies that had been implemented previously—namely, "conscription to supply sisal estate labour as necessary; guaranteed prices and other inducements to encourage settlers; the use of force to direct African peasant production; and state farming in the form of the Groundnuts Scheme."[129]

Even though the stated British policy was the maintenance of traditional agricultural policies, this policy was not implemented. In fact, from the mid-1930s, force was used to make small farmers change their agricultural techniques. Through the amended Native Authorities Ordinance, by-laws were passed for the enforcement of soil-conservation measures and other agricultural practices, and post-WWII legislation gave the government control over the production and marketing of virtually every crop.[130] As Mueller notes:

> The policy of promoting smallholder production while discouraging primitive accumulation by either Europeans or Africans was full of other contradictions. These contradictions eventually destroyed "traditional" agriculture without transforming it.[131]

In 1961, the Tanganyika African National Union (TANU), under the leadership of Julius Nyerere, inherited from the British a country dependent upon the export of a select group of primary products and the importing of basic manufactured products. While the traditional land tenure policy for the most part had been retained under colonial rule, the traditional agricultural sector had been destroyed. The "nondevelopment" strategy pursued by the British was to have serious implications for post-independence governance.

NOTES

1. See Bernard Magubane, *The Political Economy of Race and Class in South Africa* (New York: Monthly Review Press, 1979); Martin Legassick, "Gold, Agriculture, and Secondary Industry in South Africa, 1885 – 1970: From Periphery to Sub-Metropole as a Forced Labour System," The *Roots of Rural Poverty in Central and Southern Africa*, ed. Robin Palmer and Neil Parsons (Berkeley: University of California Press, 1977), pp. 175-200.

2. Magubane, *Race and Class*, p. 20.

3. Khoikhoi and San are the appropriate names for these two groups of people. When the Europeans arrived, they referred to the Khoikhoi as Hottentots and to the San as Bushmen. These names reflected the derogatory nature in which the settlers referred to these groups. Many South African scholars today use the appropriate names—Khoikhoi and San.

4. Magubane, *Race and Class*, p. 23.

5. *Ibid.*, p. 24.

6. Martin Legassick, "South Africa: Capital Accumulation and Violence," *Economy and Society*, Vol. 3, 1974, pp. 257-58.

7. *Ibid.*, p. 258.

8. Legassick, "Gold, Agriculture," p. 177.

9. Magubane, *Race and Class*, p. 102.

10. Legassick, "South Africa," p. 260.

11. *Ibid.*, p. 262.

12. Magubane, *Race and Class*, pp. 196-97.

13. *Ibid.*, p. 197.

14. *Ibid.*, p. 43.

15. *Ibid.*

16. Legassick, "South Africa," p. 260.

17. Bethuel Setai, *The Political Economy of South Africa* (Washington, D.C.: University Press of America, 1977), p. 38.

18. Legassick, "South Africa," p. 260.

19. Setai, *Political Economy*, pp. 107-8.

20. Legassick, "Gold, Agriculture," p. 186.

21. Magubane, *Race and Class*, p. 71.

22. *Ibid.*, pp. 81-82.

23. Legassick, "Gold, Agriculture," pp. 183-84.

24. Ann Seidman and Neva Makgetla, *Outposts of Monopoly Capitalism* (Westport, Conn.: Lawrence Hill & Co., 1980), pp. 4-5.

25. *Ibid.*, p. 8.

26. *Ibid.*, p. 57.

27. Andre Gunder Frank, *Crisis in the Third World* (New York: Holmes & Meier Publishers, 1981), p. 56.

28. Magubane, *Race and Class*, p. 195.

29. Margaret Lee, "The Historical Development of the South African Bantustans: Their Domestic and International Implications" (Master's thesis, University of Pittsburgh, 1980), p. 54.

30. Magubane, *Race and Class*, p. 96.

31. Richard P. Stevens, "The History of the Anglo-South African Conflict Over the Proposed Incorporation of the High Commission Territories," *Southern Africa in Perspective: Essays in Regional Politics*, ed. Christian P. Potholm and Richard Dale (New York: The Free Press, 1972), p. 99.

32. *Ibid.*

33. Frank Baffoe, "Some Aspects of the Political Economy of Cooperation and Integration in Southern Africa: The Case of South Africa and the Countries Botswana, Lesotho, and Swaziland," *Journal of Southern African Affairs*, Vol. 3, 1978, p. 332.

34. *Ibid.*, p. 333.

35. Christopher Colclough and Stephen McCarthy, *The Political Economy of Botswana: A Study of Growth and Distribution* (London: University of Oxford Press, 1980), pp. 8-9.

36. Stevens, "History," p. 98.

37. Colclough and McCarthy, *Botswana*, pp. 12-13.

38. *Ibid.*, pp. 19-20.

39. *Ibid.*, p. 21.

40. *Ibid.*, p. 22.

41. *Ibid.*, pp. 32-33.

42. Stevens, "History," p. 98.

43. Palmer and Parsons, *Roots*, p. 21.

44. James Cobbe, "The Changing Nature of Dependence: Economic Problems in Lesotho," *Journal of Modern African Studies*, Vol. 21, No. 2, 1983, p. 294.

45. Palmer and Parsons, *Roots*, p. 22.

46. Cobbe, "Changing Nature," p. 294.

47. Palmer and Parsons, *Roots*, pp. 24, 27.

48. Jonathan Crush, "The Parameters of Dependence in Southern Africa: A Case Study of Swaziland," *Journal of Southern African Affairs*, Vol. IV, No. 1, 1979, p. 55.

49. Stevens, "History," p. 99.

50. Crush, "Swaziland," p. 55.

51. *Ibid.*

52. Palmer and Parsons, *Roots*, pp. 17-18.

53. Crush, "Swaziland," p. 56.

54. Palmer and Parsons, *Roots*, p. 18.

55. Crush, "Swaziland," p. 56.

56. William Minter, *Portuguese Africa and the West* (New York: Monthly Review Press, 1972), p. 13.

57. John S. Saul, *The State and Revolution in Eastern Africa* (New York: Monthly Review Press, 1979), p. 13.

58. Minter, *Portuguese*, p. 16.

59. *Ibid.*, p. 17.

60. Saul, *State*, p. 26.

61. Minter, *Portuguese*, p. 20.

62. John Marcum, "Angola: Perilous Transition to Independence," *Southern Africa: The Continuing Crisis*, ed. Gwendolen M. Carter and Patrick O'Meara (Bloomington: Indiana University Press, 1979), p. 177.

63. Minter, *Portuguese*, p. 20.

64. *Ibid.*, p. 24

65. *Ibid.*, p. 23.

66. *Ibid.*, pp. 23-24.

67. Marcum, "Angola," p. 178.

68. Minter, *Portuguese*, p. 23.

69. James Mittleman, "Mozambique: The Political Economy of Underdevelopment," *Journal of Southern African Affairs*, Vol. III, No. 1, 1978, pp. 35-36.

70. *Ibid.*, p. 36.

71. Allen Issacman and Barbara Issacman, *Mozambique: From Colonialism to Revolution, 1900–1982* (Boulder, Colo.: Westview Press, 1983), p. 35.

72. *Ibid.*

73. Minter, *Portuguese*, p. 24.

74. Mittleman, "Mozambique," p. 36.

75. *Ibid.*, pp. 31-32.

76. *Ibid.*, p. 32.

77. Saul, *State*, p. 36.

78. Mittleman, "Mozambique," pp. 37, 42.

79. See Minter, *Portuguese*, ch. 5.

80. Saul, *State*, pp. 33-35.

81. Munhamu Botsio Utete, *The Road to Zimbabwe: The Political Economy of Settler Colonialism, National Liberation and Foreign Intervention* (Washington, D.C.: University Press of America, 1979), p. 52.

82. *Ibid.*, p. 52.

83. *Ibid.*, p. 54.

84. Patrick O'Meara, "Rhodesia/Zimbabwe: Guerrilla Warfare or Political Settlement?" *Southern Africa*, ed. Carter and O'Meara, p. 27.

85. *Ibid.*, p. 20.

86. Colin Stoneman, ed., *Zimbabwe's Inheritance* (New York: St. Martin's Press, 1981), p. 2.

87. O'Meara, "Rhodesia," p. 20.

88. Stoneman, *Inheritance*, p. 3.

89. O'Meara, "Rhodesia," p. 21.

90. Utete, *Road to Zimbabwe*, p. 12.

91. *Ibid.*, pp. 12, 15.

92. *Ibid.*, p. 17.

93. *Ibid.*, pp. 18-19.

94. *Ibid.*, p. 19.

95. *Ibid.*, pp. 19-20.

96. *Ibid.*, p. 21.

97. Seidman and Makgetla, *Outposts*, p. 259.

98. *Ibid.*, p. 261.

99. O'Meara, "Rhodesia," p. 27.

100. See John Sprack, *Rhodesia: South Africa's Sixth Province* (London: International Defence and Aid Fund), 1974.

101. Sam C. Nolutshungu, *South Africa in Africa: A Study in Ideology and Foreign Policy* (New York: Africana Publishing Co., 1975), p. 174.

102. Utete, *Road to Zimbabwe*, pp. 79-80.

103. *Ibid.*, p. 23.

104. Seidman and Makgetla, *Outposts*, p. 27.

105. *Ibid.*, pp. 261-62.

106. *Ibid.*, p. 262.

107. O'Meara, "Rhodesia," p. 28.

108. Seidman and Makgetla, *Outposts*, pp. 286-90.

109. Andrew Roberts, *A History of Zambia* (New York: Africana Publishing Co., 1976), pp. 174-75, 185-94.

110. Philip Daniel, *Africanisation, Nationalism and Inequality: Mining, Labour and the Copperbelt in Zambian Development*

(Cambridge: Cambridge University Press, 1979), p. 63.

111. Roberts, *Zambia*, p. 177.

112. *Ibid.*, p. 182-83.

113. *Ibid.*, p. 185.

114. *Ibid.*, pp. 186, 190.

115. *Ibid.*, p. 196.

116. *Ibid.*, p. 222.

117. Timothy M. Shaw, "Zambia: Dependence and Underdevelopment," *Canadian Journal of African Studies*, Vol. X, No. 1, 1976, p. 11.

118. H. M. Tapela, "Labor Migration in Southern Africa and the Origins of Underdevelopment in Nyasaland, 1891-1903," *Journal of Southern African Affairs*, Vol. IV, No. 1, 1979, pp. 68-70.

119. *Ibid.*, p. 71.

120. *Ibid.*

121. Gus Liebenow, "Malawi's Search for Food Self-Sufficiency. Part I: Resource Endowment and Development Constraints" (UFSI Reports, 1982), pp. 4-5.

122. Tapela, "Nyasaland," pp. 74-75, 77.

123. Andrew Coulson, *Tanzania: A Political Economy* (Oxford: Clarendon Press, 1982), pp. 44-45.

124. *Ibid.*, p. 43

125. Susanne D. Mueller, "The Historical Origins of Tanzania's Ruling Class," *Canadian Journal of African Studies*, Vol. 15, No. 3, 1981, p. 468.

126. *Ibid.*, p. 464.

127. *Ibid.*, pp. 466-67.

128. *Ibid.*, pp. 471-72.

129. Coulson, *Tanzania*, p. 50.

130. *Ibid.*, p. 52.

131. Mueller, "Historical Origins," pp. 475-76.

CHAPTER 3

The Political Economy of Southern Africa: Post-independence

The incorporation of the SADCC member states into the capitalist world-economy as peripheral nations during colonial rule has had serious implications for post-independence development. These nations have remained economically dependent upon South Africa and other advanced capitalist nations to supply a large percentage of their internal needs. As a consequence of their relegated status in the capitalist world-economy, they have continued to be major exporters of primary goods and importers of manufactured products.

In addition to maintaining the economic structural links of dependency established during colonial rule, the SADCC countries have found it difficult to alter the internal patterns of underdevelopment begun during that period. Such underdevelopment was fostered by, for example, the destruction of the subsistence agricultural sector, land expropriation, and the introduction of forced labor and taxation. The degree of underdevelopment that presently exists in these nations is evident in the inability of the governments to provide for the basic needs of the majority of their populations.

In this chapter the current level of dependency and underdevelopment within the SADCC states will be explored. It is precisely because of that dependency and underdevelopment that SADCC was formed. Therefore, in order to assess SADCC's potential for fostering regional structural transformation, an in-depth analysis must be undertaken of these structures. The first part therefore explores the issue of external dependency; the second part, the question of internal distortions, or underdevelopment. In order to provide the reader with current information about the economic status of the SADCC countries, a part entitled "1987/88 Update" has been added to this chapter.

EXTERNAL DEPENDENCY

The extent of the SADCC member states' economic dependence both on South Africa and on the advanced capitalist nations will be examined by exploring the issues of external trade, private direct investment, foreign economic assistance, and the servicing of foreign debt.

External Trade

Dependency theorists generally agree that foreign trade, especially trade highly concentrated by export commodity and trading partner and characterized by the exchange of exports at low levels of processing for imports at higher levels, is one of the most important mechanisms of external dependence. One contention is that trade relations of this sort tend to offer LDCs [least developed countries] ever less value for their exports relative to the prices they must pay for goods they import, an assertion based on the familiar structuralist argument that world trade, at least since the 1950s, had been marked by a secular tendency for the prices of primary products to decline relative to those of manufactured goods.[1]

Since the SADCC states remain exporters of low-priced primary products and importers of high-priced manufactured products, trade deficits are consistently recorded as Table I indicates. In some countries, however, trade surpluses are recorded, which on the surface indicate a positive and healthy economic growth. With the exception of Botswana, however, these surpluses are not indicative of such growth, as the current account balance (Table 5) reveals in the section on servicing of foreign debt.

As exporters of low-priced primary products and importers of high-priced manufactured products, the SADCC states continue to remain in a subordinate position in relationship to South Africa and the advanced capitalist nations. The SADCC strategy of regional cooperation and development aims to alter this structural linkage, in general, by enhancing the region's development potential, but more specifically, by increasing intra-regional trade among its members. However, in the *Annual Progress Report*,

July 1986 – August 1987, the SADCC Secretariat reported:

> The SADCC member states . . . face deteriorating terms of trade. The prices of primary products have declined by 1% between 1985 and 1986, while the price of manufactured goods rose by 18%. The prices of manufactures are expected to increase by 11%, while the non-oil-commodity prices are expected to decline by 5% during 1987. [2]

Botswana, Lesotho, and Swaziland

The economies of Botswana, Lesotho, and Swaziland are strongly oriented toward external trade with South Africa, an orientation that dates back to the 1910 formation of the South African Customs Union (SACU). Botswana, for example, imports 76 percent of its goods from South Africa. This figure, however, represents a recent decrease from 86 percent, as a result of the government implementation of a policy to buy more from other countries, especially European.[3] Botswana is a major exporter of diamonds, copper/nickel matte, meat and meat products, and textiles, only 17 percent of which are exported to the Common Customs Area (mainly to South Africa). Botswana's overall trade deficit (see Table 1) until 1985 reflected the fluctuations in the world market price for her major exports—diamonds and meat. Thus, for example, in 1981 the trade (visible) deficit increased because the value of diamond sales fell by P100m, while imports continued to rise.[4] However, in 1985 there was an increase in diamond revenues of almost P57m over 1984, as a result of an increase in the world market price,[5] and by 1986 the trade balance was a record P324.3m surplus.

For Lesotho, at least 90 percent of the external trade (imports and exports) is with South Africa. The country's "large and growing deficit on visible trade is balanced by growing inflows of funds from migrant labour remittances, aid inflows and in recent years private capital flows." [6] Lesotho's major exports are wood and mohair.

At least 90 percent of Swaziland's imports come from South Africa, although only approximately 20 percent of her exports go to that country. The United Kingdom and the EEC countries receive a large percentage of primary products such as sugar, wood pulp, chemicals, iron ore, asbestos, citrus, canned fruit, meat, coal, and fertilizer.[7] Swaziland's growing trade deficit (see Table 1) is an indication of her dependence on the importation of high-cost manufactured and other products (i.e., oil from South Africa).

Angola and Mozambique

Angola's foreign trade surplus reflects large amounts of revenue accumulated from the export of oil. "In 1985, crude oil, refined products and natural gas accounted for approximately 95 percent of total exports." Diamonds and coffee accounted for the remaining 5 percent. Major imports include food, military equipment, consumer goods, agricultural inputs, and equipment for the oil industry. The majority of these items are imported from Portugal, the United States, France, and Brazil. The majority of Angola's export goods go to the United States. Other significant trading partners for exports include the United Kingdom, Brazil, France, and Spain.[8]

Mozambique's large foreign trade deficit is a reflection of the decline in the total value of her exports. For example, by 1985 the total value had declined to less than a third of the 1981 level. Mozambique's principal export products—cashewnuts, sugar, and cotton—have been particularly hard hit. Prawns, however, have not been as adversely affected.[9] Other exports include tea, timber, coal, cement, and petroleum products. The largest percentage of Mozambique's exports go to East Germany. Other significant trading partners for exported goods include Portugal, the United Kingdom, and the Netherlands. Mozambique's main imports include consumer goods, raw materials, spare parts, and equipment. Major trading partners for imported goods are East Germany, South Africa, Portugal, and France.[10]

While for more than three decades Mozambique's exports have generally amounted to about half of her imports, the deficit usually has been made up from invisible exports. Such invisibles include port and railway charges on international traffic, transfers, deferred payments from migrant workers, and profit from tourist trade. Although from 1956 to 1973 these invisible exports did not compensate for the adverse balance of trade, there usually was only a small deficit each year. However, since independence and the earnings from these sources has declined, the balance of payments has increased alarmingly (see Table 1). The decline in the earnings from port services and remittances from migrant labor have had particularly adverse effects on the trade balance. The decrease in port services is a result of the effect of internal destabilization by the antigovernment insurgency group, Mozambique National Resistance (MNR), and South Africa's policy of undercutting Mozambican traffic. With respect to remittances from migrant labor, South Africa's decision to cut back the number of Mozambicans recruited to work in the mines, as well as ending its "gold premium" payment, has resulted in a decrease in earning from this source.[11]

Malawi, Zambia, and Zimbabwe

Malawi's trade deficit is indicative of the country's dependence on the importation of manufactured goods, low production levels, and the world market condition for exported commodities. Recently, the swings in export earnings have been exaggerated by transport problems caused by MNR destabilization. Major imported commodities include consumer goods, plant and equipment, transport means, building materials, and industrial inputs. The majority of these goods are imported from South Africa (48 percent in 1985) and the United Kingdom. Other import partners include Japan, Zimbabwe, France, and the United States. Malawi's major commodities for export are tobacco, tea, sugar, and maize. The country's major trading partner for exports is the United Kingdom. Other partners include West Germany, the United States, South Africa, the Netherlands, and Zimbabwe.[12]

The majority of Zambia's foreign trade earnings accrue from one commodity—copper. Fluctuations in the world price for copper have a tremendous impact on Zambia's trade balance (see Table 1). The majority of Zambia's exports go to Japan, China, West Germany, and the United Kingdom. Zambia's major imports include machinery, transport equipment, manufactures classified by material, foodstuffs, electricity, mineral fuels, chemicals, and miscellaneous manufactured articles. South Africa provides approximately 11.8 percent of imported goods, while approximately 21.4 percent come from the United States. Other trading partners for imported commodities include the United Kingdom and West Germany.[13]

In 1980, when Zimbabwe trade figures were published for the first time, they indicated that a positive trade balance had been maintained during UDI by restricting imports. The first deficit, however, occurred in 1981, and was followed in 1982 by a larger deficit. The current trade surplus is largely a reflection of an extremely low level of import allocations. Imported goods include petroleum products, chemicals, machinery, manufactured goods, and transport equipment. A large percentage of imported items come from South Africa and the United Kingdom. However, while in 1981 Zimbabwe imported 27.4 percent of its goods from South Africa, by 1985 this figure had declined to 18.9 percent. Other significant trading partners for imports include the United States, West Germany, Japan, and France. Zimbabwe exports a variety of agricultural, mineral, and manufactured products. Major trading partners for these commodities include South Africa, the United Kingdom, West Germany, and the United States.[14]

Tanzania

Tanzania's growing trade deficit is largely a consequence of the decline in the world market price for coffee. In 1976 and the first half of 1977, for example, there was an improvement in coffee prices, and this, along with careful import controls, resulted in a decrease in the trade deficit. The subsequent decline in coffee prices and rise in oil prices once again caused the trade deficit to increase (see Table 1). Although import controls have been stringent since 1979, the country's terms of trade continue to deteriorate significantly.[15] While the value of imports increased by 12 percent in 1985, export earnings fell by 22 percent. In 1986, although Tanzania's trade balance deficit was $669 million, this did represent a decrease from the 1985 deficit of $713 million.[16]

A large percentage of Tanzania's exports (mainly coffee and cotton) go to West Germany, the United Kingdom, Indonesia, and Singapore. Imported items (machinery and equipment, mineral fuels, manufactured goods, chemicals, food) come mainly from the United Kingdom, Japan, Italy, West Germany, and Iran.[17]

TABLE 1

SADCC Member States
FOREIGN TRADE BALANCE

	Botswana Pm	Lesotho Mm	Swaziland Em	Angola Kzm*	Mozambique MTm
1971	-28.6	—	7.3	—	—
1972	-33.4	—	8.5	—	—
1973	-31.0	-59.4	4.7	—	—
1974	-43.4	—	31.8	—	—
1975	-54.3	-107.8	-2.8	—	—
1976	-28.0	-164.9	-7.9	356.5	—
1977	-80.0	-189.0	-37.9	98.5	-5,898
1978	-114.0	-211.0	-99.9	164.7	-11,854
1979	-71.0	-265.7	-170.7	144.7	-10,265
1980	-147.0	-315.5	-199.6	353.6	-16,825
1981	-332.0	-407.0	-179.1	104.6	-18,392
1982	-236.0	-528.0	-194.0	11,021.0	-22,918
1983	-109.0	-602.0	-270.0	17,785.0	-20,285
1984	-42.0	-685.0	-260.0	20,850.0	-18,843
1985	304.7	-780.0	-318.0	17,753.0	-14,98
1986	324.3	-759.0	-238.0	6,482.0	—

* The original currency of Angola was the Kw. It has, however, been declared nonconvertible in the international market by the Angolan government. The figures in the the table for 1976 to 1981 are therefore in Kw, while the remaining figures are in Angola's current currency, the Kz.

TABLE 1 continued on next page

	Malawi MKm	Zambia ZKm	Zimbabwe Z$m	Tanzania TShm
1966	—	247.3	—	421.0
1967	—	163.7	—	332.0
1968	-18.1	219.2	—	94.0
1969	-17.5	454.7	—	270.0
1970	-21.8	374.3	—	-234.0
1971	-18.5	85.9	—	-579.0
1972	-25.8	137.9	—	—
1973	-34.7	395.1	—	-729.0
1974	-56.7	398.5	—	-2,314.0
1975	-97.0	-76.7	—	-2,699.0
1976	-40.0	—	—	-828.0
1977	-29.5	87.0	—	-1,697.0
1978	-122.1	96.0	—	-5,129.0
1979	-143.1	652.0	151.4	-4,977.0
1980	-126.2	-29.0	99.8	-6,116.0
1981	-69.5	-172.0	-46.0	-5,033.0
1982	-69.9	-166.0	-113.4	-6,355.0
1983	-93.1	-240.0	88.6	-4,739.0
1984	64.7	-98.0	252.3	-7,195.0
1985	-628.0	542.0	349.0	-13,002.0
1986	-27.1	-192.0	636.0 *	—

* January – October

Sources: QER of Southern Africa, 1977, 1978 • QER of Namibia, Botswana, Lesotho, Swaziland, 1982, 1983 • QER of Angola, Guinea-Bissau, Cape Verde Islands, Sao Tome and Principle, 1983 • QER of Tanzania, Mozambique, 1983 • QER of Rhodesia, Malawi, 1974, 1979 • QER of Zimbabwe, Malawi, 1983 • QER of Tanzania, Zambia, 1971, 1977 • QER of Zambia, 1983, 1985 • Country Profile: Malawi, 1986-87 • QER of Zimbabwe, Malawi, 1983 • Country Report: Zimbabwe, Malawi, 1986 • Country Profile: Zimbabwe, 1986-87, 1986 • QER of Tanzania, Zambia, 1971 • QER of Tanzania, Mozambique, 1983 • Country Profile: Botswana, Lesotho, Swaziland, 1987-88, 1987 • Country Profile: Malawi, 1987-88, 1987 • Country Profile: Zambia, 1987-88, 1987 • Country Profile: Tanzania, 1987-88, 1987 • Country Profile: Mozambique, 1987-88, 1987 • Country Profile: Angola, Sao Tome & Principle, 1987-88, 1987

Private Direct Investment

During colonial rule in the Southern African region, the replacement of the precapitalist mode of production with the capitalist mode required capital investment from corporations located in advanced capitalist nations. The sectors of the economies of the SADCC states that were highly developed and export-oriented, such as the mining, secondary industrial, and settler-controlled agricultural, usually were dominated by foreign capital. This pattern of foreign penetration and dominance still exists today. In fact, the penetration has become more pervasive and extends to all segments of society. This includes education, religion, culture, even the thought processes of the people. The extent specifically of private direct investment, however, is difficult to ascertain.

Arguments within the dependency school vary with respect to the impact of private direct investment on the economic, political, and social structures of Third World countries. Vincent Mahler identifies four important arguments:

> A first argument is that foreign investment in LDCs, far from serving as a conduit for the transmission of capital from developed to underdeveloped countries, actually results in a net drain of capital from host to investor . . . A second line of argument is that the emergence of the multinational corporation as an important international actor has fostered the development of an integrated global hierarchy in which executive decision making and advanced technology are largely confined to a "center" based in the industrial nations, with "co-opted" LDC nonelites largely excluded from influence . . . A third argument is that foreign investors play an important and negative role in conditioning internal political structures and policies in LDCs . . . A fourth argument is that domestic investment patterns in LDCs tend to be distorted by large-scale foreign investment patterns.[18]

Although direct private development in the SADCC states has contributed in some degree to development, it has resulted in these nations' further dependency either on South Africa or on the Western advanced capitalist nations. Since for the most part the government does not control such investment, it has proved to be counterproductive to economic liberation. In fact, one of the strategies pursued by the global center in an effort to maintain its hegemonic control over the global periphery is the domination of the major export industries of these countries.

In an effort to alter this pattern of economic dominance, SADCC, at its Annual Consultative Conference in 1987, instituted a program titled Investment in Production (see chapter 4). One of the major objectives of this program is to encourage more local business personnel to invest in the SADCC member states. At the same time, however, SADCC invited others external to the region to invest as well. As this section indicates, however, the economies of these states are largely dominated and therefore controlled by foreign capital.

Botswana, Lesotho, and Swaziland

South African corporations are the largest investors in these three countries. In Botswana, the majority of private direct investment is in the mining sector. The Anglo-American Corporation (AAC), through its subsidiary De Beers Botswana (Pty) Ltd. (Debswana), mines the diamonds in Botswana. In addition, the international marketing organization for diamonds, the Central Selling Organization (CSO), is controlled by De Beers. Although Debswana is jointly owned by the Botswana government and De Beers, De Beers' position in the industry is formidable.[19] During 1979, Mabrodian MV, a Belgian company, received permission to build a small diamond cutting and polishing factory; in 1980, its subsidiary, Diamond Manufacturing (Pty) Ltd., was given a diamond cutting license.[20] The significance of the dominance of South African capital in the mining industry, in terms of capital accumulation, is evidenced by the fact that in 1984, diamonds accounted for 72 percent of the country's exports, up 23 percent over 1983.[21]

In addition to controlling the diamond mines, Anglo-American, along with American Metal Climax (Amax), controls the copper-nickel mine at Selebi-Phikwe;[22] coal production is controlled by an Anglo-American subsidiary, Morupule Colliery.[23] South Africa's presence is also formidable in the meat industry, in construction, freight and forwarding, wholesale and retail, hotels, banking, and insurance. The United Kingdom has investments in construction, wholesale and retail, hotels, banking, and insurance.[24]

South African capital is present throughout all sectors of Lesotho. This includes control over Lesotho's two major natural assets—diamonds and water. The diamond mine, which closed in 1982, was controlled by the Anglo-American subsidiary, De Beers Lesotho Mining Company (Pty) Ltd.; the hydroelectric potential of Lesotho's rivers is being developed with the assistance of South African capital. Specifically, an agreement was reached between the two governments in 1983 for the development of the Highlands Water Project.[25] When completed, Lesotho will sell water to South Africa.

The major export commodity in Swaziland is sugar, grown on a large scale by 25 companies and 263 small holders. This conglomerate is under the British-owned Commonwealth Development Corporation (CDC) Vuvuland Irrigated Farms Scheme. Lonrho (British), through its subsidiary, Swaziland Sugar Milling Company, and the Mhlume (Swaziland) Sugar Co., owns two mills—Big Bend and Tsaneni. A third mill, Simuyne, is owned by Royal Swaziland Sugar Corporation. With respect to the latter mill, the Swaziland government and the Tibiyo Taka Ngwane Fund each hold 32 percent of the share capital. Other investors include the Nigerian government, Mitsui, Coca-Cola Export Corporation, and British Tate and Lyle (the manager of the operation).[26]

The production of wood pulp, another major commodity, also is dominated by foreign capital. The largest pulp plantation, Usutu, is British, jointly owned by CDC and Courtaulds. The third largest plantation, Shiseleweni, is also British, owned by CDC. The second largest plant, Peak Timbers, is owned by Mondi (Anglo-American); in 1984, Uniply (Barlow Rand) purchased the fourth largest, Swaziland Plantation. Other foreign capital (British, Danish, and South African) is present in the citrus fruit industry.[27]

South Africa dominates the mining industry in Swaziland. This includes control over the mining of asbestos and coal by Gencor, a mining subsidiary of Sanlam.[28] In addition, wholesaling and retailing, as well as the only cotton gin, are controlled by

South African firms. Therefore, that country controls all cotton prices. And the South African Co-operative Citrus Exchange markets all citrus products, and almost all medium- or large-scale enterprises continue to be managed by South Africans.[29]

Angola and Mozambique

Prior to independence, South African capital investment in both Angola and Mozambique was far more dominant than at present. Following independence, the majority of the agreements between these countries and South Africa were terminated. To the extent that South African capital is present, "it is in partnership with others in consortia, joint ventures or via devious ownership patterns in which the origin of capital is concealed." [30]

In Mozambique, the majority of South African capital is invested in the giant hydroelectric power scheme, Cahora Bassa, the construction of which took place under colonial rule. South African sources provided approximately 40 percent of the capital investment for the first phase. One of the most significant contributors was the Electricity Supply Commission (ESCOM) of South Africa. The participants in the ZAMCO consortium which financed the project include Anglo-American Corporation; L.T.A. Ltd., a subsidiary of Anglo-American; and Shaft Sinkers (Pty) Ltd.—all South African. In addition, two-thirds of the contracts for the construction of the dam were given to South African firms.[31] South African capital is present also in the industrial and banking sectors, as well as the freight industry.

The presence of Portuguese capital in Mozambique is significant in the industrial and energy sectors; and British capital, mainly through Lonrho, is present in industry, energy, agriculture, banking, tourism, and mining (gold). The Soviet Union has investments in the production of the mineral tantalite, and East Germany is involved in coal production. Other private investors include the United States, Belgium, Norway, and Algeria.[32]

In Angola, most foreign investment is in the oil sector. Four foreign companies are producing oil—Gulf (the largest), Petrofina (Belgian), Texaco, and Elf Aquitaine (French).[33] Petrofina (as a majority shareholder in Finapetroles de Angola, in association with Sonangol, the state oil company, and Texaco), is responsible for all onshore production in the Congo and Kwanza basins.[34]

The diamond mines in Angola are owned by Companhia de Diamantes de Angola (Diamang). The Angolan government holds 77.21 percent of the shares in Diamang, the majority of the remaining equity being held by the Belgian Société Générale.[35] Austria has investments in iron mining, and Bulgarian and Yugoslav capital is present in the mining of phosphates.[36]

In the manufacturing sector, the French firm Creusot-Loire has built two textile plants; General Tire, with two Portuguese companies, has shares in the Mabor tire-processing factory; and the largest food-processing firm is owned by Carnation's Seafoods of California. In addition, "Mitsubishi has a share in a sheet-metal factory and the British company Hull, Blyth Ltd., has a wholly owned Angolan subsidiary, Uniao, which manufactures Land Rovers." [37]

Malawi, Zambia, and Zimbabwe

South African investments in Malawi have been limited, due to the fact that the economy is predominantly agrarian. South Africa did, however, finance a sugar mill at "Chikwana near Zomba by a loan, 60% of which was tied to procurement of goods from South Africa." The sugar mill was financed by the South African Industrial Development Corporation (IDC), which is a parastatal.[38] The further development of the sugar industry took place under the direction of the Dwanga Sugar Corporation, which consists of the government, European aid groups, and the multinational group Lonrho.[39]

Other South African investments in Malawi include the 1969 financing of the initial railway connection to the Mozambican port of Nacala. And the South African chemical company, Optichem Ltd., built a fertilizer plant, of which the Malawian state holds 40 percent; South African Mutual Life Insurance, 27 percent; and Optichem Ltd., 30 percent. Also, the new Malawian capital, Lilongwe, was largely financed by South Africa, as is the Malawian tourist industry.[40] Additional foreign investors include Standard Bank (UK), Murray and Roberts (Sanlam), Unilever, African Lakes, Imperial, and Gallaher.[41]

A major area of foreign investment in Zambia is the copper industry. According to Arne Tostensen, the present shareholders of the Zambian copper mines are as follows:

The Zambian Government, through its holding company the Zambian Industrial and Mining Corporation (Zimco), holds 60.3 percent. The remainder is divided between Anglo-American Corporation through its subsidiary, Zambia Copper Investment (ZCI) with 27.3 percent and the Amax subsidiary, Roan Selection Trust International with 6.9 percent as the major shareholders, plus some minor ones.[42]

Even though the government holds 60.3 percent, Anglo-American and Amax were awarded management, sales, and technical consultant contracts.[43]

Foreign investment in Zambia is great throughout all sectors of the economy. Foreign companies have either partial or complete ownership of a variety of engineering and manufacturing companies. Also, the freight, hotel, energy, banking, and agricultural sectors contain large amounts of foreign capital.[44]

The amount of South African and Western private direct investment in Zimbabwe is also disturbing. In fact, it is estimated that at least 50 percent of the economy is foreign-controlled (South African, 26 percent; British, 21 percent; other foreign, 3 percent).[45] The most important companies in Zimbabwe are Anglo-American (S.A.), Barlow Rand (S.A.), Old Mutual (S.A.), Lonrho (British). "The eight biggest companies listed on the Zimbabwe Stock Exchange are: Delta, Hippo Valley, Zimbabwe Alloys, and Natural Foods (all controlled or dominated by Anglo), David Whitehead (Lonrho), Hunyani (Barlow), Plate Glass (Barlow), and TA Holdings (Zimbabwean)." [46]

Tanzania

The Tanzanian government has not been very successful in securing significant private direct investment. The major source of investment is concentrated in the diamond-mining industry, owned jointly by the government and De Beers Corporation, the only known South African investment in Tanzania.[47]

Foreign Economic Assistance

Dependency theorists often suggest that negative consequences are suffered by LDCs which are the recipients of large amounts of external economic assistance, particularly when this aid is received from a relatively small number of donors . . . Aid, then is seen as one part of a seamless web of dependence, as a tie that reinforces the other linkages . . . in particular it is seen as deepening trade dependence, especially when it is "tied" to purchases in the donor country; and as providing an entry for investment from firms based in the donor country, by improving the general investment climate and creating advantages for these firms over those based in other developed countries of the LDC itself.[48]

The majority of the SADCC countries are recipients of large amounts of foreign economic assistance. Ironically, SADCC is dependent on such assistance for regional development. The organization, however, anticipates that such assistance is only temporary. Is this possible? Certainly economic liberation can be forthcoming only if the structural linkage of dependency is transformed. In this section, the issue of foreign economic assistance is examined.

Botswana, Lesotho, and Swaziland

Total official development assistance (ODA) given to Botswana, Lesotho, and Swaziland from 1982 through 1985 is shown in Table 2. All three countries receive large amounts of aid, although there has been a decline in such assistance during this period. In addition, most of this aid is supplied by a select group of donors. In 1985, Botswana's major donors were the Federal Republic of Germany, the United States, Sweden, and the United Kingdom. Lesotho's major donors were the United States, Sweden, and the Federal Republic of Germany; prior to 1985, the United Kingdom had been a major donor. In addition, Lesotho is the recipient of large amounts of economic assistance from South Africa. Swaziland's major donors were the United States, the United Kingdom, and Canada.

Angola and Mozambique

Angola's major donors in 1985 were Italy, the Netherlands, and Sweden (see Table 3); Mozambique's major donors included the United States, Sweden, Italy, and the Netherlands. The $47

TABLE 2

SADCC Member States
GROSS OFFICIAL DEVELOPMENT ASSISTANCE (ODA) *
1982 – 1985

in U.S. $Millions

	OECD Countries **	Multilateral	OPEC Countries	Total Gross
Angola				
1982	40.4	19.5	0.5	60.4
1983	46.9	28.7	0.2	75.8
1984	59.6	34.3	1.2	95.1
1985	59.6	31.9	—	91.5
Botswana				
1982	84.3	12.5	6.2	103.0
1983	76.0	21.1	8.5	105.6
1984	66.5	28.4	10.5	105.4
1985	60.6	35.5	4.7	100.8
Lesotho				
1982	57.3	36.5	—	93.8
1983	64.8	40.8	2.6	108.2
1984	66.1	31.7	3.2	101.0
1985	51.7	40.6	3.4	95.7
Malawi				
1982	68.6	57.1	0.1	125.8
1983	59.2	62.0	—	121.2
1984	55.6	109.6	—	165.2
1985	61.1	61.7	—	122.8

TABLE 2 continued on next page

	OECD Countries **	Multilateral	OPEC Countries	Total Gross
Mozambique				
1982	160.6	41.3	6.3	208.2
1983	160.7	50.2	1.2	212.1
1984	190.5	69.3	2.9	262.7
1985	219.0	78.3	6.4	303.7
Swaziland				
1982	21.0	9.5	—	30.5
1983	22.7	13.1	—	35.7
1984	19.6	12.3	—	31.9
1985	20.3	7.6	—	27.9
Tanzania				
1982	489.7	188.9	15.2	693.8
1983	431.0	151.3	19.1	601.4
1984	410.6	142.6	12.4	565.6
1985	377.0	107.7	10.0	494.7
Zambia				
1982	192.8	52.3	70.0	315.1
1983	181.0	33.4	3.4	217.8
1984	183.1	57.8	—	240.9
1985	218.0	113.7	—	331.7
Zimbabwe				
1982	142.5	29.8	44.0	216.3
1983	186.2	22.8	0.2	209.2
1984	243.9	53.3	0.8	298.0
1985	214.9	25.5	0.6	241.0

TABLE 2 continued on next page

* Disbursements. Official development assistance is defined as grants (excluding technical cooperation grants) and loans with at least a 25 percent grant element, provided by OECD and OPEC member countries and multilateral agencies, and administered with the aim of promoting development and welfare in the recipient country. IMF loans, other than trust fund facilities, are excluded, as is aid from the Eastern bloc. (Economist Intelligence Unit, *Country Profile: Angola, Sao Tome and Principle, 1986,* p. 34.)

** The OECD countries: Australia, Austria, Belgium, Canada, Denmark, Finland, France, Federal Republic of Germany, Italy, Japan, Netherlands, New Zealand, Norway, Sweden, Switzerland, United Kingdom, United States.

Source: OECD, *Geographical Distribution of Financial Flows* (Paris: Organization for Economic Cooperation and Development, 1987).

TABLE 3

SADCC Member States
OFFICIAL DEVELOPMENT ASSISTANCE (ODA) BY LARGEST OECD-COUNTRY DONORS 1982 – 1985

in U.S. $Millions

ANGOLA

	Italy	Netherlands	Sweden
1982	4.2	4.4	15.2
1983	17.5	9.3	12.1
1984	11.2	16.7	14.6
1985	16.3	8.1	18.7

BOTSWANA

	Federal Republic of Germany	Sweden	U.K.	U.S.
1982	24.2	13.2	13.2	17.0
1983	20.1	11.6	15.1	13.0
1984	13.0	11.0	12.6	13.0
1985	13.2	7.3	7.9	11.0

LESOTHO

	Federal Republic of Germany	Sweden	U.S.
1982	9.8	2.1	25.0
1983	14.8	3.4	25.0
1984	11.7	2.6	32.0
1985	8.2	6.9	19.0

TABLE 3 continued on next page

MALAWI

	Federal Republic of Germany	U.K.
1982	21.7	23.8
1983	14.5	18.1
1984	14.7	17.0
1985	11.9	16.5

MOZAMBIQUE

	Italy	Netherlands	Sweden	U.S.
1982	27.4	29.5	46.3	2.0
1983	32.9	16.8	36.7	13.0
1984	34.2	29.2	30.6	16.0
1985	28.6	21.2	24.8	47.0

SWAZILAND

	Canada	U.K.	U.S.
1982	1.0	6.4	7.0
1983	2.1	4.5	10.0
1984	1.2	3.7	7.0
1985	4.4	2.7	8.0

TANZANIA

	Federal Republic of Germany	Denmark	Netherlands	Norway	Sweden
1982	59.0	39.8	57.5	51.9	73.8
1983	36.3	40.4	35.0	54.9	69.3
1984	49.9	31.6	40.8	46.4	55.1
1985	32.9	40.8	36.9	45.4	49.0

TABLE 3 continued on next page

ZAMBIA

	Canada	Federal Republic of Germany	Sweden	U.K.	U.S.	Italy
1982	17.0	29.0	27.5	22.5	22.0	1.0
1983	10.8	25.0	29.4	21.1	23.0	19.3
1984	19.2	19.2	20.4	20.1	40.0	5.0
1985	10.9	19.3	22.9	23.9	36.0	42.1

ZIMBABWE

	Federal Republic of Germany	Sweden	U.S.
1982	23.0	10.1	7.0
1983	34.1	15.3	56.0
1984	26.6	19.4	73.0
1985	27.7	23.5	56.0

Source: OECD, *Geographical Distribution of Financial Flows* (Paris: Organization for Economic Cooperation and Development, 1986, 1987).

million given by the United States represented a significant increase over the 1984 figure of $16 million. Between 1981 and 1984, Angola's ODA increased by more than $30 million, but began to decline in 1985. Aid to Mozambique increased by close to $100 million between 1982 and 1985.

Malawi, Zambia, and Zimbabwe

Malawi's major donors in 1985 were the Federal Republic of Germany and the United Kingdom. Zambia's major donor was Italy (see Table 3). Other significant donors include the United States, Canada, the Federal Republic of Germany, Sweden, and the United Kingdom. The major ODA donor to Zimbabwe in 1985 was the United States (see Table 3). Two other significant donors were the Federal Republic of Germany and Sweden.

The ODA to Malawi increased by more than $40 million between 1983 and 1984 (see Table 3), but declined by the same amount in 1985. The ODA to Zambia decreased significantly between 1982 and 1983, but by 1985 had increased once again. Zimbabwe's ODA, however, increased by more than $80 million between 1981 and 1984, but by 1985 had begun to decline.

Tanzania

Tanzania receives the largest amount of ODA of all the SADCC member states (see Table 2), although such assistance decreased significantly between 1982 and 1985. In 1985, Tanzania's major donors were the Federal Republic of Germany, Denmark, the Netherlands, Norway, and Sweden.

Servicing of Foreign Debt

> Debt service burdens of LDCs have been cited by many dependency theorists as an example of "reverse flows" of resources form LDCs to DCs. The general argument is that debt service on past loans has done a great deal to cancel out incoming flows of resources for many underdeveloped countries and has often resulted in considerable external influence, either formal or informal, on internal policy making. Much the same might be said for a related factor, the level of reserves holdings; when these are low, an LDC will find it difficult to pursue an independent economic

policy and will be highly sensitive to trade fluctuations and other short-term economic disturbances, either domestic or foreign.[49]

The majority of the SADCC countries have sizable debt-service burdens, low reserve holdings, and deficits in their current account balance. This situation does not seem to be improving, but in fact, seems to be worsening.

Botswana, Lesotho, and Swaziland

In 1985, outstanding and disbursed foreign debt in Botswana was $334.2 million, 47.3 percent of gross national product (GNP). The servicing of foreign debt as a percentage of exports of goods and services was the lowest in the region—5.4 percent (see Table 4), and international reserves in August 1987 were equivalent to two years' import coverage. This was the highest in the region. In 1985 Botswana's current account balance was $139 million (see Table 5). During 1986 Botswana continued to enjoy a surplus, mainly due to an increase in merchandise trade surplus. [50]

Lesotho's total outstanding and disbursed debt in 1985 was $172.2 million, 30.1 percent of the GNP (see Table 4). The servicing of foreign debt as a percentage of exports was 5.7, the second lowest in the region. International reserves in 1985 totaled $43.52 million, which represented only 1.5 months of import coverage. Lesotho's current account balance in 1985 was $9 million (see Table 5). Although the current account balance reflects a surplus in 1985, Lesotho had a large structural deficit in merchandise trade. The current account surplus, however, is due to positive balances on services (i.e., workers' remittances, official transfers).[51]

In Swaziland, debt figures in 1985 totaled $181.7 million, with servicing of foreign debt being 8.5 percent. Swaziland's current account balance reflected a deficit of $28.9 million (see Tables 4 and 5).

Angola and Mozambique

In 1985, Angola's external public debt totaled $2,496 million and by 1987 had increased to $4 billion. Since 1979, Angola's debt has increased tremendously. Between 1978 and 1981,

Angola borrowed heavily from abroad in an effort to finance major investments to build up the economy. Total disbursed, plus undisbursed external debt, increased 500 percent.[52] The servicing of foreign debt as a percentage of exports was 15.4 in 1985. The current account balance of 1985 reflects a $447 million deficit. International reserves in 1986 totaled $179 million.

Mozambique's external public debt doubled between 1982 and 1984, increasing from $585 million to $1.2 billion. By the end of 1986 this had increased to $3.2 billion. Mozambique consequently has the heaviest debt burden of all the SADCC countries.[53] In addition, the government continues to have a large deficit in the current account balance (see Table 5).

Malawi, Zambia, and Zimbabwe

Malawi's foreign debt in 1985 was $744.9 million, 75.7 percent of GNP. The servicing of foreign debt as a percentage of exports of goods and services in 1985 was 23.6, a significant increase over the 1984 figure of 17.7. In 1981, however, debt service was at 28 percent, which resulted in a government rescheduling of the debt for 1982 and 1983.[54] While in 1984 Malawi's international reserves were $61 million, by 1986 they had decreased to only $24.6 million, representing only one month of import coverage.

Zambia's foreign debt, like Malawi's, was rescheduled during the early 1980s as a consequence of the country's soaring debt-service ratio. The debt was again rescheduled in 1986, although in May 1987, the government abandoned the International Monetary Fund (IMF) adjustment program. In 1985 the foreign debt was $3,214 million, 150.8 percent of the GNP. Foreign debt as a percentage of exports of goods and services was 10.2. In 1986 Zambia had $70.3 million in international reserves, which represented a large decrease over the 1985 figure of $200 million.

As a result of Zambia's troublesome debt burden, in 1986 both Sweden and the Netherlands announced plans to write off portions of Zambia's debt. The agreement signed between Zambia and Sweden stipulated that ZK60 million (approximately $8.1 million) in development loans incurred from 1973 through 1977 would be written off. The Netherlands agreed to write off debts totaling $2.7 million.[55]

TABLE 4

SADCC Member States
FOREIGN DEBT
in U.S. $Millions

External Public Debt
(Outstanding and Disbursed)

	1978	1979	1980	1981	1982	1983	1984	1985	1986
Angola	378	381	614	983	2346	2358	2442	2700	3071
Botswana	121	135	152	164	211	230	277	334	—
Lesotho	33	58	63	77	118	133	139	172	—
Malawi	504	646	646	680	709	719	729	745	—
Mozambique	111	—	—	—	585	—	1217	—	3200
Swaziland	105	148	166	161	170	175	169	182	—
Tanzania	1095	1153	1360	2210	2383	2662	2758	2982	—
Zambia	1396	1559	2182	2228	2376	2616	2813	3214	—
Zimbabwe	—	—	698	880	1256	1609	1523	—	—

TABLE 4 continued on next page

External Public Debt as Percentage of GNP

	1978	1979	1980	1981	1982	1983	1984	1985	1986
Angola	—	—	—	—	—	—	—	—	—
Botswana	—	—	18.0	20.6	30.4	28.1	32.5	47.3	—
Lesotho	7.5	—	9.1	10.5	16.3	16.4	19.0	30.1	—
Malawi	36.8	33.1	52.2	59.1	63.2	62.1	64.1	75.7	—
Mozambique	—	—	—	—	—	—	—	—	—
Swaziland	16.0	—	—	—	—	30.0	—	—	—
Tanzania	25.1	25.3	27.6	28.3	32.7	58.9	68.0	—	—
Zambia	51.6	50.5	51.2	73.1	66.3	83.9	114.4	150.8	—
Zimbabwe	—	—	13.8	13.8	19.1	27.9	28.4	—	—

TABLE 4 continued on next page

Servicing of Foreign Debt
Percentage of Exports of Goods and Services

	1978	1979	1980	1981	1982	1983	1984	1985	1986
Angola	—	—	—	—	18.9	20.8	18.1	15.4	—
Botswana	2.5	1.6	1.7	1.4	2.1	2.9	3.7	—	—
Lesotho	0.5	0.9	1.3	1.2	2.2	4.5	5.4	—	—
Malawi	14.9	15.9	18.5	24.5	22.8	20.3	17.7	23.6	—
Mozambique	—	—	—	—	—	—	—	—	15.18
Swaziland	1.7	2.7	2.6	3.0	4.2	4.3	4.4	8.5	—
Tanzania	7.9	7.5	8.8	6.1	5.1	28.9	60.9	49.7	—
Zambia	27.1	18.0	22.2	24.0	19.4	12.6	12.0	10.2	—
Zimbabwe	0.8	1.2	2.6	4.4	9.2	31.6	20.0	—	30.0

Sources: *World Bank Annual Report, 1980-86* • *World Development Report, 1978-86* • *World Debt Tables: External Debt of Developing Countries, 1986* • *Accelerated Development in Sub Saharan Africa, 1981* • *QER of Tanzania, Mozambique, 1983* • *QER of Namibia, Botswana, Lesotho, Swaziland, 1983* • *QER of Zambia, 1983* • *QER of Angola, Guinea-Bissau, Cape Verde Islands, Sao Tome and Principe, 1983* • *Country Profile: Angola, Guinea-Bissau, Cape Verde Islands, Sao Tome and Principe, 1986*

TABLE 5
SADCC Member States
BALANCE OF PAYMENTS AND RESERVES
in U.S. $Millions

Current Account Balance

	1979	1980	1981	1982	1983	1984	1985	1986
Angola	—	—	-648	-240	-34	-57	-236	-447
Botswana	—	-75	-218	-66	-5	12	139	—
Lesotho	-22	-11	-49	-37	-6	19	9	—
Malawi	-185	-139	-101	-78	72	-20	—	—
Mozambique	—	-369	-410	-502	-356	-252	—	—
Swaziland	—	-92	-110	-50	-86	-21	-29	—
Tanzania	-457	-567	-410	-524	-314	-302	-428*	-450 *
Zambia	264	-537	-742	-566	-271	-153	-284	—
Zimbabwe	-61	-255	-635	-706	-459	-97	-97	—

* Provisional

TABLE 5 continued on next page

International Reserves

	1979	1980	1981	1982	1983	1984	1985	1986
Angola	—	—	116	107	112	172	204	179
Botswana	267	344	253	293	396	479	783	1198
Lesotho	22	50	43	48	67	49	44	60
Malawi	75	75	54	29	29	61	45	25
Mozambique	—	—	—	—	—	—	—	—
Swaziland	—	—	96	76	93	80	83	96
Tanzania	68	20	19	19	19	27	16	61
Zambia	193	207	143	157	137	55	200	70
Zimbabwe	—	373	327	320	300	260	345	—

TABLE 5 continued on next page

Reserves in Months of Import Coverage

	1979	1980	1981	1982	1983	1984	1985	1986
Angola	—	—	—	—	—	—	—	—
Botswana	—	—	—	—	—	6.3	11.2	—
Lesotho	—	—	1.1	1.2	1.4	1.2	1.5	—
Malawi	1.7	1.6	1.3	0.9	0.8	1.9	2.0	1
Mozambique	—	—	—	—	—	—	—	—
Swaziland	—	—	—	0.2	—	0.3	—	—
Tanzania	0.9	0.2	0.2	1.5	1.3	0.6	2.5	—
Zambia	1.8	1.3	0.9	1.7	2.0	2.0	2.1	—
Zimbabwe	—	2.4	1.7	1.7	2.0	2.0	2.1	6

Sources: *World Development Report*, 1978-79 • *Accelerated Development in Sub-Saharan Africa*, 1981 • *QER Of Namibia, Botswana, Lesotho, Swaziland*, 1982, 1983 • *Country Profile: Mozambique*, 1986-87

In Zimbabwe, the servicing of foreign debt as a percentage of exports of goods and services is currently among the highest in the region, 30 percent in 1986. Zimbabwe's external public debt in 1984 was $1,523 million, which represented 28 percent of the GNP. International reserves in 1985 totaled $345 million, representing two months of import coverage, although in 1986 international reserves increased to six months of import coverage. Even though Zimbabwe had a deficit account balance in 1985, the government recorded a surplus in 1986, largely as a result of continued import restrictions.

Tanzania

Tanzania's troublesome foreign debt problems resulted in a government-negotiated IMF agreement in August 1986. The country's foreign debt in 1985 was $2,981.7 million, with a debt-service ratio of 49.7 percent. The provisional current account balance for 1986 shows a $450 million deficit.

In May 1986, Denmark cancelled Tanzania's official debts of $83 million; and while Sweden did not formally cancel Tanzania's debts, it did provide the country with significant debt relief.[56]

INTERNAL DISTORTIONS

Although one contributing factor to internal underdevelopment is external dependency, another factor involves internal distortions such as limited economic growth, high levels of unemployment, large discrepancies in income distribution, and poor social-welfare conditions. Internal distortions are caused partially by structural linkages of dependency, but also by government developmental policies (colonial and post-independence), uncontrollable ecological calamities, political instability, and world economic crises.

Central to the theoretical framework of contemporary political economy is the contention that there exists within Third World countries a small elite (e.g., government officials, business persons, employees of multinational corporations) who, through their "alliance" with the elite from advanced capitalist nations (e.g., government officials, multinational corporations), are major actors in facilitating the maintenance of structural links of dependency as well as underdevelopment. These Third World elite, it is argued, are the major beneficiaries of economic growth. Their income and employment levels are higher than those of the masses, and their general level of social welfare is much better. Such elite thus perpetuate the phenomena of dependency and underdevelopment.

These internal distortions of the SADCC member states will be explored by looking at the questions of economic growth, employment and income distribution, and general level of social welfare.

Economic Growth and Employment

Economic growth refers to the growth rates of the gross domestic product (GDP). According to the *SADCC Annual Progress Report, July 1986 – August 1987:*

> The average real GDP growth for the region will not exceed 2.4%, compared with an average of 2.5% during the previous year. These figures hide large disparities in the economic performance of individual member States. In fact most economies have either stagnated or experienced negative growth rates; thus causing immense problems, particularly taking into account average population increases of 3.2%. Only Botswana and Swaziland recorded appreciable real growth rates, at 12% and 9% respectively.[57]

The primary reason for this performance, according to the report, "is the structure of the regional economies themselves,"

> largely characterized by an overwhelming dependence on the export of a few mineral raw materials and agricultural commodities; and the importation of capital, intermediate as well as consumer goods. The combined effects of the sluggish growth in the economies of major trading partners, shifting demand patterns in those markets, and depressed prices for the region's exports commodities, have seriously undermined regional economies.[58]

In addition to declining rates of economic growth, most SADCC member states also are faced with high unemployment levels and an unequal distribution of wealth, the wealth being concentrated among a select group of elite. As the economic conditions in the region continue to deteriorate, only the masses are adversely effected. Similarly, it is the elite who prosper during positive growth periods.

Botswana, Lesotho, and Swaziland

In its 1986 *World Development Report*, the World Bank stated that Botswana had the fastest growing economy in the world. Currently, its average growth rate is 12 percent. Botswana's economy, however, is undiversified: 83 percent of all exports consist of diamonds and minerals; 8 percent, cattle and by-products. The key to Botswana's economic growth has been diamonds. In fact, the country is presently the largest diamond source in the world, with 12.3 million carats produced in 1986.[59]

Botswana is a major importer of food, a problem that was heightened in 1987 as the country experienced its sixth consecutive year of drought, the worst the country has suffered in 65 years, reducing its cattle by a third. Although during good years Botswana is able to produce only a small percentage of its food requirements (sorghum, maize, millet and bean), between 1985 and 1987 it produced only 10 percent. Consequently, President Quett Masire has been forced once again to request food assistance from the international community.[60]

As a result of the continued drought, many rural households have remained in poverty due to the loss of crops and livestock. Of Botswana's total population of 1.15 million, approximately 85 percent "live in the rural areas and are dependent on traditional agriculture for their livelihood." [61] In the formal agricultural sector in 1985, 1,500 people lost their job as a result of the drought. This only exacerbated the growing unemployment problem in Botswana, where, although the average per-capita gross national product (GNP) is $920, "this figure masks numbers of considerably more impoverished rural people trying to work arid, marginal land." [62]

Although in 1987 Botswana had the fastest growing economy in Africa, the government is faced with a serious unemployment problem. According to a 1984-1985 government labor survey, Botswana's unemployment rate is 23.5 percent. Of a total workforce of 368,000, 93,000 were unemployed, with unemployment in the urban areas exceeding that in rural areas. It is projected that the current unemployment problem will worsen in the future unless more jobs are created. While the population is growing at a rate of 3.4 percent annually, formal-sector employment is available to only 20 percent of the population aged 15 or over.[63]

In addition to the heightening of the employment problem by the drought, it also has been increased by Pretoria's threat to repatriate Botswana migrant laborers employed in the South African mines. In 1986, approximately 21,000 people from Botswana were employed in South Africa.[64]

Although Lesotho's GDP grew by 9.4 percent in 1984 and 3.5 percent in 1985, estimates for 1986 indicate no economic growth. Of all the SADCC member states, Lesotho is the most dependent on South Africa, with over half its national income being earned by migrant workers in South Africa.[65] Deferred payments automatically transferred to Lesotho increased from M24 million in 1980 to M142 million in 1985.[66] These figures reflect the reality that "nearly as many Basotho males work in the Republic of South Africa as in Lesotho." [67] Labor migration is an integral part of Lesotho's economy, due to the limited sources of employment available in the country and because the income is higher for those who choose to migrate to South Africa for employment. Currently, an estimated 175,000 Basotho work in South Africa, and remittances from these workers are the main source of income for a significant percentage of both rural and urban households. Thus, although Lesotho's GNP per capita in 1984 was $530, this figure does not reveal the large discrepancies among urban dwellers, as well as between rural and urban dwellers.

In fact, even though 84 percent of Lesotho's population live in rural areas, agriculture is the main source of income for only about 42 percent of the households. The severity of the employment problem is even more evidenced by the fact that 25 percent "of rural households have no access to land, which is very limited because of the small size and mountainous topography of the country," and "two-thirds of these unfortunates do not have livestock either." [68]

Economic growth in Swaziland has been so rapid that it is no longer considered one of the world's least-developed countries. Gross domestic product (GDP) "doubled between 1968 and 1972, with a subsequent growth per annum of 23 percent in 1975/76." Following this peak, the growth rate slowed, averaging only 2.2 percent between 1978 and 1981. But in 1980-1981 the situation improved with a 6.5 percent increase,[69] and the economy has continued to grow, with GDP growth in 1986 of 9 percent.

In spite of the fact that Swaziland has experienced tremendous growth, the economy is undiversified and largely relies on one export crop—sugar. In addition, the country is dependent upon external structures, mainly foreign investment, for economic growth. In fact, its economic growth has been concentrated in the export sector, and foreign investors have been responsible for the development of its main exports. Besides sugar, these include wood pulp and timber, asbestos, citrus, canned fruit, and fertilizer. The country is also dependent on South African capital and employment opportunities for migrant workers.[70] Currently, approximately 17,000 Swazi are employed in South Africa. This represents a significant increase over the 1981 figure of 13,000.[71]

Notwithstanding that Swaziland's economy has grown rapidly, and the GNP per capita in 1985 was $670, the benefits of this growth have not spread to the masses of people. Most Swazis are peasant farmers who live on Swazi Nation Land; their contribution to GDP has fallen since independence. In addition, Swaziland, like all the regional countries, has a serious unemployment problem, partially attributable to the high population-growth rate. Where jobs are available in the formal sector, wages are very low for the majority of workers. For example, in a study conducted during the early 1980s, it was determined that while the poverty datum line was E228 per month for a family of five, the average monthly wage for an unskilled male worker was E125; for a female, E93.[72]

Angola and Mozambique

The continued political and economic instability in Angola since independence has had a negative impact on economic growth. The extent of the political instability is revealed by the fact that the government spends approximately three-quarters of the national budget and half the export revenues to defend the country against South Africa and UNITA insurgents.[73]

Following the 1975-1976 Angolan Civil War, productivity in all sectors except oil declined. Although the overall productivity level has improved, output levels continue to be generally far below those achieved before independence. Real growth in 1982 was 15 percent, and it is projected that there was not a change during 1983 – 1985. During 1986, however, there was a decrease in real growth as a result of a decline in oil earnings.[74]

Due to continued instability, in 1986 Angola was identified by the United Nations Office for Emergency Operations in Africa as a critically affected country. It was projected that in 1986-1987, 600,000 people would be affected by Angola's emergency crisis caused mainly by chronic internal strife. In 1986 the displaced population had reached approximately 480,000 persons, 80 percent of whom were women and children. During 1985-1986, the emergency food aid requirements totaled 120,000 tons; 198,000 tons in 1986-1987; and 200,000 tons in 1987-1988.[75]

Although employment and income distribution figures are not available for Angola, in 1987 the majority of its nine million people were engaged in subsistence agriculture.[76]

The extend of the decline in economic growth in post-independence Mozambique was worse than that in Angola. There was a breakdown of the economy, "with output falling by as much as 40 to 60 percent in many sectors." At independence, Frelimo inherited a bankrupt economy. Further deterioration of the economy was largely a consequence of the post-independence exodus of approximately 90 percent of the Portuguese, who filled virtually all the administrative and technical jobs. Many sabotaged the factories, farms, and shops they left behind. The protracted Rhodesian war also had a negative impact on economic growth, as did the drought, the widespread flooding in the south of the country during 1977 and 1978, and the continued South African destabilization efforts.[77]

Real GSP (Gross Social Product) grew by 1.8 percent in 1981 but declined to a -18 percent by 1983. Real growth for 1985 was -7.9 percent, and by 1986 economic growth had declined by more than a third in real terms.[78]

Mozambique was also declared a critically affected country by the United Nations Office for Emergency Operation in Africa in 1986. The emergency that Mozambique is experiencing has basically been caused by the South African-backed insurgency movement, the Mozambique National Resistance (MNR). By early 1988, it was estimated that as many as six million Mozambicans might be in danger of starvation. It is projected that emergency food aid requirements for 1987-1988 will total 421,400 tons.[79]

In Mozambique, at least 80 percent of the population is engaged in subsistence farming; therefore very few individuals are involved in formal-sector employment. A sizable number of those who are involved in such employment, however, work in the mines of South Africa.

Since the early 1900s, the Mozambican government has depended on South Africa to employ such workers, and post-independence development policies have not eradicated this dependency. In October 1986, however, following a "series of cross-border attacks attributed to the African National Congress," South Africa announced that it would discontinue hiring Mozambicans. In addition, the apartheid regime stated that contracts would not be renewed for Mozambicans currently employed in the country. By December, however, the government had modified that ban, indicating that experienced miners with long service would be allowed to remain in the country, but no novices would be recruited. It was estimated that approximately half the 61,000 mine workers from Mozambique would thus be allowed to stay. The government ban, however, applies also to Mozambicans who work in other sectors, and an estimated 13,000 migrants registered as farm workers were affected, as well as thousands of others. It is estimated that as many as 160,000 (legal and illegal) Mozambican migrant laborers may reside in South Africa.[80]

Given the present economic and political situation in Mozambique, the country will not be able to reabsorb these workers into the employment sector. This is likely to have serious implications for political stability. In addition, the repatriation of these workers will have an impact on government revenue and foreign exchange accrued from the migrant labor agreement.

Malawi, Zambia, and Zimbabwe

Between 1964 and 1977, GDP in Malawi grew by an annual average of 6 percent in real terms. Since that time, however, there has been a decline in economic growth, especially in 1981, when real growth (at 1978 prices) was a -5.2 percent. By 1984 there seemingly was a recovery with real growth at 4.3 percent. However, during 1986 real growth declined by 3 percent.[81] Reasons for Malawi's poor economic performance include the decline in prices for tea and sugar exports, sluggishness in the agricultural sector, and continued transport bottlenecks.[82]

By early 1988, Malawi was experiencing a severe food shortage and had appealed to the international community for 130,000 tons of maize by March. This appeal was in addition to the 48,000 tons that already had been arranged as donations and commercial imports. This food crisis was caused by several factors, including a failure of the government agricultural policy, drought, crop pests, and the influx of more than 380,000 refugees from Mozambique.[83]

The current food crisis has only served to exacerbate the large discrepancy in income between the elite and the masses. In fact, during the current crisis, the city shops reportedly are well-stocked, although most Malawians are very poor. "Nine out of 10 people live from subsistence agriculture, but many have plots of land too small to support their families. With annual per capital gross national product at about $160, Malawi is one of the poorest nations in the world." [84]

In 1985, just over 409,000 individuals were paid employees in Malawi, with 80 percent in the private sector and 20 percent in government. While this figure represented a 7.6 percent increase over 1984 employment figures, it was not anticipated that such growth would continue. While in 1985 an average agricultural employee received MK26.4 per month, an average government employee received MK82.1 per month.[85]

At one time South Africa was a major employer of Malawian workers. This changed, however, following a plane crash in 1974 that killed seventy-five workers in route to South Africa. Malawian migrant workers were repatriated by Malawi and the further recruitment of workers was banned. In 1973 an estimated 300,000 Malawians had been employed in the South African gold mines. When the workers were repatriated, the number dropped to 106,000, and by 1974 all but 207 had returned to Malawi. However, by 1977 recruitment was resumed, and in 1978, 20,000 mine workers were in South Africa.[86] In 1984, approximately 29,000 Malawians were working in the apartheid regime.

Zambia's economic growth is largely affected by the world market price of copper. Between 1964 and 1976, GDP growth was considerable due to the rise in world copper prices. In 1976 real growth was 8.4 percent; it fell in 1977, stabilized in 1978, and fell a further 9.7 percent in 1979. By 1982, real growth (at 1977 prices) had plunged to -2.8 percent. In 1985, however, Zambia experienced a 3.4 percent rate of growth, although during 1986 real GDP growth was only 0.75 percent amid foreign exchange difficulties.[87]

Zambia depends on copper for over 90 percent of its export earnings, a factor that has left the country underdeveloped. Unless the government is able to diversify the economy, Zambia's economic problem by the turn of the century will worsen further when, according to mining experts, the copper deposits will be gone. This problem will be exacerbated by the fact that the agricultural sector is not too viable, and Zambia, for more than ten years, has had to use valuable foreign exchange to import maize. With approximately 45 percent of the population residing in urban areas (the highest percentage of urbanized population in Africa), agriculture has not been a priority.[88]

The deteriorating economic situation in Zambia has left large numbers unemployed. For example, "the highly urbanized copperbelt, which alone holds one-third of Zambia's seven million people, now has a large and restive unemployed workforce as its industries operate at a fraction of their capacities due to the resulting chronic shortage of foreign currency."[89] One of the reasons for the large urbanized population in Zambia rests historically with the large discrepancy in the incomes of rural dwellers versus urban dwellers. At one point, it was speculated that rural income was less than one-third the average income of urban dwellers, with 20 percent of the households in the country claiming over 56 percent of the total income. Overall in Zambia, employment opportunities have changed very little since 1975; if anything, such opportunities have decreased.[90]

Real economic growth in Zimbabwe was over 11 percent in 1980 and 13 percent in 1981. This phenomenal post-independence growth was short lived, with zero growth in 1982 and -3.4 percent in 1983. This decline resulted from the drought, which caused the sales of maize, the main staple, to "drop by nearly 70 percent between 1981/82 and 1983/84." In addition, "mining suffered from falling world prices . . . while manufacturing was hit by . . . exchange shortages and contracting domestic demand, as the wage rises of 1980 and 1981 were eroded by inflation, and employment levels stagnated." [91] Although by 1984 the economy began to recover and in 1985 the GDP grew by 6 percent, real GDP growth for 1986 is estimated at only 0.18 percent. The main reason for this poor performance was the shortage of needed imports.[92]

As of July 1987, an estimated 1.5 million who wanted to work were unemployed in Zimbabwe. Fundamentally, there has been no real improvement in formal-sector employment since independence, and the number of workers employed in agriculture has declined. It is projected that unless more rapid economic growth occurs and substantially higher levels of job creation can be achieved, unemployment among well-educated school-leavers is likely to reach very serious proportions by 1990.[93]

Although the government, by introducing a minimum wage, attempted to bridge the economic gap between the elite and the masses, the elite continue to enjoy the fruits of economic growth in Zimbabwe. Granting that real wages for workers did improve in the early years of independence, these increases have been offset by inflation, leaving many workers no better off than before.[94] Even though some of the African elite have benefited from post-independence development, for the most part, the white minority continues to amass the wealth in this country.

Tanzania

Between 1970 and 1979, Tanzania's economic performance "was above the African and low-income country group average," with a GDP growth rate of nearly 5 percent. Between 1980 and 1985, however, GDP growth was only 0.8 percent. Tanzania's economic problems are said to be attributed to the external shocks of 1973–1976 and 1979–1981 (i.e., the falling price of coffee between 1980 and 1981) and the internal domestic policies.[95]

Of all the SADCC member states, Tanzania has been the most successful in decreasing the income disparity between rural and urban dwellers. Even so, a large percentage of the population lives in poverty, as indicated by the average GNP per capita, which in 1985 was only $290. Since only approximately 7.9 percent of the population is involved in wage employment, the country is faced with a serious unemployment problem.[96]

Level of General Social Welfare

As a result of underdevelopment and dependence, the SADCC governments have found it increasingly difficult to provide for the general welfare needs of the masses. In general, by looking at certain indicators such as infant mortality, life expectancy, access to safe water, adult literacy, and health care, an overall assessment can be made about the level of development in a country.

Botswana, Lesotho, and Swaziland

The infant mortality rate in Botswana was 48 per 1,000 live births in 1986, the lowest in the region. In Lesotho the rate was 98 per 1,000 live births in 1985; in Swaziland, 130 per 1,000 (see Table 6). In Botswana, life expectancy in 1985 was 64 years, an increase of 14 from 1980. In 1975 the life expectancy in Lesotho was 46, and by 1985 it had increased to 52. Swaziland's life expectancy in 1985 was 55 years. The adult literacy rate in Botswana in 1982 was reported to have been 35 percent; in Swaziland, 55 percent. The adult literacy rate in Lesotho in 1985 was 60 percent (See Table 6).

In Botswana, by 1985, 95 percent of the urban population had access to potable water, although the figure for the rural population remained at 39 percent. The most recent figures for Lesotho indicate that only 17 percentage of the population has access to safe water; for Swaziland, only 37 percent.[97]

In Botswana, health services are currently available for approximately 85 percent of the population, although malnutrition has become a major problem as a result of the protracted drought.[98] In Swaziland, health conditions "are poor and well below those of other countries with similar income levels." [99]

Angola and Mozambique

In a study published by the United Nations Children's Fund (UNICEF) it was reported that in 1986 the child mortality rate in Angola and Mozambique was the highest in the world, between 33 and 38 percent. In the Tete region of Mozambique, the figure was as high as 45 percent. The infant mortality rate in 1986 was 200 per 1,000 live births and the child mortality rate reported for these two countries was between 325 and 375. Regional destabilization by South African-supported rebel armies is cited as the reason for these alarming statistics.[100]

Life expectancy at birth in Angola was 43 years in 1985, an increase of only four years from the 1975 figure (see Table 6). In Mozambique, life expectancy in 1985 was 52 years. The adult literacy rate in Angola was only 30 percent in 1982; in Mozambique, 33 percent.

Health conditions in Angola are generally very poor, largely as a consequence of war and destabilization. In many areas accessibility to primary health-care facilities and referral units have been reduced due to lack of security. In addition, as a result of chronic food shortages, in 1986 it was estimated that 30 percent of the children in urban areas and 20 percent in rural villages were suffering from severe malnutrition.[101]

The present economic and political crisis in Mozambique has made it impossible to provide adequate health-care facilities. Between 1981 and 1986, 718 health centers reportedly were destroyed by MNR rebels, and health workers have been wounded, maimed, murdered, and kidnapped in order to prevent them from traveling to rural areas. Currently, an estimated three million Mozambicans do not have access to medical facilities.[102] Health problems in the country are no doubt exacerbated by the fact that reportedly fewer than 10 percent of the population has access to safe water.[103]

Malawi, Zambia, and Zimbabwe

Malawi also has a high infant mortality rate, reported to be 159 per 1,000 live births in 1985. Zambia's infant mortality rate in 1984 was 84 per 1,000 live births; Zimbabwe's, 77. Life expectancy at birth in Malawi was only 45 years in 1985; 52 years, in Zambia; 57, in Zimbabwe. Zimbabwe had the highest

TABLE 6
SADCC Member States
LEVEL OF GENERAL WELFARE

Infant Mortality (Per Thousand)

	1976	1977	1978	1979	1980	1981	1982	1983	1984	1985
Angola	—	—	—	—	154	152	—	147	144	325
Botswana	—	—	—	—	83	—	—	—	72	63
Lesotho	—	—	—	—	115	113	—	104	99	98
Malawi	—	—	—	—	172	169	164	164	158	159
Mozambique	—	—	—	—	115	113	115	115	125	325
Swaziland	—	—	—	—	—	—	142	—	133	130
Tanzania	—	—	185	—	103	101	98	97	111	110
Zambia	—	—	—	—	106	104	105	100	85	84
Zimbabwe	—	—	—	—	74	72	83	63	77	77

TABLE 6 continued on next page

Life Expectancy

	1976	1977	1978	1979	1980	1981	1982	1983	1984	1985
Angola	—	41	41	42	42	42	43	43	43	43
Botswana	—	—	—	—	50	—	—	50	61	64
Lesotho	—	50	50	51	51	52	53	53	54	54
Malawi	—	46	46	49	44	44	44	44	45	45
Mozambique	—	46	46	47	47	47	47	47	46	52
Swaziland	—	—	—	—	—	—	47	47	56	55
Tanzania	—	51	51	52	52	52	52	52	53	52
Zambia	—	48	48	49	49	51	51	51	52	52
Zimbabwe	—	—	—	55	55	55	56	56	57	57

TABLE 6 continued on next page

Adult Literacy (Percent)

	1976	1977	1978	1979	1980	1981	1982	1983	1984	1985
Angola	—	—	—	—	—	—	30	30	30	30
Botswana	35	35	35	35	35	35	35	—	—	—
Lesotho	—	52	—	55	—	—	—	—	—	60
Malawi	25	25	25	25	25	25	25	25	25	25
Mozambique	—	28	—	—	—	—	—	28	—	33
Swaziland	45	—	—	—	—	—	55	—	—	—
Tanzania	66	66	74	—	79	—	—	—	—	—
Zambia	39	44	—	—	—	—	—	—	—	54
Zimbabwe	—	—	—	—	69	—	—	—	—	—

Sources: *World Development Report,* 1978-1987 • *Country Reports on Human Rights Practice,* 1981–1985 • *The Washington Post,* December 11, 1986

adult literacy rate among these three countries, with a reported rate of 69 percent in 1980. The 1985 adult literacy figures for Malawi reflect a rate of only 25 percent; for Zambia, 54 percent.

In the rural areas of Malawi, 37 percent of the population is reported to have access to safe water; in the urban areas, 77 percent. According to the most recent figures for Zambia, 67 percent of the urban population and 66 percent of the rural population have access to safe water.[104]

In Zimbabwe, the provision of health care for the urban areas and the rural areas varies widely. While good health services are generally available to urban inhabitants, the rural population "is much less likely to have easy access to even basic medical attention, primarily because Zimbabwe lacks the personnel and infrastructure necessary."[105]

Tanzania

Tanzania's infant mortality rate in 1985 was 110 per 1,000 live births. Life expectancy was 52 years, and the latest (1980) figures for Tanzania's adult literacy rate, reported to be 79 percent, is not only the highest among the SADCC nations, but the highest in Africa.

Although a high priority is placed on medical care in Tanzania, "health care is still inadequate for the needs of the population." According to the most recent figures, more than 42 percent of the population had access to clean water.[106]

1987/88 UPDATE

As mentioned, this part of the chapter will provide an economic update on the SADCC member states. While "the performance of SADCC countries improved substantially in 1987 compared to 1986,"[107] these nations, with the exception of Botswana, continued to experience deteriorating terms of trade, foreign exchange shortages, heavy debt-service burdens, and rising unemployment. This trend continued throughout 1988.

Botswana

Gross domestic product (GDP) in Botswana increased by 14.7

percent in 1986-1987. This figure represents the highest rate of economic growth in 1987 among the SADCC member states. Botswana recorded a GDP per capita growth rate of 11.5 percent in 1986-1987, and it is projected that the GDP will grow by 8.7 percent in real terms during 1987-1988, reaching $1,500 per capita. In 1987 Botswana recorded a balance of payment surplus of Pula 950 million. This was a significant increase over the 1986 surplus of Pula 566 million.[108] "The current level of reserves would pay no less than 28 months' imports."[109]

Amidst all this prosperity, Botswana continues to be a major importer of food. Although after six years of drought the country finally received normal rainfall in 1988 (which means a significant increase in agricultural production is expected), Botswana has a deficit of 122,000 tons of maize equivalent (MGE).[110]

Lesotho

The GDP grew by approximately 1.7 percent in 1987, while GDP per capita declined by 1.1 percent. As a result of the poor performance of its economy, largely caused by adverse weather conditions, Lesotho embarked on a structural adjustment program with the IMF. Due to the drought, the country will experience a food deficit of 110,000 tons (MGE).[111]

Swaziland

The GDP grew by only 3.8 percent in Swaziland in 1987, which represented a significant decline over the 9 percent growth experienced in 1986. The GDP per capita grew by only 0.6 percent in 1987. Imported food requirements for 1988-1989 will total 30,000 tons.[112] "Foreign reserves in 1987 reached four months' import coverage, and external debt-service payments reportedly are approximately 8 percent of exports of goods and services."[113]

Angola

Angola's economy continues to be adversely affected by the war being waged against the South African- and U.S.-backed UNITA rebels. Fortunately, oil production remains relatively unaffected by the war and has, in fact, increased.[114]

However, at least 37 percent of all state expenditures go

toward the war. By 1987, according to President José Eduardo dos Santos, war damage was estimated at $12 billion. At least 1.5 million persons are displaced in Angola, and in 1987 the International Red Cross said 10,000 had been crippled, mostly by land mines.[115]

With its foreign debt having reached $4 billion in 1987, "debt-service payments were absorbing one-third of Angola's revenue, and debt arrears were up to $37 million." With the U.S. continuing to oppose Angola's IMF membership, the country cannot reschedule its debt.[116]

In 1988 the government embarked on a program of economic recovery for the period 1988-1989. "The programme encompassed fiscal, monetary, wage and price policy reform, privatisation of certain activities, rehabilitation of existing productive enterprises, and investment in new enterprises."[117] By the end of 1988, there had been no measurable improvement in the economy.

In a further effort to reverse the economic decline, during 1988 the government embarked on a campaign for a greater share of world-wide aid funds. "In April the EEC granted Angola ECU 42m to finance imports associated with rehabilitation and development of food production, trade networks, industrial and agricultural projects in Hula and Kwanza Sul Province and fisheries in Namibe."[118] In addition, $75 million for humanitarian and emergency aid was given to Angola at a May donors conference in Geneva. This was followed by an EEC grant for emergency rehabilitation of basic sanitation facilities. It is hoped that this will help control the current cholera outbreak.[119]

In order to help with its food requirements, Angola plans to import commercially 179,000 tons. Although by May 1988 the government had either received or been given pledges for 80,000 tons of food aid, the country was still in need of 350,000 tons.[120]

Mozambique

After six years of negative growth, in 1987, Mozambique recorded a positive rate of GDP growth, 4.7 percent. This improved performance is attributed to a number of economic reforms (e.g., improvement of producer price incentives, land redistribution). Mozambique initially embarked on an economic

Post-independence 113

recovery program in 1984 (Economic Action Program of 1984–1986), followed by a second program in 1987 (Economic Rehabilitation Program, 1987–89 [PRE]).[121] The PRE was developed after "extensive discussions with the IMF and World Bank during 1985 and 1986 and also formed the basis of an agreement with the Fund and Bank signed in March 1987."[122] In a further effort to reverse the current economic crisis, an emergency conference was held in Maputo in April 1988, with a view toward raising money for a two-year emergency program. At the conference, donors pledged $270 million, $60 million less than the country had asked for.[123]

Although the PRE has resulted in an improvement in the economic situation, most notable by plenty of goods on the shelves and in the market, the masses have not been the major beneficiaries. The devaluations of the Mozambique currency have been catastrophic for the majority of Mozambicans. While in January 1987, 43 Meticas (MT) were equal to one U.S. dollar, by July 1988, 580 MT equaled one U.S. dollar. Even though "wage increases of 50 percent were granted at the time of each of the first two devaluations, these have not compensated for higher consumer prices."[124]

Although in early 1987, Mozambique rescheduled its $3.2 billion debt, its "external interest debt will continue larger than gross export receipts."[125] As a result of the war, all of Mozambique's food imports will be in the form of food aid. As of July 1988, the country had received 50,000 tons of food, but still required some 675,000 tons.[126]

South Africa's continued aggression against Mozambique and its ongoing support of the Renamo terrorists is the major hindrance to economic development. In 1988 an estimated six million internally displaced Mozambicans were in danger of starvation; and a U.S. State Department release in April "indicates that more than 100,000 Mozambicans have been murdered over the last two years by the South African-backed Renamo terrorists."[127] Amidst the ongoing tragedies of war, the situation has been aggravated by South Africa's decision to repatriate migrant workers. According to Labor Minister Aguiar Mazula:

For more than a year now, the South African government

has been enforcing a "continuous process of repatriation of Mozambican mine workers" . . . and judging by the numbers of workers being expelled, between 30,000 and 40,000 Mozambican miners would have been repatriated within three years. On the other hand, no new workers have been hired.[128]

In addition, during the first six months of 1988, an estimated 20,000 illegal immigrants from SADCC member states were repatriated from South Africa. Of this number, approximately 15,600 were repatriated to Mozambique.[129] The government of Mozambique has responded to this repatriation by working with UN agencies, the Nordic countries and Non-governmental Organizations (NGOs) to create reception centers for these workers and help reintegrate them into the Mozambique economy.[130]

Malawi

The GDP in Malawi grew by 2.3 percent in 1987, but the GDP per capita declined by 1 percent. Malawi continues to be faced with food shortages, partially attributable to the 600,000 Mozambican refugees residing in that country. In addition, the drought continues to pose a serious problem. Currently, Malawi has a food deficit of 233,000 tons.[131]

During 1987 Malawi continued to experience a severe current account balance of payment deficits. The 149.2 million kwacha deficit for 1987 represented a 7 percent deterioration over 1986, due to an increasing debt burden (interest payments on external loans rose by 75 percent) and continued transport problems.[132] Malawi's debt service in 1986-1987 constituted 56 percent of GDP, and during 1987 the inflation rate rose from 15 percent to 26.7 percent.[133] As a result of severe problems with the economy:

> Malawi's facility with the IMF was cancelled in early 1986, and a new facility has been under negotiation ever since. The decision in mid-1987 to seek a further debt rescheduling appeared to clear the way for an agreement. If one is announced, its terms are likely to be harsh, including large cutbacks in public spending, and consequently substantial job losses in the public sector.[134]

Zambia

Zambia's decision to abandon its IMF structural adjustment program in May 1987 has had serious consequences for its economy. The GDP growth in real terms declined by 0.2 percent in 1987 and the rate of inflation stood at 55 percent. In addition, the drought hindered agricultural production, and the country currently faces a food deficit of an estimated 149,000 tons (MGE).[135]

On the positive side, the price of copper increased to "1,078 pounds sterling per tonne in 1987 compared to 937 pounds per tonne in 1986."[136] This was basically offset, however, by Zambia's problems with the IMF.

In January 1988, the government announced a New Economic Recovery Program with a view toward arresting the current economic malaise. As part of the program the government decided to reduce its debt payment to 10 percent of its net foreign-exchange earnings. By the end of 1987, Zambia's foreign debt was estimated to be $5 billion.[137] Neither the World Bank nor the IMF is impressed with the program, and

> before they will do business they are holding out for a downward re-adjustment of the Kwacha, a reduction in the budget deficit, a move towards control of prices, more encouragement for farmers, and of course, as condition precedent, the paying up of arrears due to them.[138]

Needless to say, Zambia recently rejected these proposals by the IMF and the World Bank "for the devaluation of the Kwacha and reduction of the budget deficit by 4% before the two institutions can help the country out of its economic problems."[139] Currently, Zambia's arrears to the World Bank total $90 million, and in 1989 this will increase to $140 million unless something is done.[140] Since Zambia is not on good terms with the World Bank and the IMF, it has found that the aid taps of most Western nations have been turned off.[141]

Zimbabwe

In 1987, the GDP grew by less than 1 percent in Zimbabwe, and the balance of payment surplus of 1986 turned to a deficit of Z$190 million in 1987. Inflation was about 11.9 percent, and even though the government plans to export surpluses of 866,000 tons of maize and 21,000 tons of sorghum during 1988-1989, 90,000 tons of wheat are scheduled to be imported.[142]

At the end of 1987, Zimbabwe's foreign debt, including short-term obligations, was estimated to be $2.7 billion, which represented a 5 percent increase over figures for 1986.[143]

Zimbabwe continues to experience a serious unemployment problem, and estimates are that if current trends continue, the unemployment level will reach 24 percent by 1990.[144]

Tanzania

The GDP in Tanzania grew by 3.9 percent in real terms during 1987, although GDP per capita remained stagnant.[145] The overall balance of payment deficit was $516.2 million in 1986, and it is projected that it will increase to $714 million in 1988.[146] The country will experience a grain surplus of 60,000 tons (MGE) for 1988-1989.[147]

As a result of Tanzania's Economic Recovery Program (ERP), which includes an agreement with the IMF signed in 1986 (an 18-month stand-by agreement, to be followed by a three-year structural adjustment program), there has been an increase in production and per capita income. In addition, the government fiscal balance has improved in real terms; and "despite large devaluations (500%+ between 1986 and the present) and the removal of price subsides, inflation has been contained."[148]

However, in social terms, it appears that the program has had an adverse effect on low-income groups. Unemployment among this group has increased, and access to social services has declined. In addition, "progress on combating major social problems," including malnutrition, "has slowed down."[149]

NOTES

1. Vincent A. Mahler, *Dependency Approaches to International Political Economy: A Cross National Study* (New York: Columbia University Press, 1980), p. 64.

2. SADCC, *SADCC Annual Progress Report, July 1986–August 1987* (SADCC, 1987) p. 4).

3. Maggie Jonas,"Botswana Survey," *African Business*, September 1986, p. 50.

4. Economist Intelligence Unit, *Quarterly Economic Review of Namibia, Botswana, Lesotho, Swaziland* (London: Spencer House, 1983) p. 28. Hereafter referred to as EIU and QER.

5. Jonas, "Botswana," p. 56.

6. EIU, *QER of Namibia, Botswana, Lesotho, Swaziland*, 1982, pp. 36-37.

7. *Ibid.*, p. 47.

8. EIU, *Country Profile: Angola, 1986–87*, (London: Spencer House, 1986), pp. 30-32.

9. EIU, *Country Profile: Mozambique, 1987-88*, 1987, p. 28.

10. EIU, *Country Profile: Mozambique, 1986-87*, 1986, pp. 25-27.

11. *Ibid*, p. 28. On the issue of the "gold premium" payment, which was crucial to the Mozambican economy, Allen Issacman and Barbara Issacman in *Mozambique: From Colonialism to Revolution, 1900-1912*, (Boulder, Colo.: Westview Press, 1983), p. 217 (n. 63) note:
    > In the last year before independence, Mozambique earned approximately $150 million from remittances of approximately 100,000 miners. By 1978 the number of Mozambicans working in the mines had decreased to 30,000, and in that year the South African government abrogated the colonial sales agreement, which stipulated that 60 percent of each worker's salary be paid directly to the Portuguese authorities in Mozambique in gold at a low fixed exchange rate. The Portuguese paid the miners in escudos and then sold the gold on the market at much higher prevailing rates, thus generating a substantial source of invisible income. This was one of the main ways in which South Africa propped up the sickly Portuguese economy.

12. EIU, *Country Profile: Malawi, 1986-87*, 1986, pp. 26-27, and *Country Profile: Malawi, 1987-1988*, 1987, p. 26.

13. EIU, *Country Report: Zambia*, No. 3, 1986, p. 2, and *Country Profile: Zimbabwe, 1987-88*, 1987, p. 34.

14. EIU, *Country Profile: Zimbabwe 1986-87*, 1986, and *Country Profile: Zimbabwe, 1987-88*, 1987, p. 32.

15. EIU, *QER of Tanzania, Mozambique*, 1983, p. 16.

16. EIU, Country Report: *Tanzania, Mozambique*, 1986, p. 17; "Tanzania Survey," *African Business*, September 1987, p. 51.

17. EIU, *Country Profile: Tanzania, 1987-88*, 1987, p. 23.

18. Mahler, *Dependency*, pp. 31-32.

19. EIU, *QER of Southern Africa*, 1981, p. 44; Arne Tostensen, *Dependence and Collective Self-Reliance in Southern Africa: The Case of the Southern African Development Coordination Conference* (Uppsala, Sweden: The Scandinavian Institute of African Studies, 1982), p. 52.

20. EIU, *QER of Southern Africa*, 1981, p. 44.

21. Jonas, "Botswana," p. 53.

22. Tostensen, *Self-Reliance*, p. 53.

23. EIU, *QER of Southern Africa*, 1981, p. 45.

24. Joseph Hanlon, *Beggar Your Neighbours: Apartheid Power in Southern Africa* (London: Catholic Institute for International Relations, 1986), p. 286.

25. EIU, *QER of Southern Africa*, 1982, p. 35.

26. *Ibid.*, p. 98.

27. Hanlon, *Beggar*, p. 99.

28. *Ibid.*, p. 98.

29. *Ibid.*, pp. 98-99.

30. Tostensen, *Self-Reliance*, p. 57.

31. *Ibid.*, p. 56.

32. Hanlon, *Beggar*, p. 295.

33. EIU, *Country Profile: Angola, 1986-87*, 1986, p. 21.

34. EIU, *QER of Angola, Guinea-Bissau, Cape Verde Islands, Sao Tome and Principle*, 1983, pp. 13-14.

35. *Ibid.*, p. 17.

36. Hanlon, *Beggar*, p. 295.

37. EIU, *QER of Angola, Guinea-Bissau*, 1983, p. 19.

38. Tostensen, *Self-Reliance*, p. 55.

39. EIU, *QER of Zimbabwe and Malawi*, 1983, p. 30.

40. Tostensen, *Self-Reliance*, p. 55.

41. Hanlon, *Beggar*, p. 291.

42. Tostensen, *Self-Reliance*, p. 54.

43. *Ibid.*, p. 54.

44. See Hanlon, *Beggar*, pp. 301-302.

45. *Ibid.*, p. 305.

46. *Ibid.*, p. 201. For a list of foreign companies in Zimbabwe, see D. H. Clarke, *Foreign Companies and International Investment in Zimbabwe* (London: Catholic Institute for International Relations, 1980), pp. 169-207.

47. EIU, *QER of Tanzania and Mozambique*, 1983, p. 9.

48. Mahler, *Dependency*, pp. 32-33.

49. *Ibid.*, p. 33.

50. EIU, *Country Profile: Botswana, Lesotho, Swaziland, 1987-88*, 1987, p. 32.

51. *Ibid.*, p. 53.

52. EIU, *QER of Angola, Guinea-Bissau*, 1983, p. 26; *Financial Times* (London) January 2, 1988.

53. SADCC, *Report*, p. 2.

54. EIU, *Country Profile: Malawi, 1986-87*, 1986, p. 29.

55. EIU, *Country Report: Zambia*, No. 3, 1986, p. 29.

56. EIU, *Country Report: Tanzania, Mozambique*, No. 3, 1986, p. 4.

57. SADCC, *Report*, p. 3.

58. *Ibid.*, p. 4.

59. Jonas, "Botswana," p. 49; Gwen Ansell, "Botswana Survey," *African Business*, October 1987, p. 43.

60. *Ibid.*, pp. 55-56; SADCC, *Report*, p. 5.

61. SADCC, "Revised Assessment of the Impact of the 1986/87 Drought in SADCC Member States," Harare, June 1987, pp. 9, 13.

62. Ansell, "Survey," p. 62.

63. Jonas, "Botswana," p. 62.

64. *Ibid.*, p. 62; *Country Profile: Botswana, Lesotho, Swaziland, 1987-88*, 1987, pp. 14-16.

65. James Cobbe, "Sanctions Against South Africa: Lesotho's Role," paper presented at the 30th Annual Meeting of the African Studies Association, Denver, Colorado, November 20, 1987.

66. EIU, *Country Profile: Botswana, Lesotho, Swaziland, 1987-88*, p. 43.

67. V. Jamal, *Rural-Urban Gap and Income Distribution: The Case of Lesotho* (Addis Ababa: International Labour Organisation, Jobs and Skills Programme for Africa, 1982), p. 2.

68. Cobbe, "Sanctions," p. 7.

69. EIU, *QER of Namibia, Botswana, Lesotho, Swaziland*, 1982, p. 30.

70. EIU, *Country Profile: Botswana, Lesotho, Swaziland, 1987-88*, 1987, p. 66.

71. Hanlon, *Beggar*, p. 297.

72. EIU, *Country Profile: Botswana, Lesotho, Swaziland, 1987-88*, 1987, p. 67.

73. Hanlon, *Beggar*, p. 169.

74. EIU, *Country Profile: Angola, Guinea-Bissau, Cape Verde Islands, Sao Tome and Principle, 1986-87*, 1986, pp. 10-11; *Country Profile: Angola, Guinea-Bissau, Cape Verde Islands, Sao Tome and Principle, 1987-88*, 1987, p. 11.

75. United Nations Office for Emergency Operations in Africa, *Status Report on the Emergency Situation in Africa as of April 1, 1986* (New York: United Nations, 1986), pp. 23-25; "War and Hunger: Angola," *Africa News*, December 7, 1987, p. 7.

76. SADCC, "Revised Assessment," p. 3.

77. Colin Legum, ed., *Africa Contemporary Record* (New York: Africana Publishing Company, 1981-82), p. B661.

78. EIU, *Country Report: Tanzania and Mozambique*, No. 4, 1986, p. 3; EIU, *Country Profile: Mozambique, 1987-88*, 1987, p. 9.

79. SADCC, "Revised Assessment," p. 35.

80. William Claiborne, "S. Africa Halts Hiring of Mozambican Workers," *The Washington Post*, October 9, 1986; EIU, *Country Profile: Mozambique 1987-88*, 1987, pp. 12-13.

81. SADCC, *Report*, p. 5.

82. "Budget Speech Confirms Negative GDP Growth," *African Business*, May 1987, p. 18.

83. *Financial Times* (London), January 7, 1988.

84. *Ibid.*

85. EIU, *Country Profile: Malawi 1987-88*, 1987, pp. 13-14.

86. Kenneth Grundy, "Economic Patterns in the New Southern African Balance," *Southern Africa: The Continuing Crisis*, ed. Gwendolen Carter and Patrick O'Meara (Bloomington: Indiana University Press, 1979), p. 307.

87. EIU, *Country Report Zambia*, No. 3, 1986, p. 2; SADCC, *Report*, p. 6.

88. Andrew Meldrum, "Going it Alone," *Africa Report*, November-December 1987, p. 40.

89. *Ibid.*

90. Department of State, *Country Reports on Human Rights Practices for 1983* (Washington, D.C.: U.S. State Department, 1984), p. 365.

91. EIU, *Country Profile: Zimbabwe, 1986-1987*, 1986, p. 8.

92. EIU, *Country Report: Zimbabwe and Malawi*, No. 3, 1986, p. 2; SADCC, *Report*, p. 6.

93. "MPs Voice Fears over Rise in Unemployment," *Herald* (Zim.), July 16, 1987; "Beating Job Shortage," *Herald* (Zim.), August 10, 1987, August 13, 1987.

94. "Beating Job Shortage," *Herald* (Zim.).

95. Legum, *Africa*, p. B272; "Tanzania Survey," *African Busi-*

ness, September 1987, p. 51.

96. "Tanzania Survey," p. 51; V. *Jamal, Rural-Urban Gap,* p. 49.

97. Department of State, *Country Reports on Human Rights Practices for 1985* (Washington, D.C.: U. S. State Department, 1986), pp. 24, 173, 337.

98. EIU, *Country Profile: Botswana, Lesotho, Swaziland, 1987-1988,* 1987, p. 9.

99. *Ibid.,* p. 63.

100. Blaine Harden, "UNICEF Blames S. Africa for Child Deaths," *The Washington Post,* December 11, 1986.

101. United Nations Office for Emergency Operations in Africa, *Status Report,* p. 27.

102. Harden, "UNICEF"; SADCC, "Revised Assessment," p. 37.

103. Department of State, "Country Reports," 1986, p. 229.

104. Ibid., pp. 199-200, 387.

105. Department of State, "Country Reports," 1984, pp. 439-40.

106. *Ibid.,* p. 380.

107. SADCC, *Draft Annual Progress Report,* 1988, p. 1.

108. *Ibid.,* p. 4.

109. "The Embarrassment of Riches," *The Southern African Economist,* February/March 1988, p. 16.

110. SADCC, *Draft,* 1988, pp. 6, 11.

111. *Ibid.,* pp. 5, 11.

112. *Ibid.,* pp. 7, 11.

113. "Tax Burden Eased in Swaziland," *The Southern African Economist,* April/May 1988, p. 16.

114. "Angola Still Waits for Reforms," *African Business*, July 1988, p. 21.

115. "Angola's Economy Needs Peace," *The Southern African Economist*, June-July 1988, p. 21.

116. *Ibid.*

117. SADCC, *Draft*, 1988, p. 4.

118. "Angola's Economy Needs Peace," June-July 1988, p. 21.

119. *Ibid.*

120. SADCC, *Draft*, 1988, p. 11.

121. *Ibid.*, p. 7.

122. Rob Davies, "Crisis Management in Mozambique," *Southern African Economist*, June/July 1988, p. 17.

123. *Ibid.*

124. *Ibid.*, p. 19.

125. "Devaluation at Work," *Southern African Economist*, February/March 1988, p. 11.

126. SADCC, *Draft*, 1988, p. 11.

127. "State Department Report Exposes Remano Atrocities," *Mozambique Update*, Embassy of the People's Republic of Mozambique, May 20, 1988, p. 2.

128. *Mozambique Update*, Embassy of the People's Republic of Mozambique, August 5, 1988, p. 5.

129. *Facts and Reports*, August 19, 1988, Vol. 19, p. 32.

130. *Mozambique Update*, August 5, 1988, p. 5.

131. SADCC, *Draft*, 1988, pp. 5-6, 11.

132. "Malawi Grasps the Nettle," *Southern African Economist*,

April/May 1988, pp. 13-14.

133. *Ibid.*, p. 15.

134. "Success and Setback," *Southern African Economist*, February/March 1988, p. 21.

135. SADCC, *Draft*, 1988, pp. 8-9, 11.

136. *Ibid.*, p. 8.

137. "Regional News," *Southern Africa: Political and Economic Monthly*, July 1988, p. 3; "Zambia Economic Indicators," *African Business*, April 1988.

138. "Eyeball to Eyeball in Zambia," *Southern African Economist*, June/July 1988, p. 16.

139. "Regional News," July 1988, p. 3.

140. "Eyeball to Eyeball," June/July 1988, p. 16.

141. *Ibid.*

142. SADCC, *Draft*, 1988, pp. 9-10, 12.

143. "Zim's Debt Now U.S. $2.76b," *Financial Gazette* (Zim.), July 29, 1988.

144. See "Swelling the Ranks of the Unemployed," *Herald* (Zim.), July 22, 1988.

145. SADCC, *Draft*, 1988, pp. 7-8, 11.

146. "Tanzania Economic Indicators," *African Business*, June 1988, p. 70.

147. SADCC, *Draft*, 1988, p. 11.

148. This information was taken from Chris Davids, "Executive Summary," a study for CIDA, July 1988.

149. *Ibid.*

CHAPTER 4

SADCC's Strategy for Regional Cooperation and Development

A review of the *SADCC Annual Progress Report, July 1987 – August 1988* will leave the reader quite impressed with SADCC, although some questions might be raised about the ever expanding list of projects, old and new, that have yet to be implemented. Visiting the SADCC Secretariat in Gaborone, Botswana, is even more impressive. The highly competent staff includes individuals from the various SADCC member states who greet visitors with open arms. That they are serious about SADCC and committed to its success is obvious. It is also obvious that the Secretariat is rapidly outgrowing its current home. Under the leadership of Dr. Simba H. S. Makoni, SADCC's executive secretary, the office has grown tremendously from its original two-person staff.

As a review of chapters 2 and 3 indicate, however, the problems of development with which the SADCC states are confronted are formidable. Faced with these problems, which are worsening daily due to South Africa's regional destabilization, one must ask, Can SADCC really be a conduit for regional structural transformation? Can SADCC really begin to alter the structural linkages of dependency and underdevelopment in the region? Certainly a review of the Lusaka Declaration, in which SADCC's objectives are outlined, indicate that structural transformation is crucial to the member states. This includes the decreasing of economic dependence on South Africa; the reduction of dependence in general; the forging of links to create a genuine and equitable regional integration; the mobilization of resources to promote the implementation of national, interstate, and regional policies; and concerted action to secure international cooperation within the framework of the strategy outlined for economic liberation. The specific program calls for regional cooperation to develop seven sectors: transport and communications; food, agriculture, and natural resources; industry and trade; energy; mining; manpower; and tourism.

Each sector identifies projects that will serve to enhance the potential for regional structural transformation. Project implementation, however, is almost totally dependent upon economic assistance from Western nations. Such assistance has resulted in increased dependence on the global center, which fundamentally is a major contradiction, which SADCC officials themselves acknowledge. It is precisely this contradiction, however, that SADCC's harshest critics point to when noting that SADCC is not a success. For example, Moeletsi Mbeki of the *Herald* (Zim.) argues:

> The imperialists, alarmed by the inroads being made into Southern Africa by the socialist bloc, especially through Angola and Mozambique, also began to re-think their policies in the mid-70s in particular in the economic sphere where the imperialists are strongest in Southern Africa. The rethinking was to lead to the formation of .... SADCC, in 1980 . . . Several African students of Southern Africa are now coming to the view that SADCC was in fact inspired by the imperialists themselves, the objective was to entice Angola and Mozambique back from their attempts to link up with the socialist Council for Mutual Economic Assistance, CMEA of COMECOM, headquartered in Moscow, through the promise of Western aid. Secondly while purporting to help the government of these countries to disengage from South Africa, the imperialist powers hoped to strengthen and broaden their influence over the economic and social policies of the nine countries, through financial and technical assistance.[1]

The SADCC officials and supporters, on the other hand, argue that SADCC was created by the independent nations of Southern Africa. With respect to the contradiction inherent in increased dependency on the West, Nkwabi Ng'wanakilala, SADCC information officer, agrees that:

> there is a contradiction . . . Right now it is true that we might be looking kind of desperate, but I think more and more the countries are seeing the mobilization of resources in their own countries as being the only, most viable thing to do. That if you can put up the dollars, then put them up, rather than depend on someone else. This is

actually what SADCC is doing now. To sort of encourage these countries to think inwardly. Originally . . . we thought our major function was to stand on the platform and plead for assistance from donors. Actually, the other task is even more important: to tell the SADCC countries that you can't develop unless you have been able yourself to coordinate your own programs and to mobilize resources from within the nine countries . . . I can assure you that a lot of people are looking inwardly and if you see the communique of the 1987 Summit . . . we are better to go on with our poverty rather than accept money with strings attached.[2]

Unfortunately, there is no such thing as untied economic assistance, and there is no simple solution to the problem of dependency and underdevelopment in Southern Africa. Currently, the SADCC member states are caught in a vicious cycle; one that will not be solved by simply rejecting economic assistance from the West. The deteriorating regional security situation, as a result of South Africa's destabilization, is causing unimaginable suffering in the region, and as Ng'wanakilala further notes, "when you get five billion from the Western countries, and the cost of destabilization comes to five billion (which the West is supporting) . . . you don't make any progress . . . you're caught in a vicious cycle." [3]

Needless to say, it appears that the Western imperialist powers are not currently interested in regional development that will lead to structural transformation. After all, such transformation would alter their economic and political hegemony over the region. This discussion, however, is reserved for chapter 7.

The objective of this chapter is to explain SADCC's Program of Action and to investigate the degree to which it can potentially lead to regional structural transformation, if all the 571 SADCC projects are implemented (see Table 7). This chapter is divided into five sections, representing five of the seven sectors: transport and communications; food, agriculture, and natural resources; industry; energy; and manpower. The other two sectors, mining and tourism, are still in the early stages of development. Among these seven sectors, however, all nine countries are responsible for coordinating one or two areas. An area may include an entire

TABLE 7
SADCC PROJECT FINANCING STATUS BY SECTOR, 1988
(in US$ millions)

Sector	No. of Projects	TOTAL	OF WHICH Foreign	%	Local	%	FOR WHICH Secured	%	Negotiation	%	Gap	%
ENERGY	68	308.14	291.55	94.6	16.59	5.4	153.69	49.9	15.67	5.1	138.79	45.0
FOOD, AGRICULTURE AND NATURAL RESOURCES												
Agriculture Research	15	103.79	91.44	88.1	12.35	11.9	70.51	68.0	1.92	1.8	31.36	30.2
Food Security	32	397.98	356.07	89.5	41.91	10.5	77.05	19.4	9.66	2.4	311.27	78.2
Fisheries	13	21.16	19.99	94.5	1.17	5.5	7.52	35.5	7.55	35.7	6.09	28.8
Forestry	23	94.12	90.92	96.6	3.20	3.4	44.02	46.8	14.14	15.0	35.96	38.2
Wildlife	19	15.66	14.38	91.8	1.28	8.2	2.11	13.5	9.44	60.3	4.11	26.2
Livestock Production and Animal Disease Control	14	73.47	62.50	85.1	10.97	14.9	57.92	78.8	8.30	11.3	7.25	9.9
Soil and Water Conservation and Land Utilisation	19	53.81	50.15	93.2	3.66	6.8	18.25	33.9	17.47	32.5	18.09	33.6

TABLE 7 continued on next page

Sector	No. of Projects	TOTAL	OF WHICH Foreign	%	Local	%	FOR WHICH Secured	%	Negotiation	%	Gap	%
INDUSTRY AND TRADE	92	1271.91	1009.64	79.4	262.22	20.6	313.23	24.60	540.11	42.50	418.73	32.9
MANPOWER DEVELOPMENT	32	37.46	37.30	99.6	0.16	0.40	8.73	23.30	2.00	5.30	26.73	71.4
MINING	53	73.38	66.27	90.3	7.11	9.7	33.29	45.40	1.90	2.60	38.19	52.0
TOURISM	10	12.33	11.72	95.0	0.62	5.0	7.02	56.90	2.22	18.00	3.10	25.1
TRANSPORT AND COMMUNICATIONS	181	4719.60	4216.30	89.3	503.30	10.7	1882.30	39.90	199.60	4.20	2637.70	55.9
	571	7182.81	6318.22	88.0	864.58	12.0	2675.62	37.25	829.98	11.55	3677.21	51.2

NOTES: (1) The column Secured includes both local and foreign resources.

(2) The column Negotiation refers to resources for which there is a clearly identified funding source and a high probability of concluding a funding agreement within a specified period.

(3) The totals do not include completed or withdrawn projects.

SOURCE: *SADCC Annual Progress Report,* July 1987-August 1988.

FIGURE 3

ALLOCATION OF COORDINATION WITHIN THE SADCC PROGRAM OF ACTION

Energy

Livestock Production and Animal Disease Control; Agricultural Research

Soil and Water Conservation and Land Utilization; Tourism

Fisheries, Wildlife, and Forestry

Transport and Communications

Manpower

Industry and Trade

Mining

Food Security

Strategy for Regional Cooperation and Development 133

sector, as is the case with Angola, Mozambique, Swaziland, Lesotho and Tanzania; or subsectors within sectors, as is the case with Botswana, Lesotho, Malawi, Zambia, and Zimbabwe (see Figure 3).

Each section will include an overview of the sector, as well as an analysis of its prospects for decreasing regional dependency and fostering development. The process by which projects are identified and implemented will be discussed in the next chapter, which examines SADCC's institutional framework.

TRANSPORT AND COMMUNICATIONS

The regional sector that has received the highest priority within SADCC is transport and communications, for the SADCC states all agree that "a reliable and efficient transport and communications system is a prerequisite for an intensified and concerted development of the region." [4] In 1987, capital investment project priorities were identified as:

— rehabilitation of existing facilities;

— projects that reduce economic dependence and promote regional trade.

Special emphasis has been put on projects that will enhance the capacity of the regional transport network to handle all international trade through SADCC ports.[5]

In addition to capital investment projects, the program for this sector has two other areas: operational coordination and training. Within each subsector of the transport and communications sector, operation coordination and training projects have been identified. These subsectors are: Port Transport Systems, intra-regional surface transport systems, civil aviation, telecommunications, meteorology and postal services (see Table 8). In 1980, the Southern Africa Transport and Communications Commission (SATCC) was established in Mozambique to coordinate the development of this sector.

As of August 1988, this sector consisted of 181 projects, at a total estimated cost of $4,719 million. Of the total funding needed, 44 percent had been secured or was under negotiation (see Table 8). At least nineteen capital investment projects have been completed, and numerous others were underway.

Surface Transport Systems

Capital investment projects under the surface transport plan are centered around establishing viable transportation to the regional ports. Consequently, various port, railway, and road projects are combined and included in one of the five Port Transport Systems: the Maputo Port Transport System, the Beira Port Transport System, the Nacala Port Transport System, the Dar es Salaam Port Transport System and the Lobito Port Transport System (see Appendix B, Figure 7). Capital investment projects included in the regional surface transport plan, but not related to one of the five Port Transport Systems, are classified as intra-regional surface transport projects.

The intra-regional surface transport system consists of intra-regional railway projects and intra-road transport projects (see Appendix B, Figure 8). The intra-regional surface transport system, combined with the five Port Transport Systems, serves all internal and external transport needs of the region. In addition, the intra-regional projects include future road and railway links to independent Namibia.[6]

Progress is being made on four of the five Port Transport Systems. Maputo Port is currently being rehabilitated, and studies have been completed for the rehabilitation of the Maputo-Swaziland railway. Rehabilitation in Mozambique is scheduled to start before the end of 1988. Progress continues on the rehabilitation of the Limpopo line, and it is anticipated that the line will reopen to commercial traffic before the end of 1988 or by early 1989.[7] A Limpopo Technical Conference was held in Maputo July 27-28, 1988, and donors, along with Botswana, pledged about $60 million toward work on the railway. The donors include the United States, Germany, Canada, and Portugal.[8]

The rehabilitation of Beira Port is in progress, and the track rehabilitation of Zimbabwe-Dondo has been completed. There has been a significant increase in traffic between Beira and Zimbabwe, and the "rehabilitation of the Beira-Malawi railway has

TABLE 8
TRANSPORT AND COMMUNICATIONS FINANCING BY SUB-SECTOR, 1988

Subsector	No.	Total Cost US$	Foreign US$ MIL	Local US$ MIL	Funding Secured US$ MIL	%	Funding Under Negotiation	%	Funding Gap US$ MIL	%
Regional Operational Coordination Projects	23	55.9	55.2	0.7	24.5	44	5.4	10	26.0	47
Training Projects	15	60.6	57.4	3.2	37.3	62	8.0	13	15.3	25
Maputo Port Transport System Projects	19	812.4	710.5	101.9	271.0	35	35.0	4	506.4	62
Beira Port Transport System Projects	7	612.0	552.5	54.6	278.1	45	98.2	16	235.7	39
Nacala Port Transport System Projects	5	277.9	234.2	43.7	261.1	94	0.0	0	16.8	6
Dar-es-Salaam Port Transport System Projects	6	592.0	516.4	75.6	404.7	68	15.0	3	171.3	29

TABLE 8 continued on next page

Subsector	No.	Total Cost US$	Foreign US$ MIL	Local US$ MIL	Funding Secured US$ MIL	%	Funding Under Negotiation	%	Funding Gap US$ MIL	%
Lobito Port Transport System Projects	7	594.8	588.7	6.1	31.1	5	0.0	0	563.7	95
Intra-Regional Surface Transport Projects	32	713.4	594.3	119.1	223.0	31	25.0	4	465.4	65
Civil Aviation Projects	19	260.6	242.4	18.2	45.9	18	0.0	2	214.7	82
Telecommunications Projects	34	688.6	620.7	67.9	290.3	42	10.5	2	387.8	56
Meteorology Projects	10	19.8	19.6	0.2	2.7	14	2.5	13	14.6	74
Postal Services Projects	4	31.6	19.5	12.1	12.6	40	0.0	0	19.0	60
TOTAL	181	4719.6	4216.3	503.3	1882.3	40	199.6	4	2637.7	56

Source: SADCC Annual Progress Report, July 1987–August 1988.

been covered by pledges." [9]

The rehabilitation of the first phase of the Nacala Port has been completed, and plans are being finalized for a second phase. "The first phase of rehabilitation of the Nacala-Malawi railway has also been completed and the second phase is being completed." Plans are being made for the line to be reopened to international traffic.[10]

Traffic on both the Dar es Salaam and the Beira Port Transport Systems is increasing. Both the ports and the TAZARA line are being rehabilitated and upgraded.[11]

A 10-year Development Plan for the Lobito Port Transport System was presented at the 1988 Annual Consultative Conference. A Technical Coordination Conference on the Lobito system will be held in Lobito during the latter part of 1988. "It will follow the same pattern as the earlier conferences on TAZARA, the Beira Port Transport System, and the 10-year Development Plan for Telecommunications."[12]

If it appears that SATCC has assigned high priority to the development of the Port Transport Systems, Mugama Matolo, director of SATCC, is quick to point out that this is not the case; in fact, all the systems are extremely important. Instead, he argues, the SADCC strategy has been to highlight a Port Transport System each year, with the exception of the year the focus was on the telecommunications subsector.[13]

Civil Aviation

The immediate objective of the civil aviation program is the upgrading of regional airports located in SADCC member countries. Of particular concern is the upgrading of airports located in the regional capitals (see Appendix B, Figure 9), and those that are crucial for the intra-regional network and for intercontinental operation.[14] Successes in this sector to date include the opening of airports of Lilongwe (Malawi) and Gaborone (Botswana); completion of the new airport at Maseru (Lesotho); completion of the rehabilitation of airport lights and navigation, and the approach and landing aids at the airports of Maputo and Beira. In addition, there has been an increase in the number of flight connections between member states by national carriers (currently there is at least one flight connection each week between every SADCC capital); connections via Johannesburgh are being reduced.[15]

Telecommunications

The program of action for the development of the regional telecommunications subsector is related to the overall plan to provide Africa with a high-capacity telecommunications network, PANAFTEL (Pan African Telecommunications), which pre-dates the establishment of SADCC (see Appendix B, Figure 10). "The main emphasis in the PANAFTEL plan is the provision of a terrestrial network," which the SADCC states are committed to implementing.[16] Work in this subsector is being undertaken within the context of the Southern African Telecommunications Administration (SATA). As a result, most SADCC states now have telecommunications systems that are independent of South Africa. Less than five years ago, most intra-region and international calls had to be routed through Capetown, London, or Lisbon. In addition, Botswana, Lesotho, Swaziland, Zimbabwe, and Mozambique now have new earth stations.[17]

Meteorology and Postal Services

Both these subsectors were added to the activities of SATCC in January 1985. The major objective of the meteorological subsector is to decrease dependency on South African services; the objective of the postal services subsector is the development of an efficient regional postal system.[18]

Prospects for External and Internal Structural Transformation

Increased intra-regional interdependency in the area of surface transport not only would decrease regional dependency on the South African transport system, but also would decrease regional trade dependency on South Africa. Thus, at the subsystem (regional) level, a northward-bound transport system would increase intra-regional trade; enhance external trade, increasing the amount of available foreign exchange for respective SADCC member states; and decrease external debt, since transport through less expensive routes than South Africa would be available. But at the international level, the economic assistance received for project development, coupled with recurrent costs (i.e., maintenance, personnel, equipment, etc.) will result in the SADCC member states deepening their economic dependence on the imperialist nations of the global center.

In terms of internal structural transformation, a developed surface transport system would improve intra-country transportation, increasing the prospects for farmers in remote rural areas to transport their products to urban markets. A viable regional surface transport system would also make it possible for food and relief aid to be transported to desolate regional areas which presently are not easily accessible. While it is difficult to ascertain the overall effect of an improved regional surface transport system on internal development, in the long run, the gross domestic product (GDP) of specific SADCC member states should be increased as a result of improved efficiency in getting agricultural products to market.

As a result of regional destabilization by South Africa and South African-backed rebels, however, the SADCC states have had limited success in implementing the program of action for this subsector. In fact, by early 1987, these nations found they were more dependent on the South African transport network than in 1980, although by mid-1987, progress once again had been made in decreasing dependency (see chapter 6).

In the civil aviation subsector, proposed structural transformation includes decreased dependence on the South African network and greater interdependence among the SADCC states. Similarly, structural transformation within the telecommunication, meteorological, and postal subsectors would include decreased dependency on South Africa and increased intra-country and intra-regional efficiency. However, at the international level, the economic assistance received for project development, coupled with recurrent costs, will result in these nations deepening their economic dependence on the global center.

FOOD, AGRICULTURE, AND NATURAL RESOURCES

Since the majority of the population of SADCC states lives and works in the rural areas, the development of this sector is critical, as is evident in the fact that:

> from 1980 to 1986, agriculture contributed 34 percent of the region's GNP, employed up to 80 percent of the total labour force and accounted for about 26 percent of total foreign exchange earnings. In the member States that are not dominated by mining, agriculture contributed about 60 percent of total foreign exchange earnings.[19]

Accordingly, the overall goal of this sector is to:

> achieve food security at the household, national and regional levels; defined as ensuring that all members of a household, nation or region have access to an adequate diet to lead an active and normal life. Its two essential elements are food availability through expanded production, storage and trade; and the access by people to an adequate diet.[20]

To this end, SADCC realizes that "income and employment generating projects in rural areas are essential components of the strategy to increase national food security."[21]

This sector, coordinated by Zimbabwe, is divided into two areas: (1) Food and agriculture, which includes the following subsectors: food security; agricultural research; and livestock production and animal disease control. (2) Natural resources and the environment, which is divided into the following subsectors: soil and water conservation and land utilization; fisheries; forestry; and wildlife. As of August 1988, 135 projects, at a total estimated cost of $758.035 million had been presented for funding (see Table 7).

Food And Agriculture

Food Security

The overall responsibility for determining how best the SADCC states can rid themselves of regional food insecurity rests with the food security subsector. Food security, according to K.J.M. Dhliwayo, food security sector coordinator, "is defined as a situation whereby a member state can assure members of its population, regardless of their status, of adequate food and good nutrition throughout the year." [22] Projects in this sector have been placed within the context of an overall program which addresses such issues as agricultural resources and food production; food marketing; storage and processing; intra-regional and international trade; nutrition; and employment.[23]

Achieving food security at the regional level, Dhliwayo argues, is possible. Eventually, it is hoped with the grain surpluses in certain nations, there will be enough food to feed everyone in the SADCC states. In many cases, however, according to Dhliwayo, food is not accessible, due to "the failure of our marketing institutions to enable the food to be moved from one point to another." The regional food-marketing infrastructure project is designed to begin correcting this problem. Another project is being implemented with a view toward salvaging the amount of food lost between the initial stage of production (field and harvesting) and the final stage (storing, transportation, milling, and marketing).[24]

This subsector is faced with the real challenge of achieving food security at the household level. The focus of the program currently is on achieving such security, because, according to Dhliwayo, "When you have achieved food security at this level, you have achieved food security on all other levels." The subsector must now "look at income generating activities which will encourage small farmers to increase their food production, including poultry production, piggery, livestock, and so on." As a result of criticism that the strategy for increasing regional food production was elitist and therefore not designed to help the average small farmer, Dhliwayo acknowledges that food security developed a new strategy to deal with this weakness. No longer is the average small farmer being treated as peripheral to the program. Instead, new projects, such as the feasibility study on regional seed production and supply, are designed specifically for the small farmer. This project, for example, will determine how best to distribute seed to small farmers.[25]

Special emphasis also is being placed on the early warning

system project, designed to monitor regional food production so as to warn SADCC member states in advance of prospective food surpluses as well as of shortages. The SADCC governments, it is hoped, will therefore be able to prevent food crises.

Dhliwayo is quick to point out that the food security subsector does not actually implement agricultural projects, but instead assists member states on the best ways to use the information that food security gathers, both to secure financial resources and to develop projects to deal with their specific needs. In addition, training courses are provided for member states, to allow them to study, for example, how best they can achieve food security.[26]

Agricultural Research

Projects in the area of agricultural research, under the direction of the Southern African Centre for Cooperation in Agricultural Research (SACCAR), established in 1986 and located in Botswana, focus on:

— development of high-yielding food and cash crops, and livestock adapted to various conditions;

— development of efficient rainwater harvesting techniques;

— development of high-income-generating crops and livestock;

— conservation and development of the natural resources of soil, water, natural vegetation, wildlife, and fisheries; and

— development of irrigation.[27]

Research on various crops, especially sorghum and millet, has begun to show results. "High yields and adaptable varieties and hybrids, which last year were still at the experimentation stage, are now being bred." In addition, an office and laboratory building at Matopos, Zimbabwe, was completed for agricultural research and began work "to breed different varieties of these crops for specific utilization for baking, animal feed and brewing."[28]

Livestock Production and Animal Disease Control

In addition to concentrating on disease control, with emphasis on rinderpest and foot-and-mouth disease, the expanded livestock production and animal disease control subsector also will:

— elaborate programs for improved livestock production, including dairy and pasture management, and improving stock breeds and breeding methods;

— improve efforts to develop a regional industry for the production of veterinary products and stock feeds.[29]

As of July 1988, the subsector had eight projects, all in different stages of implementation. In addition, six projects had been completed.[30]

Natural Resources and the Environment

The objectives of the natural resources and environment area are to:

— ensure the conservation of natural resources, not only for sustainable production, but also in order to maintain and enhance the quality of the region's environment and natural heritage;

— relate the conservation and utilization of natural resources to sustainable development, particularly with a view to maintaining and increasing the productivity of the land for the benefit of the rural population and the society at large; and

— highlight the outstanding economic, nutritional, scientific, educational, cultural, and aesthetic values inherent in the natural resources of the region.[31]

Soil and Water Conservation and Land Utilization

These subsectors, coordinated by Lesotho, have eighteen projects. Of these, funding has been secured for seven; commitments for funding have been made for three; seven are under review; and one has not attracted any funding.[32]

Fisheries, Forestry, and Wildlife

The fisheries, forestry, and wildlife subsectors are coordinated by Malawi. There are thirteen projects in the area of fisheries, seven of which are under implementation. Funding for two other projects has been secured, and they are scheduled to be implemented soon. Funding has not been secured for four projects.[33]

In the forestry subsector, nine projects have been either fully or partially funded, and negotiations are underway for the funding of an additional ten. This subsector is working in collaboration with the energy sector to increase the production of fuelwood, since it is the region's most important source of energy. "To this end, efforts have been made to develop community forestry and village fuel wood plantations, in addition to the urban fuel wood projects already under implementation." [34]

Only one project is currently under implementation in the wildlife subsector, although pledges have been received for an additional ten projects. Funding for the remaining eight is being sought.[35]

Prospects for External and Internal Structural Transformation

At a SADCC conference convened in London in July 1984, Denis Norman, Zimbabwe minister of agriculture, "estimated that if present trends continue, grain imports . . . would rise from their present 1.8Mt to a horrific 8Mt by the end of the century." [36] As several of the SADCC states experienced their sixth year of drought in 1987 and increased South African regional destabilization, there continued to be a decline in the per-capita growth rate in food production, with the volume of food imports increasing. The prognosis for 1988 is not promising, and many of the SADCC states will continue to be net importers of food, much of which will be provided by international donor agencies and South Africa. Regional dependence on South Africa for food supplies is shown in Table 9.

Given the overall status of the regional agricultural sector, it is difficult to speculate on the prospects for decreased dependency on South Africa with completed project development. It appears that even with project development, the SADCC states

TABLE 9

SADCC CEREAL IMPORTS FROM SOUTH AFRICA, 1984-85

	Wheat	Coarse Grain
Botswana	100%	95%
Lesotho	81%	100%
Malawi	100%	100%
Mozambique	49%	—
Swaziland	1/3 of all cereal requirements	—
Zambia	100%	—
Zimbabwe	44%	—

Source: Chris Davids, *The Impact of Economic Sanctions Against South Africa on the SADCC States* (Ottawa: Canadian International Development Agency (CIDA), February 1986), pp. 65-67.

will remain dependent on food imports from the South Africa and Western nations for some time to come. In addition to remaining dependent on food imports, these nations are likely to remain dependent on financial assistance for project development for years. The United States' program of action for this sector, for example, is not scheduled to be completed until the year 2000.

With respect to internal structural transformation, as previously indicated, planned regional development has been criticized for ignoring the small rural farmer, in that proposed project development has been designed for developing the modern subsector. Specifically, in a paper presented at the Lusaka Conference in February 1984 by the Nordic countries (Denmark, Finland, Norway, and Sweden), it was suggested that:

> actions that indiscriminately favour the modern subsector within agriculture . . . will endanger equity and thereby the necessary basis for sustained long term economic

growth. They will contribute to rendering income distribution more skewed by employment only to some selected few while ignoring the mass of rural dwellers.[37]

Currently, SADCC is addressing this problem by concentrating on increasing production in the rural areas.

With project development reoriented to include the participation of the small-scale farmers in the region, structural transformation in the area of employment and income distribution, and in the general level of social welfare, is possible. In addition, an overall improvement in the regional sector will have a positive affect on the gross domestic product (GDP) of specific SADCC member states.

Although the idea of an early warning system is good, unless the regional security system improves, SADCC states may not benefit from the information generated. For example, during 1987-1988, Zimbabwe, with its grain surplus, is supposed to be a major source of needed food for Mozambique. However, due to transportation difficulties caused by South African-backed MNR destabilization, Zimbabwe has been able to transport only a small percentage of the grain destined for wartorn Mozambique. Therefore food security is not likely to become a reality in the region until apartheid is dismantled.

INDUSTRY AND TRADE

In June 1986, SADCC's industrial sector was expanded to include the issue of trade. The overall goal of the industrial component "is to promote self-reliance among SADCC countries by ensuring production of goods and services to satisfy the basic needs of the people." To this end, it is projected that SADCC states must:

— reduce external dependence on imports of industrial products and inputs from outside the region, especially from South Africa;

— increase the size, scope, and diversity of the industrial sector both nationally and regionally;

— increase linkages within the national and regional economies as a means of creating an integrated and self-reliant regional economy.[38]

The program of action for industrial development is divided into two major areas: projects for manufactured goods and projects for industrial support services.

As of August 1988, the sector was comprised of 92 projects, costing an estimated $1.271.91 billion, of which $313.23 million (or 25 percent) had been secured (see Table 10). As of July 1988, eight projects had been completed, twelve were being implemented, and negotiations were underway for funding of six.[39]

The overall constraints to regional industrial development, according to E.P.A. Simwela, senior economist for the SADCC Industry and Trade Co-ordination Division, include: the low level of investment in resources; the limited markets of individual countries; the structure of the regional economies which are not self-supporting and are externally dependent; the international investment climate; and deteriorating terms of trade. Simwela admits that there has not been much progress made in this sector and that the current strategy is being reviewed with a view toward enhancing regional participation in industrial development.[40]

Projects in the industry and trade sector are divided into thirteen subsectors: cement and cement products; chemicals; electrical goods, farm implements and equipment; fertilizer, insecticides, and pesticides; food and food processing; iron and steel, and engineering; leather and leather goods; pulp and paper; salt; textiles; trade promotion; and trade financing.

The overall objective of the trade component is to increase intra-SADCC trade. Specifically, the program "aims at increasing existing trade flows as well as identifying and facilitating new product flows, especially in connection with industrial cooperation projects." [41]

In an effort to increase regional production and intra-regional trade, the theme of the 1987 Annual Consultative Conference was "SADCC: Investment in Production." Fundamentally, this is a new initiative to involve the private sector in regional development. According to SADCC executive secretary Dr. Makoni:

Until now the main focus of SADCC has been the integration and the upgrading of infrastructure so as to facilitate the delivery of goods and services. We've been specifically improving transport and communications in this regard. But what use are these improved infrastructures without goals to make the goods that can be handled by the infrastructure? That is why we are opening the door to co-operation with the business community. It is a recognition that while there are many things governments can do, there are also important things that private business can contribute.[42]

Investment in Production

The Investment in Production program envisages as a crucial part of its plan increased investment by local entrepreneurs in regional enterprises, for, as Emang Motlhabane Maphanyane, SADCC economist notes, "foreign investment can only come if there is an active regional business community." To this end, SADCC is currently attempting to address the daily problems of the regional business community and determine what would contribute to a more conducive business environment. In terms of attracting foreign investors, Maphanyane admits that currently, the prognosis is not promising, given the fact that many have the impression that the region is too unstable.[43]

Prospects for External and Internal Structural Transformation

The successful completion of project development in this sector at the subsystem level would result in decreased dependency on South Africa, which presently supplies the SADCC countries with "73% of their machinery and equipment, 55% of their chemicals, 89% of their plastics and rubber products, and 73% of their transport machinery." [44] Estimated projections with respect to decreased external dependency include regional self-sufficiency in salt production, the production of polyester and cotton-polyester blended fabrics, wool scouring and spinning facilities, tractor production, fertilizer production, the production of pulp and paper needs, and cement production. It is also projected that project development could contribute toward meeting regional

TABLE 10

INDUSTRY AND TRADE FINANCING BY SUBSECTOR, 1988

Subsector	No.	Total Cost US$ MIL	Foreign	Local	Funding Secured & Source	%	Funding Under Negotiation	%	Funding Gap	%
Cement and Cement Products	4	25.40	25.40	0.00	6.40	25.20	19.00	74.80	0.00	0.00
Chemicals	7	3.74	2.24	1.50	2.24	59.90	1.50	40.10	0.00	0.00
Electrical Goods	1	0.25	0.25	0.00	0.25	100.00	0.00	0.00	0.00	0.00
Farm Implements and Equipment	10	23.34	10.85	12.49	15.42	66.10	0.00	0.00	7.92	33.90
Fertilizer, Insecticides, Pesticides	15	806.11	720.68	85.43	103.68	12.90	514.00	63.70	188.43	23.40
Food and Food Processing	2	0.30	0.30	0.00	0.30	100.00	0.00	0.00	0.00	0.00

TABLE 10 continued on next page

Subsector	No.	Total Cost US$ MIL	Foreign	Local	Funding Secured & Source	%	Funding Under Negotiation	%	Funding Gap	%
Iron and Steel and Engineering	7	1.61	1.61	0.00	0.62	38.50	0.00	0.00	0.99	61.50
Leather and Leather Goods	1	0.11	0.11	0.00	0.11	100.00	0.00	0.00	0.00	0.00
Pulp and Paper	7	339.06	198.50	140.56	143.06	42.20	0.00	0.00	196.00	57.80
Salt	8	21.01	13.67	7.34	13.34	63.50	2.66	12.70	5.01	23.80
Salt Support Services	12	0.95	0.95	0.00	0.62	65.30	0.00	0.00	0.33	34.70
Overall Coordination	0	0.00	0.00	0.00	0.00	0.00	0.00	0.00	0.00	0.00
Textiles	12	48.96	34.01	14.95	26.37	53.90	2.75	5.60	19.84	40.50
Trade Promotion	4	0.87	0.87	0.00	0.62	71.30	0.20	23.00	0.05	5.70
Trade Financing	2	0.20	0.20	0.00	0.20	100.00	0.00	0.00	0.00	0.00
TOTAL	92	1271.91	1009.64	262.27	313.23	24.60	540.11	42.50	418.57	32.90

Source: *SADCC Annual Progress Report, July 1987-August 1988.*

demand with respect to needed chemicals and farm implements. Seemingly, this production would result in increased intraregional trade. South Africa, however, will continue to prevent these states from developing a viable regional industrial and trade sector (see chapter 6).

To the extent that SADCC countries are successful in securing funds for continued project implementation and investment in production, they will remain economically dependent on foreign investors. This strategy will only reinforce the linkages of dependency established during colonial rule. To date, that has not contributed toward economic liberation, and therefore it is not likely that new foreign investment will alter this phenomenon. Can SADCC really expect that entrepreneurs in the global center would invest in Southern Africa for any reason other than continued imperialist control?

In terms of internal development, since the majority of projects will be funded by foreign private investors, it is highly unlikely that such industries would contribute substantially to altering the present pattern of regional underdevelopment. The majority of capital surplus accrued from such industries will be exported out of the SADCC countries, and industrial development will be concentrated in the modern subsector. These industries will contribute minimally to eradicate unemployment, equalize income distribution, or to improve the general level of welfare of the masses. Even if such investment in production were initiated by local entrepreneurs, it is doubtful that the condition of the masses would be improved, given the current economic structures of these countries.

ENERGY

The energy sector is being coordinated by Angola within the Technical and Administrative Unit (TAU) of its Ministry of Energy responsible for regional coordination. The short- and medium-term objectives of this sector are to:

— reduce the drain on foreign-exchange reserves caused by extensive import of petroleum products;

— reduce the depletion of wood fuel resources;

— develop expertise in energy technologies and promote technology transfers to the region;

— establish detailed knowledge of the energy situation and its interrelation with macro economic development in the region;

— strengthen regional cooperation in the various energy subsectors;

— establish emergency supply and distribution mechanisms;

— promote better knowledge of the capital and technological requirements of the region; and

— continue rehabilitation programs.[45]

This sector is divided into six subsectors: petroleum, coal, electricity, new and renewable sources of energy, wood fuel and conservation.

By August 1988, sixty-eight projects, at a total estimated cost of $308.143 million had been presented for funding (see Table 11). Of the total funding needed, 50 percent had been secured. "Eighteen projects are fully funded and support is fully or partly being sought for 40 projects." [46]

The majority of projects in both the petroleum and the coal subsectors are studies designed to explore regional reserves and potential, possible substitutions, and, in the case of coal, potential for conversion.[47]

The electricity subsector, on the other hand, is more developed and, in fact, has thirty-six projects which represent the majority of the total sector funding requirements. Since this subsector is characterized by a surplus of generating capacity, projects are designed to facilitate better use of the region's electrical system, versus adding substantial capacity.[48] As of August 1987, the development of a small hydroelectric plant in Lesotho was at an advanced stage of implementation, and in northern Botswana, two rural townships had been connected to

TABLE 11
ENERGY FINANCING BY SUBSECTOR, 1988

Subsector	No.	Total Cost US$ MIL	Foreign US$ MIL	Local US$ MIL	Funding Secured	%	Funding Under Negotiation US$ MIL	%	Funding Gap US$ MIL	%
Overall	6	15.921	12.021	3.900	14.916	93.7	—	—	1.005	6.3
Petroleum	9	55.555	50.655	4.900	22.625	40.7	—	—	32.930	59.3
Coal	5	4.413	4.018	0.395	—	—	—	—	4.413	100.0
Electricity	36	215.427	208.427	7.624	103.937	48.4	15.02	7.0	95.846	44.6
N.R.S.E.	4	2.750	2.680	0.070	1.520	55.3	—	—	1.230	44.7
Woodfuel	6	9.197	9.152	0.045	6.585	71.6	0.654	7.1	1.958	21.3
Conservation	2	4.880	4.600	0.280	3.480	71.3	—	—	1.400	28.7
GRAND TOTAL	68	308.143	291.553	17.214	153.063	49.8	15.674	5.1	138.792	45.1

Source: *SADCC Annual Progress Report, July 1987-August 1988.*

the Zambian/Zimbabwe electrical network. A 100MW interconnection between Zimbabwe and Botswana was out to tender and the rehabilitation of the Kafue Gorge hydroelectric power station in Zambia was underway, with the aim of guaranteeing a reliable supply. "Financing for other grid interconnections, or for cross-border cooperation between Mozambique, Malawi, and Tanzania," had been secured, and efforts were underway "to promote enhanced cooperation between the region's electricity utilities."[49] In 1988, the Botswana-Zimbabwe-Zambia interconnection was commissioned, and the Botswana-Zimbabwe interconnection contract was awarded.[50]

The new and renewable sources of energy subsector has begun to focus attention on identifying alternate sources of energy, with the objective of reducing the pressure on traditional energy sources. Alternatives currently being considered include wind and solar energy, biogas, and ethanol.[51] In addition, "an energy conservation office, which will develop programmes to encourage conservation in industry and mining, is being established in Harare."[52]

The SADCC region faces a potential serious wood fuel problem as a result of the depletion of wood resources. Since three-quarters of the regional population depend on wood as the major source of energy, the development of this sector is crucial. Projects in this subsector include forestation programs, the development and introduction of efficient stoves, and programs for substitution of fuel wood with charcoal.[53]

Prospects for External and Internal Structural Transformation

Prospects for decreased dependency on South Africa for the supply of oil to Botswana, Lesotho, and Swaziland are not likely in the near future. In the case of Zimbabwe, since independence there has been a general improvement in its fuel position; it no longer must rely exclusively on South Africa for oil supplies.[54] Presently, neither Botswana, Lesotho, Swaziland (the BLS states), Malawi, nor Zimbabwe have the capacity to refine oil.[55] Therefore, in order for the oil-exporting countries (Angola and Mozambique, although Angola is the only oil-producing country in the region) to

Strategy for Regional Cooperation and Development 155

accommodate the oil needs of regional countries presently dependent on South Africa, a complete oil product transport system would need to be installed between the various SADCC countries.[56] Currently, regional destabilization would prevent the development of such a system (see chapter 6).

In the electricity subsector, BLS (Botswana, Lesotho and Swaziland) and Mozambique have increased their dependence on imports from South Africa. However, Angola, Zambia, Malawi, and Tanzania have continued to be self-sufficient in electrical supply.[57]

Limited potential exists for the development of the coal subsector and coal's subsequent potential as a major source of energy for the region, despite "the very vast coal resources available to the region." According to the findings of the regional energy survey:

> apart from Zimbabwe and Botswana, the contribution from the sector to regional energy supplies will remain limited, at least up to 1990. But during this period it will be necessary to clarify longer term prospects, both on the regional and international markets . . . These objectives will have to take account of new uses for coal such as they are envisaged for the last decade of this century. The substitution of coal for oil, which is already far advanced in electricity, could in the future be extended to the production of synthetic materials and to that of motor fuels.[58]

The actual development of the regional coal subsector over the next few years will be dependent largely upon the opportunities for the external exporting of coal, provided transport, infrastructure, and production constraints are overcome.[59]

Development in this sector in terms of external dependency could thus contribute toward enhanced regional self-sufficiency in oil and electricity production. In addition, if coal becomes a regional exported commodity, it could enhance accessibility to increased foreign exchange and result in a decrease in regional external debt. With respect to internal development, the development of the coal subsector for export would contribute toward an increase in the gross domestic product (GDP) for respective countries.

TABLE 12

SADCC ENERGY IMPORTS FROM SOUTH AFRICA
(as % of total energy consumed)

	Oil	Electricity
Botswana	100%	27%
Lesotho	100%	100%
Swaziland	100%	60%
Mozambique *	none	55% of Maputo's supply
Zimbabwe	aircraft fuel	none
Zambia	occasional imports	none
Malawi	30-40%	none

* Exports heavy crude oil from the Maputo refinery and until recently electricity from Cahora Bassa Dam.

Source: Chris Davids, *Impact of Economic Sanctions,* February 1986, p. 15.

Finally, progress in both the renewable sources of energy and wood fuel subsectors could help to prevent a major crisis likely to develop if alternatives to wood fuel are not discovered.

MANPOWER

The major objectives identified for regional manpower development, coordinated by Swaziland, include:

— training to support the activities of the other SADCC sectors specifically with regard to the execution, operation, and maintenance of projects;

— training in management and public administration;

— without detracting from the need for high-level personnel, the training of subprofessional cadres, especially agricultural and engineering craftsmen, technicians, and trainers;

— foundation training in scientific, technical, and mathematical subjects at both the elementary and secondary school levels;

— language training to ensure that personnel from all SADCC member states can fully participate in all training programs;

— project formulation and design and the mobilization of technical resources in support of the above activities.[60]

Projects have been identified to address each of these objectives. As of August 1988, thirty-two projects at a total estimated cost of $37.46 million had been presented for funding. Of the total funding needed, 23 percent of total cost has been secured, and 5 percent was under negotiation (see Table 7).

Projects in this sector have been rated as first priority and second priority. Four of the eighteen first-priority projects have been completed. An additional four are under implementation; two are under implementation, although they are only partially funded; funding for two is under negotiation; and funds for the remaining six are being sought.[61]

Prospects for External and Internal Structural Transformation

The SADCC information officer, Ng'wanakilala, admits that manpower is the weakest SADCC sector, although it is central to the SADCC Program of Action. If the SADCC countries are to become self-reliant and decrease their dependency on expatriate workers, it is imperative that appropriate skilled job training is implemented. With project implementation, SADCC could make a significant contribution toward this endeavor. Project development in this sector will contribute little, however, to decreased regional dependency on South Africa for the employment of the estimated 250,000 to 300,000 migrant workers from SADCC countries. Nor will development in this sector enhance the prospects for SADCC member states to reabsorb repatriated South African migrant laborers. Needless to say, Ng'wanakilala does remind us that job training, not employment creation, is the focal point of the sector.

NOTES

1. Moeletsi Mbeki, *Profile of Political Conflicts in Southern Africa* (Harare, Zimbabwe: Nehanda Publishers, 1987), pp. 34-35.

2. Interview with Nkwabi Ng'wanakilala, SADCC information officer, August 1987, Gaborone, Botswana.

3. *Ibid.*

4. SADCC, *SADCC Maseru* (SADCC, 1983), p. 135.

5. SADCC, *SADCC Transport and Communications*, paper presented at SADCC Conference, Lusaka, February 2-3, 1984, p. 5.

6. *Ibid.*, p. 37.

7. SATCC, "Transport and Communications Progress Report," Maputo, Mozambique, July 1988, p. 6.

8. "Donors Fund Rail Link," *Independent* (Britain), July 30, 1988.

9. SATCC, "Report," July 1988, p. 6.

10. *Ibid.*

11. *Ibid.*

12. SADCC, *Draft Annual Progress Report*, 1988, p. 34.

13. Interview with Mugama M. Matolo, director of SATCC, Maputo, Mozambique, July 1988.

14. SADCC, *SADCC Transport*, 1984, p. 41.

15. SADCC, *SADCC Transport and Communications*, paper presented at SADCC Conference, Harare, January 30-31, 1986, pp. 35-36; *SADCC Annual Progress Report, July 1986 – August 1987*, p. 16; SADCC, *SADCC: Development of Infrastructure and Enterprise*, paper presented at SADCC Conference, Arusha, January 28-29, 1988, p. 7.

16. *SADCC Transport*, 1984, p. 46.

17. *Southern Africa Report*, August 29, 1986, p. 16; SADCC,"SADCC Links Up—Telecommunications Success" (SADCC, 1985); SADCC,*SADCC: Development of Infrastructure*, 1988, p. 7.

18. *SADCC Transport*, 1986, pp. 42-43.

19. SADCC, *SADCC Food, Agriculture and Natural Resources*, paper presented at the SADCC Conference at Gaborone, February 5-6, 1987, p. 6.

20. *SADCC Report, July 1986 – August 1987*, p. 17.

21. *Ibid.*

22. Interview with K.J.M. Dhliwayo, SADCC food security coordinator, August 24, 1987, Harare, Zimbabwe.

23. *SADCC Food*, 1987, p. 60.

24. Interview, Dhliwayo.

25. *Ibid.*

26. *Ibid.*

27. SADCC, *Draft*, 1988, p. 20.

28. *Ibid.*

29. *SADCC Food*, 1987, p. 22.

30. SADCC, *Draft*, 1988, p. 24.

31. *Ibid.*, p. 18.

32. *Ibid.*, p. 25.

33. *Ibid.*, p. 21.

34. *Ibid.*, p. 22.

35. *Ibid.*

36. *Africa Research Bulletin*, July 15 – August 14, 1984, p. 7364.

37. "Policies in Agriculture and Rural Development — A Nordic View," position paper presented to SADCC Conference, Lusaka, February 1-3, 1984, pp. 2-3.

38. SADCC, *SADCC Industry*, paper presented at SADCC Conference, Gaborone, February 5-6, 1987, p. 3.

39. Based on an interview with E.P.A. Simwela, senior economist, SADCC Industry and Trade Co-ordination Division, Maputo, Mozambique, July 1988.

40. *Ibid.*

41. *SADCC Industry*, 1987, p. 11.

42. "SADCC Plan Will Back Private-Sector Partners," *African Business*, February 1987, p. 10.

43. Interview with Emang Motlhabane Maphanyane, SADCC economist, August 1987, Gaborone, Botswana.

44. United States Agency for International Development (USAID), *Country Development Strategy Statement, FY 1986 Southern Africa* (USAID, May 1984), p. 4.

45. SADCC, *SADCC Energy*, paper presented at SADCC Conference, Harare, January 30-31, 1986, pp. 6-7.

46. SADCC, *Draft*, 1988, p. 18.

47. SADCC, *SADCC Energy*, paper presented at SADCC Conference, Gaborone, February 5-6, 1987, pp. 26-27.

48. *Ibid.*, p. 27.

49. *SADCC Report, July 1986 – August 1987*, p. 27.

50. SADCC, *Draft*, 1988, p. 17.

51. *SADCC Energy*, 1986, pp. 28-29.

52. *SADCC Report, July 1986 – August 1987*, p. 27.

53. *SADCC Energy*, 1986, pp. 24, 29-30.

54. EIU, *Quarterly Economic Review of Zimbabwe and Malawi*, 1983, p. 14.

55. Chris Davids, *The Impact of Economic Sanctions Against South Africa on the SADCC States*, (Ottawa: Canadian International Development Agency (CIDA), 1986), p. 15.

56. See SADCC, *SADCC Energy*, paper presented at SADCC Conference, Lusaka, February 2-3, 1984, p. 16.

57. SADCC, *SADCC Macro-Economic Survey* (SADCC, 1986), p. 55.

58. *SADCC Energy*, 1984, p. 39.

59. *Ibid.*, p. 39.

60. SADCC, *SADCC Manpower*, paper presented at SADCC Conference, Gaborone, February 5-6, 1987, p. 1.

61. SADCC, *Draft*, 1988, p. 27.

CHAPTER 5

SADCC's Institutional Framework

When SADCC was formed, the member states determined that in order for the organization to be viable, a unique strategy would need to be pursued to address the diverse needs of the regional countries. In addition to developing a program of action that would allow each member state to be directly responsible for some aspect of implementing regional development projects, the countries also determined that a decentralized institutional framework must be created in order to allow each member state equal weight in the decision-making process. This framework has served both as a conduit for and as a hindrance to regional development. The purpose of this chapter is to describe SADCC's institutional framework and analyze its weaknesses and strengths, within the context of SADCC's ability to implement its program of action. The chapter is divided into four sections: SADCC organizational structure; SADCC project cycle; SADCC annual conference; and implementation of the SADCC program of action.

SADCC ORGANIZATIONAL STRUCTURE

The organizational structure contains the Summit, the Council of Ministers, the Standing Committee of Officials, the Sector Coordinators (Sectoral Commissions), and the SADCC Secretariat (see Figure 4). This structure is outlined in the *Memorandum of Understanding on the Institutions of the Southern African Development Co-ordination Conference* (see Appendix A).

Summit

At the top of SADCC's hierarchical structure is the Summit, which consists of the heads of state and government of the member countries. "The Summit is the supreme institution of SADCC and is responsible for the general direction and control of the functions of SADCC and the achievement of its objectives."[1] The Summit meets once a year during July, and in most cases, only

FIGURE 4

SADCC ORGANIZATIONAL STRUCTURE

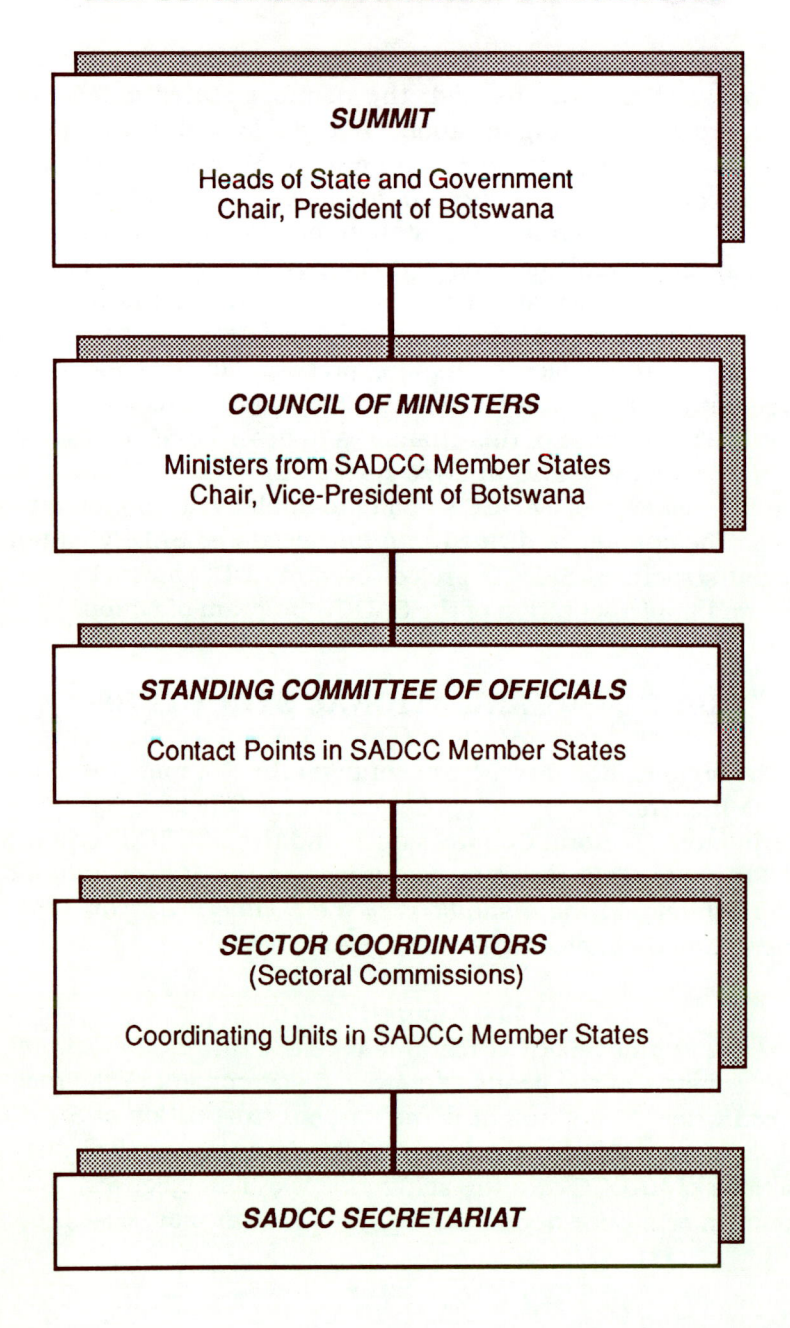

SUMMIT

Heads of State and Government
Chair, President of Botswana

COUNCIL OF MINISTERS

Ministers from SADCC Member States
Chair, Vice-President of Botswana

STANDING COMMITTEE OF OFFICIALS

Contact Points in SADCC Member States

SECTOR COORDINATORS
(Sectoral Commissions)

Coordinating Units in SADCC Member States

SADCC SECRETARIAT

to receive the SADCC Annual Progress Report.[2]

Council of Ministers

The Council of Ministers contains at least one minister from each of the member states. This group is responsible "for the overall policy of SADCC, its general coordination, the supervision of its institutions, and the supervision of the execution of its programs." The Council meets at least twice a year, before the Summit and before the Annual Consultative Conference.[3]

Standing Committee of Officials

The real functioning units of SADCC, according to Nkwabi Ng'wanakilala, SADCC information officer, are the Standing Committee of Officials and the Sector Coordinators. The Committee, for example, makes recommendations to the Council, and the Council in turn makes recommendations to the Summit. In many cases, however, decisions are made by the Council, and certain issues are never addressed at the Summit level. Overall, the Committee consists of SADCC contact points, who are senior officials in various member countries. "The Committee may appoint sub-committees of officials for programs in functional areas and may designate SADCC member Governments to convene meetings and coordinate the work of such sub-committees; such sub-committees report to the Standing Committee." Since the Committee is directly responsible to the Council of Ministers, it usually meets three times a year to prepare for meetings of the Council of Ministers.[4] The SADCC development projects are initially reviewed by SADCC contact points before being presented for funding.

Sector Coordinators

The Sector Coordinators are the experts responsible for planning and developing strategies within each of the SADCC sectors, known also as the coordinating units. Ng'wanakilala notes that the SADCC Program of Action is really based on these units, since one starts with the coordinators and goes up.[5] The coordinators are those directly responsible for each regional sector or subsector. In order to effectively coordinate development, Sectoral Commissions can be created by the Council of Ministers. To date, only one commission has been established—the Southern Africa Transport and Communications Commission (SATCC), located in Mozambique.

SADCC Secretariat

The SADCC Secretariat, located in Gaborone, Botswana, is "responsible for the general servicing of and liaison with SADCC institutions and coordination of the execution of the tasks of SADCC." It is headed by an executive secretary who is appointed by the Summit.[6] A detailed description of the Secretariat's responsibilities are outlined in Figure 5.

SADCC PROJECT CYCLE

As chapter 4 revealed, the SADCC Program of Action consists of 571 projects. In order for a work to qualify as a prospective SADCC project, it must be either a national project that will have a regional impact, or a regional project that involves more than one country. To be approved, a project must go through several phases, outlined below:

Phase 1 (National Level)

Ministries in all SADCC member states identify projects for implementation and present them to the Ministry of Finance in their respective countries.

Phase 2 (National Level)

Ministry of Finance reviews projects and accepts or rejects them.

Phase 3 (Regional Level)

Each sector or subsector coordinator convenes a meeting with relevant technical subcommittees (the food security coordinator, for example, works directly with representatives from the other eight SADCC member states within their Ministry of

Agriculture who serve as food security contact points and members of the food security technical subcommittee). At each sectoral meeting projects are reviewed to determine if they meet the necessary criteria to qualify as a SADCC project. Projects that meet SADCC guidelines are then evaluated with a view toward determining possible international and/or SADCC funding.

Phase 4 (Regional Level)

The relevant ministers from all SADCC states review projects pertaining to their respective ministry approved at the sectoral meetings. Each respective group is known as the Sectoral Committee of Ministers (e.g., one sectoral committee consists of Ministers of Agriculture from SADCC member states).

Phase 5 (Regional Level)

Projects recommended for funding are reviewed by the Standing Committee of Officials. Members of the Committee consist of representatives from the Ministry of Finance or the President's office of each SADCC member state. The national contact point for each SADCC country is located either in the Ministry of Finance or the office of the president. The Committee evaluates the economic and/or political feasibility of projects recommended for funding by the SADCC Ministers. Projects approved are recommended for funding.

Phase 6 (Regional Level)

Projects are reviewed by the Council of Ministers. Projects approved are presented for funding at the Annual Consultative Conference.

Phase 7 (Regional Level)

Projects are presented for funding at the Annual Consultative Conference.

The SADCC national projects usually go through phases 1 through 4, and then phase 7, unless there are serious financial or political considerations that must be addressed at a higher level. In the event of such a situation, projects must also go through phases 5 and 6.

Regional projects usually start at phase 3, since most are submitted by SADCC sector or subsector coordinators and therefore have a regional orientation. Most regional projects go through phases 3, 4, and 7 in the SADCC project cycle. Again, if there are significant financial or political considerations that must be addressed, such projects must go through phases 5 and 6.

ANNUAL CONSULTATIVE CONFERENCE

According to the Lusaka Declaration, *Southern Africa: Toward Economic Liberation* (see Appendix A), among SADCC's objectives is the "concerted action to secure international cooperation within the framework of the strategy outlined for economic liberation." To this end, SADCC has international cooperating partners—governments and international agencies. Most of these are Western, although recently several Eastern nations have expressed interest in the organization. However, their commitment to regional development has been very limited. Some speculate that this is because the Soviet Union has not made a commitment to SADCC, since it does not like to work with a multilateral organization. It does not have the same influence as when it works directly with individual countries on a bilateral basis. Given the Soviet Union's control over the Eastern bloc, it is speculated that other nations which might be interested in supporting SADCC are constrained from doing so.

The cooperating partners meet once a year with SADCC officials at the Annual Consultative Conference and make financial pledges to the organization for project development. These pledges consist of both grants and loans. In addition, at the con-

FIGURE 5
OFFICE OF THE EXECUTIVE SECRETARY

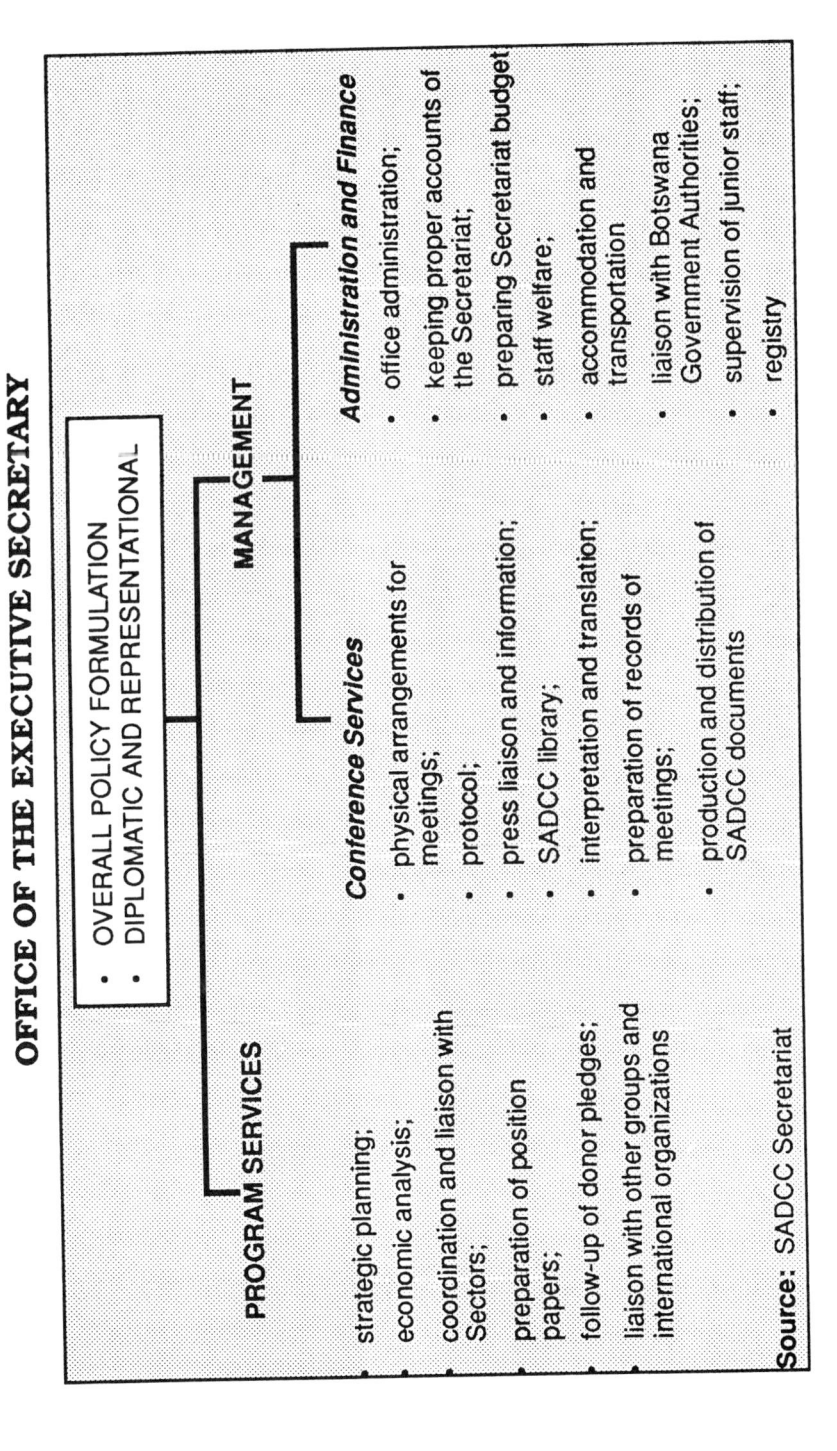

- OVERALL POLICY FORMULATION
- DIPLOMATIC AND REPRESENTATIONAL

MANAGEMENT

PROGRAM SERVICES

- strategic planning;
- economic analysis;
- coordination and liaison with Sectors;
- preparation of position papers;
- follow-up of donor pledges;
- liaison with other groups and international organizations

Conference Services

- physical arrangements for meetings;
- protocol;
- press liaison and information;
- SADCC library;
- interpretation and translation;
- preparation of records of meetings;
- production and distribution of SADCC documents

Administration and Finance

- office administration;
- keeping proper accounts of the Secretariat;
- preparing Secretariat budget
- staff welfare;
- accommodation and transportation
- liaison with Botswana Government Authorities;
- supervision of junior staff;
- registry

Source: SADCC Secretariat

ference, "invited guests are updated on progress in regional cooperation; projects and studies are presented for funding; and problems and bottlenecks are ironed out." [7]

At the January 1988 Annual Consultative Conference held in Arusha, Tanzania, approximately 1,000 delegates were present, the largest SADCC meeting to date.[8] The SADCC member states alternate as host of the Annual Conference.

IMPLEMENTATION OF THE SADCC PROGRAM OF ACTION

There is no doubt that SADCC has before it a mammoth task in its struggle to foster regional cooperation among nine independent nations, particularly since all have diverse economic and political structures. This task is made even more challenging by the fact that seven sectors and five subsectors must be coordinated among the nine member states. This part of the chapter is divided into two sections: decentralized institutional framework and sector coordinating units.

Decentralized Institutional Framework: A Conduit for, or a Hindrance to Regional Development?

The decentralized institutional structure of SADCC, on the whole, has facilitated regional cooperation and development. It becomes clear in talking with SADCC officials from throughout the region that the organization has served to politically unify the member states. They point out, for example, that as a result of SADCC, the regional nations have an open dialogue with one another (including Malawi). In addition, because the nations are working collectively to develop the various regional sectors, information is shared about problems as well as achievements. Members openly criticize others' economic policies, with a view toward encouraging the implementation of alternative strategies. According to numerous SADCC officials, many improvements in development policies have grown out of this sharing of information.[9]

Since each member state has the responsibility for coordinating a sector or subsector, all feel they are benefiting from regional cooperation. And since projects presented for funding originate from each member state's national development plan, a decision does not need to be made to participate in regional development to the neglect of national development.

At the same time, however, this decentralized structure has posed problems for the organization, two of which will be discussed below. The first concerns the issue of whether SADCC's Program of Action is really oriented toward regional development; the second concerns the issue of autonomy for sector coordinators.

National, or Regional Development?

Although one of SADCC's strengths as a regional unifying force rests with the fact that its decentralized organizational structure means that the national development objectives of its member states are not compromised by planned regional development, some argue that the structure is, in fact, too loose, and therefore is not a conduit for regional development. According to Daniel Ndlela:

> The origins of SADCC are more political than economic, and political considerations run strongly through all major SADCC decisions. Despite its claim to political strength and unity, the very framework of cooperation chosen indicates the shaky foundation on which SADCC is built. Desire for collective independence from South African domination is one thing but commitment to regional integration is another. SADCC member states are unwilling to substitute one dependence with another. Consequently, cooperation in SADCC is a loose arrangement from which a member state can opt out without any serious repercussions on its domestic economy. Thus SADCC's claim to political strength and unity is its economic weakness.[10]

Ndlela further argues that "while preservation of national and economic sovereignty is an indisputable demand, it should not be synonymous with a weak and uncoordinated decision-making which weakens the regional organization."[11]

The food security subsector is clearly an example of SADCC's national orientation, according to Clever Mumbengegwi:

Food production is deemed a national responsibility. While the benefits from specialization and intra-regional food trade are recognized, SADCC prefers the nationalistic route to regional food security and self-sufficiency, irrespective of the efficiency costs involved. Thus cooperation is merely an attempt to reinforce each nation's capacity to produce food "in accordance with national policies and priorities." . . . This nationo-centric approach may have some adverse long-term implications for the achievement of SADCC's goals.[12]

The implications of this nationalistic versus regional approach to food self-sufficiency, and therefore SADCC's failure to enter into agricultural production coordination, are that (1) South Africa will remain a cheaper source of supply for food imports and that (2) since SADCC members do not appear to be willing to replace South African dependency with dependency among themselves, this leaves "room for lucrative bilateral dealings" with South Africa, "where an individual member state stands to be advantaged by such deals."[13] The involvement of Botswana, Lesotho, and Swaziland in helping the apartheid regime evade sanctions, and the intra-regional competition that exists (see chapter 6), further point to problems often associated with SADCC's national versus regional orientation.

Those directly involved with implementing the SADCC Program of Action offer a different perspective on the issue of national versus regional development. It is often very difficult, they argue, to make sector projects regional. In many cases, projects can be nationally oriented only insofar that the specific problem to be addressed pertains to a given country. Even though this is the case, sector coordinators work directly with technical assistants in all member states regarding the specific problem. While on the surface it may appear that regional cooperation is not taking place, these officials argue that in reality, such cooperation is occurring.[14]

The loose organizational structure of SADCC, designed to address the national needs of its member states, does leave the states vulnerable to control by their international cooperating partners. Specifically, SADCC's strategy allows donors to choose which sectors and which countries will receive funds. Thus very often, specific countries are rewarded for "good behavior," while others are punished for "bad behavior." The SADCC officials themselves point out that often money for projects is not forthcoming if a project addresses a specific need in only one country, although addressing the problem would lead to development of the regional sector. As Ibbo Mandaza points out:

> All this only helps to highlight the weakness of the SADCC structure and, as is evidenced by the small SADCC Secretariat, the absence of a strong supranational body that would in turn mobilize and coordinate local efforts at genuine regional cooperation. This has exposed SADCC members to the machinations of aid donors, who in many instances are able to exercise direct or indirect control of their economies.[15]

The donors, it has been suggested, are pleased that the Secretariat is not a powerful entity, because "in the absence of a strong supranational body, the foreign experts will hold sway in each speciality assigned to them with no corresponding regional expertise and institutional set up to 'interfere' in their work."[16]

The solution to these problems, according to Ng'wanakilala, does not rest, however, with the development of a strong centralized bureaucratic structure similar to that of other regional organizations. Instead, he argues, SADCC must improve the level of cooperation among its member states.[17] Historically, regional cooperation and development strategies that have had strong centralized bureaucratic structures have not proved to be a successful alternative to a loose structure.

Perhaps as a middle ground between these two extremes, SADCC's sector coordinators could be given more autonomy. Such autonomy could perhaps result in a greater regional orientation for the organization and greater control over regional development.

Autonomy for Sector Coordinators?

According to Ng'wanakilala, one of the problems with implementation of the SADCC Program of Action rests with the fact that SADCC sector coordinators are actually government officials, freely employed as directors of departments or undersecretaries, while at the same time they also have the task of coordinating SADCC. This means that SADCC responsibilities are superimposed on their ministerial duties. Ideally, according to Ng'wanakilala, these individuals should be given as much autonomy as possible. This would allow them, as SADCC officials, to have both administrative and financial strength, so that they could operate more efficiently. Even though Ng'wanakilala feels it would be advisable for these coordinators to work only for SADCC, he admits this would pose a problem because of SADCC's decentralized organizational structure:

> In a system of decentralization . . . the system itself, by which we have given each country a responsibility, is a strength of the organization. We have an apparent contradiction which we always have to explain; that is, you have a decentralized system with the officials being full-time employees on their own in their respective governments, and they are at the same time responsible to SADCC for certain coordination. Where do they get the time to do it? This in-build factor that the program of SADCC is part and parcel of those governments gives it the strength that it has. If you had a different system you might have problems of coordination.[18]

For K.L.M. Dhliwayo, SADCC food security coordinator, the decentralized system has been a serious hindrance to the development of this subsector. Food security is under the Ministry of Agriculture in Zimbabwe:

> We as sector coordinators really feel that our current Ministers should do more by way of support in terms of some degree of flexibility in the way we are organized . . . The problem is that we are undertaking regional activities . . . but we are still very much a part of a national structure . . . We really want to be treated as an entity slightly different from the Ministry, although we are still under the Ministry . . . We need some form of autonomy . . . it seems our Council of Ministers has been made aware of the problem and they have urged the current Ministries of all member states to try as much as possible to give us as much support as we think we need and also to try and give us some form of flexibility.[19]

Institutional Framework

Since food security is under the Ministry of Agriculture, Dhliwayo must seek approval through the centralized bureaucratic structure of this Ministry in order to implement his food security program. This means, for example, that if he, or one of his officials, needs to make a special trip to Swaziland, the trip must first be approved by the Ministry; then a formal application must be made through the Zimbabwe Reserve Bank for allocation of foreign exchange. This is the case because the SADCC food security money is given to the Reserve Bank by donors, and is then placed in a special fund administered by the bank through the Ministry of Finance. Dhliwayo feels that if this bureaucratic system were corrected, the food security subsector could make far more progress.

For Dhliwayo, the system is so centralized that reproduction of documents must be done through the government printing office.

> The way we are structured now is such that we are even offending some of our donors. Like the financial reports we are to submit to our cooperating partners are not often done on time—sometimes six months later . . . Sometimes our progress reports are not submitted on time because we have to go through the government printing office, and sometimes we have a six-month delay. So we feel we should be free to go even to a private printer . . . But our monies are locked in the national structure.[20]

While this seemingly is a problem throughout SADCC coordinating units, thus contributing to the weakness of these units, this may not be the case for the Standing Committee of Officials. For example, one official in the Ministry of Finance, who is part of the Zimbabwe delegation to the Committee, does not feel confined by having to go through the centralized channels of the bureaucratic system of the Ministry of Finance.[21] Perhaps these differences exist because the Committee and the sector coordinators assume different responsibilities within SADCC, with sector coordinators being directly responsible for implementing the SADCC Program of Action.

Sector Coordinating Units

The SADCC Secretariat is currently working to strengthen SADCC's coordinating units, since the foundation of the organization rests with these entities. "The program of action of SADCC is really based on the coordinators. You start with the coordinators and go upwards. So if you have weak coordinating units, it means you have weak implementation." [22]

The Secretariat is involved in helping the units define their objectives clearly and develop more appropriate sector strategies. Overall, it is agreed that the SADCC sectors need more specialized manpower and more equipment to help in the implementation process. Currently the Secretariat is helping to streamline the sectors and bring about some sense of equality in terms of strength.[23] Clearly, the strongest sector is transport and communications, followed by energy. The weakest sector is manpower, which poses a serious problem for SADCC because appropriately trained personnel is a prerequisite for ongoing regional development.

The issue of the weakness of the manpower sector has raised many questions about the responsibility for coordination of sectors or subsectors. Does Swaziland, for example, have the resources and expertise needed to develop the regional manpower sector? Does Tanzania have the necessary resources and expertise to develop the industry and trade sector? In answering these questions, Ng'wanakilala reminds us that the first criteria for determining coordination rests with the desire to be responsible for a particular SADCC area. He notes, for example, that there have been no complaints about Tanzania's coordination of industry and trade. With respect to the weakness of certain sectors or slow progress in development, Ng'wanakilala argues that SADCC is very flexible and therefore will see how things go. If no progress is made, the Council of Ministers will call a meeting to discuss the issue.[24]

Even though a particular country may not be the most qualified to coordinate a sector or subsector, the SADCC Program of Action is designed to draw upon the expertise and resources of all member states. Consequently, theoretically, Swaziland works with all member states in its endeavor to develop the manpower sector. In reality, however, there exist constraints to such development.

For Dhliwayo, for example, communications is a serious problem. In the beginning, there was no official contact point in the member states he could call or telex about food security requests, and particularly about information.

> But now it has slightly improved because we have set up what we call a technical subcommittee on food security, which is made up of individuals at the level of chief economists appointed by their member state in their Ministry of Agriculture that act as the official contact point. So that if we need information, I just have to pick up the phone and call and address my letters or telexes to him and it is his responsibility to ensure that if we are in need of information he provides it to us.[25]

In the area of communications, SADCC is also faced with the problem of disseminating at the national level the information that has been presented at the regional level.

> When we organize a workshop or a seminar, or a short-term training course, we assemble all these people, two from each country . . . We discuss, we identify certain problems, we make some firm recommendations as to what should be done. At a regional level it seems we have achieved our purpose. But now it is the responsibility of these two representatives from these countries, when they go back to their industries, to also ensure that whatever was recommended is now translated into practical action, by disseminating those recommendations to the right institutions. That area is lacking, and I'm sure there is still more to be done if we are to gain anything from that which we have invested in and that which we're doing . . . We need someone actually on the ground to start to implement those decisions.[26]

Perhaps one of the reasons SADCC, eight years later, is continuing to experience problems of implementation rests with the fact that there are too many sectors and subsectors as well as projects to coordinate. In fact, SADCC has been accused by numerous cooperating partners of having a "shopping list" of projects. This "shopping list," which consists of too many studies and not enough actual planned implementation, provides Western nations with the opportunity to pursue a policy of "selective" funding, based on their own interests, versus that of SADCC. In response to this criticism, SADCC's information officer argues:

> On the question of studies, I think it's unfair. Most of the studies have been on agreed areas of project implementation. In terms of a shopping list, I think what they're trying to imply is that SADCC has not come up with concrete strategies or programs in the different sectors which are acceptable as a strategy . . . Therefore, if you don't have a concrete directional approach, then you will have a list of projects which might even seem to be duplicated sometimes . . . While I can say that the criticism is fair, I think the process of coordination development in these nine countries needs much more time and much stronger coordinating units, especially in manpower . . . I can assure you that of all the programs which have been drawn out by the sectors, I don't remember any that has been rejected because it conflicts with the economic and political policies of the nine countries. The main objective of these projects is to fulfill felt needs.[27]

For SADCC, the issue may be that certain projects should, at this point anyway, be left to the respective national governments to implement, in an effort to begin to solve the above problem and enhance project implementation. For example, SADCC might consider eliminating the regional mining and tourist sectors and the following subsectors: meteorology and postal services; soil and water and land utilization; fisheries; forestry; and wildlife. These sectors, at this juncture, should perhaps be coordinated by the nine nations at the national level. This would allow for the sharing of responsibility for the development of the remaining sectors and subsectors. A case can certainly be made for their elimination, since, according to the Secretariat, these projects will be implemented with or without economic assistance from SADCC's cooperating partners, since they are part of the national development plans of the SADCC countries.

Within the remaining SADCC Program of Action, the organization might then streamline the current sectors and begin to limit new projects presented to its international cooperating partners for funding. Although the Secretariat feels there is no duplication within the sectors (even though there are, for example, similar industrial projects identified for several member states), there is overlapping. It has been suggested that SADCC should work with the Preferential Trade Area of Eastern and Southern Africa (PTA) in the area of regional trade, as opposed to having a separate program within SADCC for intra-regional trade.

Dhliwayo agrees that SADCC is taking on too much. "We are probably overstretching ourselves . . . We have this psychological feeling that we are doing a lot, but we are not doing much . . . We probably need focusing. It's a manageable problem, but manpower is a problem." He further notes that because there are so many projects for SADCC's international cooperating partners to fund based on their interests, SADCC is never able to secure enough money to complete much of anything.[28] This concern is also voiced by Nelson Moyo, chair of the Department of Economics at the University of Zimbabwe. Moyo has worked with SADCC.

> One thing about SADCC—they went beyond the issue of trade to talk about planning production as a whole, planning the unit as a whole, talking about investment. So that was the positive thing. But again I think the problem, which Makoni is talking about, we want to talk production now . . . So far again nothing really has happened concretely. And I think even in the transport and energy sectors, SADCC has been concerned really with coming up with projects which need funding, hundreds of them. But the actual implementation is lagging behind the program of action. So I'm beginning to be worried now that perhaps we will not see much again in the way of actual implementation of SADCC programs, because of the geopolitics of the region. What SADCC is talking about now is collaboration in production; I think it's also going to remain on paper.[29]

Currently SADCC is taking very seriously the need to evaluate its institutional framework within the context of implementing the Program of Action more efficiently. In addition to the support being given to the SADCC sector coordinators, with the objective of helping them both strengthen and streamline their sectors, the Council of Ministers has developed "project performers" which serve as a guideline for selecting and reviewing projects, within the context of the strategy for project implementation of each sector or subsector.

NOTES

1. SADCC, *SADCC: A Handbook* (SADCC Secretariat, 1984), p. 6.

2. Interview with Nkwabi Ng'wanakilala, SADCC information officer, Gaborone, Botswana, August 1987.

3. SADCC, *Handbook*, p. 6.

4. *Ibid.*

5. Interview, Ng'wanakilala.

6. SADCC, *Handbook*, p. 7.

7. *Ibid.*

8. "Donors Boost Front-Line Assistance," *Africa Economic Digest*, February 5, 1988.

9. Based on interviews with numerous SADCC officials during the 1988 Annual Summit, Maputo, Mozambique, July 1988.

10. Clever Mumbengegwi, "Food and Agriculture Cooperation in the SADCC: Progress, Problems and Prospects," *SADCC: Prospects for Diengagement and Development in Southern Africa*, ed. Samir Amin, Derrick Chitala, and Ibbo Mandaza, (London: Zed Books, 1987), pp. 79-80.

11. Daniel B. Ndlela, "The Manufacturing Sector in the East and Southern African Subregion, with Emphasis on the SADCC," *Prospects*, ed. Amin et al., p. 37.

12. C. Mumbengegwi, "Food and Agriculture," p. 71.

13. *Ibid.*, p. 83.

14. Interviews, July 1988.

15. Ibbo Mandaza, "Perspectives on Economic Cooperation and Autonomous Development in Southern Africa," *Prospects*, ed. Amin et al., p. 220.

16. *Ibid.*, p. 14.

17. Interview, Ng'wanakilala.

18. *Ibid.*

19. Interview with K.J.M. Dhliwayo, food security coordinator, Harare, Zimbabwe, August 1987.

20. *Ibid.*

21. Interview with official in the Ministry of Finance, Harare, Zimbabwe, August 1987.

22. Interview, Ng'wanakilala.

23. *Ibid.*

24. *Ibid.*

25. Interview, Dhliwayo.

26. *Ibid.*

27. Interview, Ng'wanakilala.

28. Interview, Dhliwayo.

29. Interview with Nelson Moyo, chair, Department of Economics, University of Zimbabwe, August 1987.

CHAPTER 6
SADCC and South Africa

When SADCC was established in 1980, the organization identified its major objective as decreasing its economic dependence on South Africa. This chapter will examine the problems SADCC has experienced in achieving this objective in light of the geopolitics of the region—namely, South Africa's determination to maintain regional economic and political hegemony. Chapter six is divided into two parts. The first, "Structural Transformation of South Africa's Regional Hegemony," places the position of South Africa and the SADCC member states in theoretical perspective. Part two, "SADCC's Program of Action," analyzes the constraints to regional cooperation and development that exist at the regional level. The focus of analysis is therefore on the dynamics of the relationship between South Africa and the SADCC member states.

STRUCTURAL TRANSFORMATION OF SOUTH AFRICA'S REGIONAL HEGEMONY

In chapter 1, two orders of dependency were identified within the capitalist world-economy: the regional or subsystem (first order) and the international (second order). The dynamics of the relationship between South Africa and the SADCC member states have been classified as the first order of dependency (see Figure 1, chapter 1), since the SADCC countries have identified as their major objective the decreasing of regional economic dependence on South Africa.

At the regional or subsystem level, South Africa operates as the "regional center"; the SADCC states, as the "regional periphery." As the regional center, the apartheid regime's major objective is regional economic and political hegemony. In an effort to obtain this objective, South Africa has adopted imperialist strategies that parallel those of the imperialist powers of the global center. In order for the apartheid regime to ensure its continued economic dominance, it must maintain the relationship between itself and the SADCC members that is characterized by unequal economic relationships, identified by structural linkages of trade, direct private investment, economic assistance, foreign debt, transport and communications, migrant labor, and energy. For the SADCC countries, in order for regional structural transformation to occur, leading to regional development and decreased economic dependence on South Africa, it is precisely these historical linkages that must be altered. The successful alteration of these linkages would result in:

— limited economic interaction between South Africa and the SADCC member states;

— symmetrical economic interaction between the SADCC member states; and

— expansion of economic interaction among the SADCC member states.

Economically, there would exist greater regional interdependence among the SADCC countries, with these nations being more dependent upon one another rather than on the apartheid regime. But is such a structure possible in Southern Africa?

The ability of the SADCC countries to alter their present pattern of economic dependence is made even more complex by the varying degrees of vulnerability these countries have in relationship to South Africa. They can be categorized as totally encapsulated by South Africa, as are Botswana, Lesotho, and Swaziland; moderately encapsulated, as are Malawi, Mozambique, Zambia and Zimbabwe; and nonencapsulated, as are Angola and Tanzania. Although these vulnerabilities may vary to some degree when the strengths of each nation are analyzed within the context of SADCC's strategy for regional cooperation and development, overall, the present regional economic and political turmoil has prevented the moderately encapsulated and nonencapsulated nations from developing their strengths.

Specifically, in keeping with its imperialist regional objectives, when SADCC was established, South Africa commenced disruption through a strategy of regional destabilization. In creating SADCC, the nine independent regional nations completely rejected South Africa's idea of regional cooperation via a Constellation of Southern African States (CONSAS). This CONSAS was part of the apartheid regime's "total strategy." Specifically, in 1977, following a series of domestic, regional, and international events that served to threaten the survival of the apartheid regime (including the independence of Angola and Mozambique in 1975),[1] the South African Department of Defense argued that the government faced a "total onslaught." As a result of this conclusion, Pretoria developed a strategy which "sought to restructure specific aspects of apartheid capitalism in order to preserve its basic parameters, to defuse developing mass unrest, and to reduce South Africa's international isolation." The strategy had both domestic and regional components.[2]

The domestic component entailed the introduction of "reforms" in South Africa that were to indicate to the black majority, as well as to the international community, that the government was in the process of dismantling apartheid. The masses of blacks dismissed the so-called reforms as inconsequential; they understood that they were designed only to further consolidate white control over the country. With the exception of a few Western leaders, such as President Ronald Reagan who congratulated President P.W. Botha for his timely restructuring of the apartheid regime, the international community rejected these reforms and continued to condemn South Africa.

In an effort to maintain its hegemonic regional control, the implementation of the regional component of the total strategy consisted of a mixture of the carrot and stick. As Dan O'Meara notes:

> Through the carrot of what can be termed "formative action," it sought to create a network of economic, political, and security relationships that would persuade neighboring states that it was in their interest to cooperate with Pretoria. However, the stick of destabilization was used frequently against countries that would not cooperate. The adoption of any particular mix of formative and destabilizing measures toward specific states between 1978 and 1984 depended on various factors, the most important of

which were the rhythm of the struggle in the region and the pattern of internal relations within the target states.[3]

Outlined by Botha in 1979, CONSAS was designed to include white South Africa, the ten Bantustans, and the independent regional nations. South Africa, through CONSAS, was to promote "South African technology and know-how as the key to regional co-ordination." [4]

In addition to the establishment of CONSAS, the total strategy aimed to: (1) prevent regional states from supporting the liberation struggle led by the South West Africa People's Organization (SWAPO) of Namibia and the African National Congress (ANC) of South Africa; (2) prevent any communist (Soviet Union and Cuba) presence in the region; (3) prevent the regional states from advocating mandatory sanctions against South Africa; and (4) decrease anti-South African rhetoric.[5]

Until SADCC was formed, the South African government attempted to implement CONSAS. However, after SADCC came into existence, the apartheid regime realized that CONSAS would never be implemented. Continuing to provide carrots to a few regional states, South Africa began to pursue regional destabilization in an effort to force its regional "periphery" to discontinue its rebellion against the regional "center." The extent and various phases of South Africa's regional destabilization have been thoroughly recounted:[6] military invasions; bombings of capital cities, the development projects, the regional transport sector, and so on; support for dissident groups; assassinations and attempted assassinations (including President Robert Mugabe of Zimbabwe and the former leader of Lesotho, Chief Jonathan Leabua). Hundreds of thousands of blacks have been killed, and the economic structures of several member states have been devastated.

In response to South Africa's aggression, both domestically and regionally, the international community was called upon by SADCC to impose comprehensive, mandatory sanctions against the apartheid regime (see chapter 7).[7] Although it was anticipated that the SADCC nations would be adversely affected by sanctions against South Africa, ironically, South Africa has used the situation to increase its economic control over the regional periphery.

What has become increasingly clear is that South Africa is

dependent upon the SADCC member nations for its continued economic survival. For example, as a result of the economic relationship with SADCC states, the minority-ruled regime has an estimated trade surplus of $2.5 billion per year. In addition, "the net foreign exchange earnings from the SADCC countries roughly equals the amounts needed to pay interest on South Africa's outstanding debt." [8] These economic realities, as well as others, point to the significant role the SADCC states play in South Africa's economy, particularly amidst its current economic crisis, and therefore it is extremely vulnerable to any alterations in the historical linkages of dependency.

Throughout SADCC's existence, as this chapter will show, South Africa has effectively used the carrot or the stick to maintain its imperialist grip over the region and effectively undermine SADCC's objective of decreasing regional economic dependence on the apartheid regime.

SADCC'S PROGRAM OF ACTION

Constraints to develop at the regional level will be discussed within the context of four SADCC sectors: transport and communications; food, agriculture, and natural resources; industry and trade; and energy.

Transport and Communications

Although currently several SADCC member states are extremely dependent on the South African transport network for external trade, this has not always been the case. In fact, until the early 1960s most of their goods were carried via Angola and Mozambique. This practice, however, was disrupted when the indigenous populations of Angola and Mozambique began their fight for independence against Portuguese colonial rule, thus making it impossible to use these outlets to the sea. The practice of exporting via the SADCC states was further disrupted in 1975 when Mozambique closed its border with the white minority-ruled regime of Rhodesia. The long and protracted struggle resulted in the SADCC member states being forced to redirect their trade through the South African transport network.

Consequently, when SADCC was formed, the member states determined that the establishment of a viable regional surface transport system was a prerequisite for effective cooperation and development, particularly since six of the members are landlocked. However, such a system poses a threat to South Africa's regional hegemonic position. This is evident in the fact that South Africa has consistently attacked vital surface transport systems that connect SADCC member states:

> In the field of transport, the apartheid regime has used its military and paramilitary forces to delay the carrying out of SADCC projects. Acts of sabotage with this intent have been carried out against Beira port, Mozambique railways and in Angola the port of Lobito and the Benguela Railway line, as well as many other sabotages of bridges and roads vital to the economies and trade of countries concerned.[9]

For South Africa, the successful redirection of trade away from its ports could mean the loss of $350 million a year, including $225 million from Zimbabwe alone.[10]

As a result of South Africa's destabilization of the regional transport network, by early 1987 the Nacala and Lobito Port Transport Systems were inoperative, and the Maputo and Beira systems were only partially operative. This resulted in the SADCC states being more dependent on the South African transport system than in 1980, with 85 percent of all external trade traveling via South Africa. Although by mid-1987 the situation had begun to change (see below), South Africa has used a unique strategy to undermine the real potential of these states for delinking in this sector. The strategy has included direct military intervention, support for insurgency rebels, disinformation, political sabotage, and threats of economic leverage. The result is that SADCC has a greater challenge before it now than in 1980.

Zimbabwe

In 1982, for example, 33 percent of Zimbabwe's external trade was shipped through SADCC ports and 63 percent through South Africa. By 1986, however, approximately 93 percent of Zimbabwe's external trade was shipped through South African ports, but only 7 percent through SADCC ports. It was not until mid-1987 that Zimbabwe's use of South Africa's transport system declined to less than 70 percent.

Zimbabwe, however, paid dearly for that increased dependency on South Africa's transport network. In 1983 SADCC had projected that between 1985 and 1990, Zimbabwe would increase its use of the port of Maputo by 45 percent; Beira, by 14.2 percent. As a result of the destabilization of these two lines by the South African-backed MNR (Renamo), Zimbabwe is not likely to meet its targeted deadlines, particularly with respect to the Maputo port. Mozambique was forced to close the Zimbabwe-Maputo line (Limpopo) in 1985, and with the exception of a small percentage of local traffic on certain portions of the line, it has basically remained inoperative since.

It was not until April 1988, according to Pedro Figueiredo, a Mozambican engineer directing the rehabilitation of the Limpopo line, that all bridges were repaired and trains could once again move up and down the line. Although the line is open to local traffic (largely relief assistance), it is not currently open to commercial traffic. Figueiredo predicts the Limpopo line will be reopened to commercial traffic before the end of the year. Progress on the rehabilitation of the line has been largely made possible by the protection provided by both Mozambican and Zimbabwean troops.[11]

In terms of the Beira to Zimbabwe line, MNR attacks totaled seven in 1982, thirteen in 1984, and six in 1985. Throughout 1986, the MNR continued to destabilize the Beira line, so that the only route to the sea for Zimbabwe that remained unscathed was the direct railway line through Rutenga and Berthridge to South Africa.[12] During 1987, Renamo continued to disrupt the Beira line, although the level of disruption had decreased significantly. In fact, a great deal of progress was made on the development of this line during 1987 and throughout 1988, although the MNR continued its disruptive tactics.

The most obvious evidence of progress on the Beira Corridor, according to Rui Fonseca, executive director of the Beira Corridor Authority (BCA), rests with the fact that during the first six months of 1988, use of the port increased 15.6 percent over the first six months of 1987. While during the first six months of

TABLE 13

PERCENT DISTRIBUTION OF ZIMBABWE'S EXTERNAL TRADE BY ROUTE, 1981-1987

Year	SADCC Ports	South Africa
1981	33%	67%
1982	37%	63%
1983	24%	76%
1985	15%	85% (min)
1986	7%	93%
1987	31%	69%

Source: Chris Davids, *The Impact of Economic Sanctions Against South Africa on the SADCC States,* Canadian International Development Agency (CIDA), Ottawa, February 1986, p. 20; *Southern Africa Report,* August 15, 1986.

1987, 866,000 tons of goods were handled at the port, during the first six months of 1988, 1 million tons were handled. In addition, Fonseca noted that Zimbabwe's use of Beira increased by 34 percent during this same period.[13]

The destabilization of the Zimbabwe transport network has posed serious political and economic problems. As a landlocked country, Zimbabwe's nearest access to the sea is through the port of Beira; second, through the port of Maputo (see Figure 6). Since currently Beira can handle only a limited percentage of Zimbabwe's exports and imports, and those handled at Maputo must first travel to South Africa, Zimbabwe remains dependent on the longer and more expensive South African network. Goods being transported through South Africa must travel 1,921 km to East London or 2,521 km to Cape Town, compared to only 592 km to Beira. It has been estimated that the disruptions are costing Zimbabwe $100 million per year in invisibles and higher transport costs.[14] Additional problems include lost orders, the destruction of property by bandits, and lost investment and tourism.[15]

Currently, the Beira line is opened to Zimbabwe partially because the Zimbabwean government has deployed approximately seven thousand troops along the route to prevent further destruction. These troops ride the trains and supply trucks, and patrol the road on foot and in armored personnel carriers. In addition, troops are stationed approximately every half-mile along the Zimbabwe pipeline, which runs parallel to the road most of the distance. Further protection is provided by an air force base established by Zimbabwe.[16]

Without such protection, Zimbabwe would be forced to rely totally on South African ports. The continued presence of troops in Mozambique is costly, but President Mugabe sees the protection of both the Beira line and Mozambique as being central to Zimbabwe's political and economic survival. Therefore, following President Samora Machel's death, Mugabe pledged increased support to the Mozambique government to fight against heightened MNR destabilization. In fact, in November 1986, Zimbabwe extended a $30 million loan to Mozambique as a supplement to the troops.[17] It is estimated that it costs Zimbabwe $Z1 million a day to maintain troops in Mozambique.[18]

The apartheid regime always manages to display to Zimbabwe, either through the carrot or the stick, that delinking is not advantageous. In 1981, when South Africa withdrew locomotives that had been loaned to the previous government of Rhodesia, the transport system was so disrupted that lost export earnings were estimated at Z$7 million a week.[19] Then following the August 1986 announcement by President Kaunda and President Mugabe that their countries would impose limited sanctions against South Africa, the apartheid regime responded by imposing transit fees and slowing down traffic from Zambia and Zimbabwe.

In respect to use of the carrot, Pretoria has been involved in ratecutting, so that often it is less expensive for Zimbabwe to send goods via Durban than through Beira. The desire to delink from South Africa and the ability to do it are made more complex by the fact that the freight-forwarding agencies who control the shipment of goods are owned by South African private and parastatal enterprises. Therefore, neither Mozambique nor Zimbabwe

CHART I

DESTABILIZATION OF THE TRANSPORT AND COMMUNICATIONS SECTOR

1980

- With the exception of a short period in 1980, South African and UNITA attacks on the Benguela railway have made it inoperative since 1975.

- South Africa imposed a railway embargo on cargo to Maputo for two weeks.

1981

- The embargo on South African cargo to Maputo continued.

- During three months, South Africa imposed rail embargoes on Botswana and Zimbabwe.

- MNR began attacking the Beira-Zimbabwe railway.

- SA planted a mine on the Beira-Zimbabwe railway.

- SA hit two bridges 50 km from Beira, destroying the bridge carrying the road and the oil pipeline, and damaging the railway, thus cutting all traffic between Beira and Zimbabwe.

- SA destroyed the marker buoys in Beira harbor.

- The only road linking Beira and Maputo was closed.

1982

- MNR raided the Limpopo line (Maputo-Zimbabwe) 25 times (line was closed 75 days).
- MNR raided the Beira-Zimbabwe line 7 times (line was closed 24 days).
- MNR began to attack the line between Beira and Malawi (by the end of the year the line was closed).
- SA attacked road and rail bridges near the port of Namibe in Angola.
- SA blew up the depot that held fuel for the Zimbabwe pipeline and for Malawi.

1983

- MNR raided the Limpopo line 38 times (line was closed 144 days).

1984

- MNR raided the Limpopo line 30 times.
- MNR raided the Beira-Zimbabwe line 13 times (line was closed 32 days).
- Two cargo ships in Luanda harbor were sunk by SA limpet mines.
- UNITA rebels destroyed 12 locomotives in the Benguela railway yard.
- MNR began to attack the Malawi-Nacala line.

- MNR damaged a railway bridge on the Maputo-South African line.

- MNR attacked the Maputo to Swaziland road and railway.

1985

- Mozambique was forced to close the Limpopo line.

- MNR damaged two bridges on the Maputo-South African line.

- The Malawi-Nacala line was closed due to MNR attacks.

- MNR attacked rail links between South Africa and Swaziland.

- MNR raided the Beira-Zimbabwe line six times (line was closed 24 days).

1986

- SA and the MNR continued to attack the Beira Port transport system.

1987

- MNR continued to disrupt the Beira Corridor.

- Maputo-Swaziland line was closed to regional traffic in October due to MNR attacks.

- The destruction of a bridge on the Maputo-Swaziland line in December closed the line again until January 3, 1988.

1988

- Maputo-Swaziland line was closed again during the second week of January as a result of the MNR.

- MNR continued to disrupt the Beira Corridor.

- A vital bridge carrying the Benguela line across the Cuanza river was blown up by UNITA.

Sources: Economist Intelligence Unit, (various documents); Joseph Hanlon, *Beggar Your Neighbours: Apartheid Power in Southern Africa* (1986); *Destructive Engagement: Southern Africa at War,* ed. Phyllis Johnson and David Martin, (1986); *Facts and Reports; Washington Post; Africa Economic Digest.*

FIGURE 6

Figure 6 - Africa Railroads

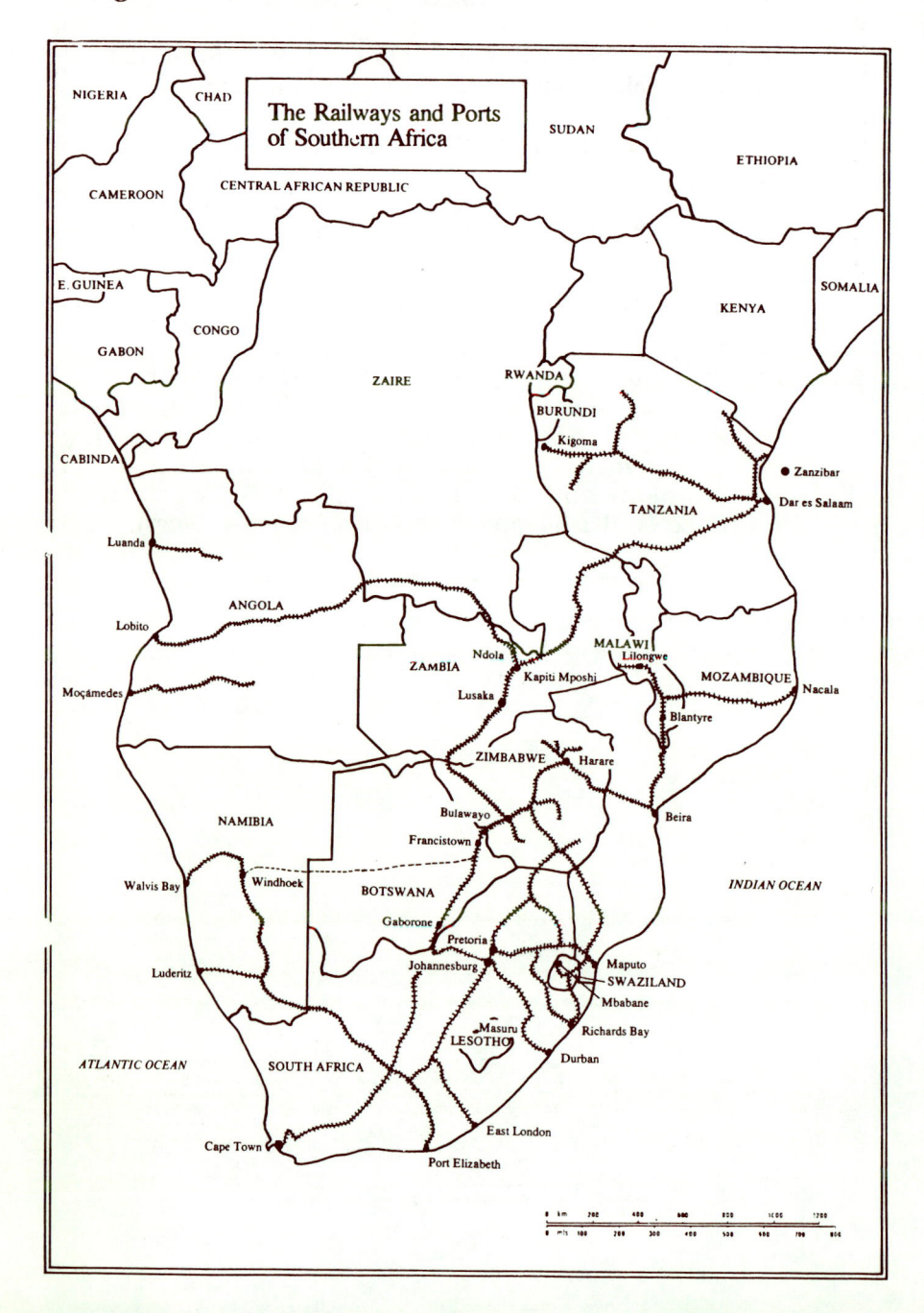

is directly involved in decision making.[20]

In what is likely to result in a boost for Beira Port, the chairman of the Shipping and Forwarding Agents Association of Zimbabwe, Rhette Hill, reported in June 1988 that "under the new General Agreement on Tariffs and Trade system, introduced at the beginning of this year, transport costs are included in the value of the goods when duty is levied. Thus, Beira gives the lowest transport and duty costs to importers." This new system consequently makes Mozambican routes less expensive.[21]

Another reason for Zimbabwe's increased use of the Beira line rests with the BCA's commitment to rehabilitate the entire Beira Port transport system (the Beira Corridor). The BCA was created by the Mozambican government in 1985, after the 10-year plan for the development of the Corridor was completed. The BCA has "the role of mobilizing the capital and the human and material resources from the international community and of conceiving, planning, designing, monitoring and managing the implementation of this 10-year programme." [22]

In order to keep those informed who have a vested interest in the development of the Beira Port transport system, the Ministry of Transport and Communications of Mozambique decided to reestablish the Beira Port Advisory Committee (BPAC). The first meeting to accomplish this was held on May 18, 1988, in Beira. In his welcoming address, Fonseca noted that the BPAC was being reestablished:

> . . .with the aim of creating an adequate forum where views can be exchanged and the required coordination created between all the parties involved in trade and traffic flows, to increase communication and dessiminate accurate information, to promote operational planning and co-operation in order to secure needed harmonization between trade demand and required transport capabilities . . . In doing so we will enhance the efforts being undertaken on a regional basis in the framework of SADCC and thus effectively contribute to the maximization of the utilization of SADCC transport routes.[23]

Appointed members of the BPAC include "one government representative and one railway administration representative from each of the following countries: Botswana, Malawi, Zambia, Zimbabwe and Mozambique." In addition, elected representatives on the BPAC are from these same countries.[24]

Currently in Southern Africa, there exists a great deal of controversy over the development of the Beira Port transport system. This controversy centers around a group of white Zimbabwe businessmen who in 1985 created an entity known as the Beira Corridor Group (BCG), with the stated objective of involving the business community in the development of the Corridor.[25] Currently, the BCG consists of 246 Zimbabwe-based companies that have purchased shares in the BCG at Z$12,000 a share. These investors, as well as people in the region and SADCC's international cooperating partners, were led to believe that the BCG would invest the money in the development of agricultural and industrial projects along the Corridor, as well as in the tourist sector of Mozambique. As of July 1988, however, according to Fonseca, the BCG had not invested one penny in the development of the Beira Corridor.[26]

Not only has the money not been invested in the Corridor, which of course raises the issue of what is being done with the money, but the BCG's chairman, Denis Norman, and its managing director, Eddie Cross, continue to present themselves as officials directly involved in the development of the Corridor. In June 1988 in Zimbabwe, during a TV interview on a program called "The Nation," when pressed to give specifics about the progress the BCG has made to date, Denis Norman responded by listing the various successes experienced by the Beira Corridor Authority, and then noted, "We have assisted in these exercises with the government. As far as the private sector is concerned, we have many projects which look as if they have attracted sufficient funding to begin in the near future." [27]

In a further misrepresentation of the role of the BCG, Norman commented, "In addition, we just established with the Mozambicans a Beira Port Advisory Committee." [28] As previously noted, the BPAC was established by the Ministry of Transport and Communications prior to 1988.

As investors, as well as some SADCC officials, request information about what the BCG is doing, to no avail, Fonseca has had to contend with the disinformation campaign waged by both

Cross and Norman about developments at Beira. Eddie Cross reported to the media that by March the situation in Beira had deteriorated, causing a reduction in exports through the port over the previous six weeks by 40 percent. He further noted, "We are diverting these exports to South African routes, which is very disappointing, because we were hoping for a sustained growth in Beira." [29] This disinformation campaign was potentially so catastrophic that Fonseca had to personally wage his own campaign to inform users of the port, as well as SADCC's cooperating partners, that while problems of congestion did exist, there was no need to divert traffic from Beira to South Africa.

Questions about the motives of the white Zimbabwe business community in establishing the BCG were raised before 1988. Hasu Patel, a professor at the University of Zimbabwe in the Department of Political and Administrative Studies, noted in an interview in 1987 that for some private-sector business people, the Beira Corridor has become a major instrument for maintaining their role on state decisions. Since the white business community has shown that within Zimbabwean society it is very powerful, it feels it has political access and therefore is involved in state decisionmaking. Patel further argues that the private sector really feels that the state cannot move without "us whites." This attitude is also taken with respect to Mozambican development.

> Mozambique cannot do very much, so let us teach them what to do; let us take over the Corridor as if it belongs to us. It does not belong to us. It's Mozambique's sovereign territory. But if you talk to some of these business guys, they will talk as if the Beira Corridor belongs to us.

Patel also suggested that as a result of the perceived motives of the more than two hundred Zimbabwean companies that have invested in the BCG, there exists ambivalence in Zimbabwe about their plans to increase production and tourism along the Corridor. Why, for example, is the business community of Zimbabwe now interested in developing Mozambique? "So that they can prove that capitalism works; that, in fact, destabilization is not the real problem in Mozambique, but socialism is." [30]

In 1987, Eddie Cross noted that "up to 1985, every Zimbabwean businessman, and that included me, had not taken any interest in Mozambique at all. For us, Mozambique was a write-off. It was a Marxist state on our boundaries. It was in shambles; Renamo was growing in strength every day, and we really didn't even think about Mozambique." Once the BCG was established, Cross argues, he became involved in anti-Renamo lobbying, in both South Africa and the United States.[31]

Given the activities of the BCG, one must ask, Is the white business community really interested in developing the Beira Corridor? This question must be raised within the context of the knowledge that the business community has a reputation of being pro-South African and of maintaining a "kith and kin" relationship with the apartheid regime. The misrepresentation by Norman and Cross of the BCG as a conduit for development on the Corridor points to the fact that in reality, they could be working in the best interests of the apartheid regime, which obviously does not want Beira to become a success. The depth of these feelings between Cross and the Afrikaners was recently expressed by Cross in an editorial, "Distasteful Attack on Afrikaans": "When the system of apartheid is removed from Africa, the Afrikaner will take his rightful place as one of the 'great ethnic groups' of the continent. In the interim, we can achieve little by attacking those things of which they can be justly proud." [32] It appears that the SADCC member states and SADCC's international cooperating partners would do well to forget that the BCG ever existed.

Given the complexity of the economic and political dynamics, the SADCC member states continue to find it necessary to involve South Africa in the development of the regional transport network. Consequently, during the latter part of 1987, the National Railways of Zimbabwe (NRZ) was forced to request ten locomotives from South Africa. A shortage of Zimbabwe locomotives was caused by the government's lack of the necessary foreign exchange to import spare parts to repair over half of NRZ's diesel locomotives.[33]

Swaziland

For both Zimbabwe and Swaziland, the Mozambique port of Maputo is an alternative to the South African transport network. Ideally, the majority of Swaziland's external trade should travel via the port of Maputo, and in 1981 and 1982, roughly 67 percent of Swazi's trade did travel this route.[34] According to 1983 SADCC projections, it was anticipated that between 1981 and 1985, Swaziland would increase its use of the port of Maputo/Matola by 50 percent, and between 1985 and 1990, another 33 percent. Instead, by 1985, Swaziland's use of the port had dropped to 30 percent as a result of MNR destabilization, the cessation of iron-ore exports, and the construction of a South African-financed railway line across Swaziland to connect the Eastern Transvaal with the port of Richards Bay.[35] The line was completed in early 1986, and, as the general manager of South African Railways at the time boasted,

> Such a connection will make it possible to divert traffic coming from northern Transvaal over this route to Richards Bay and Durban. Mozambique is fully aware that we may, at any time now, be diverting this traffic from Maputo. Furthermore, the diversion of traffic opens spare capacity to carry traffic to Durban from Zimbabwe and Zambia which, in line with SADCC's aims, should flow through Maputo and Beira. S.A. can keep this traffic moving south by rate cutting, or by using the MNR to attack competing rail lines.[36]

According to Figueiredo, the Maputo-Swaziland line (Goba Line) has always remained open, although destabilization has resulted in the line being periodically closed.[37] Reportedly, "People from Swaziland have dubbed the road to Maputo a 'hell run,' and their authorities have warned that Swazi citizens using the road do so at their own risk." [38] Figueiredo, however, suggests that this is an exaggeration of the dangers, particularly since Mozambican troops protect the line, and 80 to 90 percent of all trains pass safely.[39]

Swaziland is definitely not a major user of the Maputo Port. In fact, only approximately 20 percent of the goods handled have a Swazi or Mozambican origin. Most of the Swazi goods handled consist of sugar.

Malawi

In 1981, 70 percent of Malawi's external trade was shipped through the Mozambican port of Nacala; only 5 percent, through the port of Durban. By 1986, however, approximately 97 percent of Malawi's external trade was being shipped via Durban; the remaining 3 percent, via Dar es Salaam. In 1983, SADCC had projected that Malawi would have increased its use of Nacala by 100 percent between 1985 and 1990.

Of all the regional nations, Malawi, to the consternation of other SADCC states, has always maintained strong diplomatic relations with South Africa. Thus when the Renamo terrorists destroyed the marker buoys in Beira harbor—only days before Malawi was scheduled to host the SADCC Annual Conference during November 1981, and at a time in which Malawi was the major user of the port—it was obvious that South Africa was warning Malawi that the decreasing of economic dependence was not a viable alternative.[40] The message became even more clear when Renamo began to attack the transport line between Beira and Malawi in 1982. By the end of 1982, this line was closed and more than 50,000 tons of sugar was stockpiled. This figure had risen to 130,000 tons by the end of 1983. And during the latter part of 1982, Malawi experienced shortages of fuel and fertilizer, since such essential products were normally imported through Beira.[41]

After South Africa had been successful in closing the Beira-to-Malawi line, its next objective was to make the Nacala-to-Malawi line inoperative. Initially the line was subjected to a disinformation campaign waged by the South African-owned Manica Freight Services, designed to discourage client usage of the line. The Nacala line, however, continued to be used by Malawi through 1983, to South Africa's disappointment. Consequently, by 1984 the MNR began to attack the line, costing Malawi K100 million in higher freight charges and lower export prices.[42] The line was closed by 1985. In the meantime, the routes used to carry South Africa's trade to Zambia remained unscathed.[43]

After destroying these vital transportation links, South Africa began to offer Malawi new economic alternatives. When Malawi found it impossible to transport the needed fertilizer stuck in Beira, a South African soft loan of K5 million provided for the purchase of South African fertilizer to be trucked to Malawi. Then in 1984, following a visit by Foreign Minister Pik Botha to Malawi to discuss an appeal by President Kamuzu Banda for transport

TABLE 14

PERCENT DISTRIBUTION OF MALAWI'S EXTERNAL TRADE BY ROUTE 1981-1987

Country	Port	1981	1982-1984	1985	1986	1987
Mozambique	Beira	70%	5%	—	—	—
	Nacala	25%	35%			
South Africa	Durban	5%	60%	95%	97%	97%
Tanzania	Dar es Salaam	—	—	5%	3%	—

Sources: Davids, *Impact of Economic Sanctions,* p. 19; *Country Profile: Malawi 1986-87, 1987-88.*

assistance because of the disruption of the Nacala line, the two countries signed an agreement that resulted in a further reduction in the prices of tea, tobacco, and fertilizer sent by road. Malawi/South African economic ties were further strengthened in 1985 when the apartheid regime granted a K1.1 million soft loan to upgrade the railway and telecommunications sector, and South African Transport Services offered lower trucking rates if Malawi agreed to send the majority of its exports by road.[44]

This new economic assistance, however, has not relieved the Malawian government of the more than $50 million yearly increase in transport costs as a result of using the South African transport network, rather than the shorter, more convenient Mozambique network. While the distance between Malawi and Beira is only 640 km and that between Malawi and Nacala is 815 km, the distance between Malawi and Durban is between 2600 and 3500 km. Other costs to Malawi include the loss to the Malawian railway network of its international traffic and the increased dependency on South Africa for transport and imports.[45] When Malawi first joined SADCC, South Africa's share of its imports dropped from 41 percent in 1979 to 32 percent in 1981. In an effort to circumvent this decline, Pretoria, for the first time in almost a decade, responded in 1980 by offering Malawi new development aid—R12 million. The apartheid regime further provided R11 million in export credits for a massive grain silo in Lilongwe. By 1983, South Africa's share of Malawi's imports had risen to 39 percent.[46]

In an effort to decrease the South African stranglehold, Malawi signed a preliminary agreement in April 1986 with Tanzania, which was designed to give Malawi greater access to the Tanzanian port of Dar es Salaam. The new agreement called for the two nations to work collectively to secure foreign financing for a 50-km highway from the Malawi town of Karonga to Ibanda in Tanzania, and for the resurfacing of the Kyela-Uyole road in the Tanzanian region of Mbeya. This road was opened in 1983, but it has been plagued by problems of inefficiency; thus only 2 to 3 percent of Malawi's external trade travels via this route. Although currently this represents only 300,000 tons annually, projections are that this will increase to 800,000 tons.[47]

While the SADCC states have abhorred Malawi's economic and political relationships with South Africa, the military relationship between the two nations prior to December 1986 was considered incomprehensible. Between 1982 and December 1986, Malawi provided military bases in order for Renamo to launch attacks against Mozambique. Ironically, Renamo is the same insurgency group that forced Malawi to seek alternative trade routes and prevented oil from reaching the country. Prior to December 1986, the Mozambique government had failed to convince Malawi to discontinue its support of Renamo, but by 1986, the situation had become so catastrophic for regional security that the Frontline States joined together in an effort to convince President Banda of Malawi to stop supporting the rebels. Only a month before his fatal plane crash, President Machel threatened to close the 1,500-km Malawi-Mozambique border and to station troops, artillery, and missiles along it.[48]

Finally, in December 1986, Banda responded to the Frontline States by signing a pact with Mozambique, agreeing to dispatch troops to help protect the Beira Corridor.[49] Currently, Mozambican and Malawian troops are stationed along the Nacala line, and Tanzanian troops are fighting alongside Mozambican troops throughout the country.[50]

Zambia

In August 1986, at the time Zimbabwe and Zambia announced they would impose sanctions against South Africa, Zambia's transportation difficulties had been complicated by inefficiency on the Tanzania-Zambia Railway (Tazara) and the continued closure of the Benguela Railway to the port of Lobito. Nonetheless, the Zambian government ordered Zambia Consolidated Copper Mines (ZCCM) to re-route copper through the ports of Beira and Dar es Salaam.[51] Prior to 1987, there had been a slight increase in Zambia's use of the South African transport network. In fact, in 1986 Zambia shipped most of its copper by way of South Africa. Currently, none goes through the apartheid regime; 84 percent of exports are shipped via Dar es Salaam and some copper is exported via Beira. In fact, according to Fonseca of the Beira Corridor Authority, although 37,000 tons of Zambian copper were handled at the port during the first six months of 1987, by the end of the first six months of 1988, this had increased to 68,000 tons, representing a 34-percent increase in Zambia's use of the port.[52] Prior to that, South Africa and Zambia had agreed on a special road-haulage service which allowed Zambia to pay transport fees in Zambian kwacha, and a flight service between Lusaka and Johannesburg begun in 1980 by Zambia offered a discount on air freight.[53]

In 1983, SADCC projected that between 1985 and 1990, Zambia would increase its external trade through the port of Lobito by 100 percent. Given the geopolitics of the region, however, it is not likely that this target date will be met.

Zambia's increased use of the Tazara route, however, has proved to be a viable alternative, as a result of the tremendous progress made on upgrading the Dar es Salaam Port Transport System through the implementation of a ten-year rehabilitation plan begun in 1985. Currently, Zambian exports and imports account for over 50 percent of Tazara's traffic.[54]

Tazara, according to President Kaunda, has become "a target for South Africans," since Zambia rerouted its traffic away from the apartheid regime. Therefore, "Zambia has mounted a security

TABLE 15

DISTRIBUTION OF ZAMBIA'S EXTERNAL TRADE BY ROUTE, 1981-1984

Year		SADCC	South Africa
1981		64%	36%
1982		67%	33%
1983	imports	30%	70%
	exports	60%	40%
1984	imports	35%	65%
	exports	60-65%	35-40%

Source: Davids, *Impact of Economic Sanctions,* p. 20.

alert on all bridges along the Tanzania-Zambia Railway (Tazara) to protect Zambia's major outlet to the sea from South African attacks."[55]

Botswana and Lesotho

The carrot and stick have been used by South Africa to warn Botswana and Lesotho against attempts to disengage from the South African transport network. About 95 percent of Botswana's exports travel either to or through South Africa by rail.[56] The landlocked country is particularly dependent on South African refrigerator cars to transport beef to the European Economic Community (EEC). When the apartheid regime desires to threaten Botswana with its economic leverage, it withholds these rail cars. In an effort to remind Botswana of its leverage, in 1987 South Africa caused Botswana to postpone, "at considerable expense and inconvenience, its plans to take over from Zimbabwe the railway running through its own territory."[57]

In an effort to begin to disengage from South Africa's network, the government of Botswana, at the 1988 Annual SADCC Summit held in Maputo during July, announced a pledge of $3.5

million to Zimbabwe for the rehabilitation of the Limpopo railway. (A portion of the railway runs along Botswana's border.) This is the first such investment by one SADCC country in another.[58] In addition, this move is historic since it could serve as a precedent for greater self-reliance among the member states.

Being completely surrounded by South Africa, Lesotho is forced to use South Africa's transport network and thus is totally dependent on the apartheid regime. South Africa has consistently attempted to disrupt Lesotho with long delays in transporting goods. In 1982, for example, South Africa left British aircraft tires and small arms stranded in Durban and Johannesburg. An Italian helicopter and oil from Maputo were later blocked. Border closures and disruptions which began in 1983 caused shortages of meat, milk, and other foodstuffs in the capital of Maseru.[59] Then, in January 1986, a South African border closure that caused shortages in needed supplies resulted in a coup d'etat.

Mozambique

The effects of destabilization have been far-reaching in Mozambique, which is facing perhaps the worst economic crisis of all the SADCC states. South Africa's objective of totally destroying Mozambique's transport sector can be understood, since it is the key to the development of a successful SADCC transportation system and, ultimately, to decreased dependency on South Africa. The overall strategy of SADCC for liberation has thus been undermined by South Africa and the MNR.

Destabilization has had a catastrophic affect on Mozambique's economy. The inability of the surrounding nations to transport their goods via Mozambique's transport systems deprives that country of crucial foreign exchange. In fact, before twenty years of guerrilla warfare and economic collapse reduced it to a dilapidated and barely functional outlet, the port of Beira handled 80 percent of the region's trade.[60] In addition, South Africa deliberately began to decrease its use of the port of Maputo, so that between 1980 and 1985, port revenues paid to Mozambique dropped from $92.6 million to an estimated $20 million.[61] Then, in 1987, income from transport services was

> lower than forecast because South Africa diverted even

more traffic from Maputo than previously (traffic through Maputo was 35% lower than the same period of 1986). This drop was partly compensated for by an increase of 50% in traffic from other neighbors, mainly Zimbabwe using the railway to Beira.[62]

In fact, according to Figueiredo, Mozambican engineer for the Limpopo line, for the first time in history, more Zimbabwean than South African traffic is being handled in Mozambique's ports (including Beira and Maputo). The Zimbabwean traffic handled at Maputo represents 30 percent of all traffic. The goods, however, must first travel to South Africa and then to Maputo, since the Limpopo line is closed.[63]

Additional damage done to Mozambique's economy is evidenced by the fact that during a three-year period, as a result of destabilization, 93 locomotives and 250 rail cars were either destroyed or damaged, and 150 workers were killed. "In dozens of horrific massacres, MNR guerrillas derailed trains and wrecked buses, then shot the passengers as they climbed from the wreckage and burned the vehicles with the wounded still inside." [64] This strategy of destabilization continues.

Another serious problem for Mozambique is that South African companies control the freight-forwarding industry in the region and have corporate links with shipping companies that operate out of South Africa. Thus there is a great incentive to redirect regional shipping away from Mozambique to South Africa. This rerouting is made easier by the fact that discounts offered by the South African Transport System (SATS) on rail, port, and shipping charges make it cheaper to send a container of coffee from Mutare to Durban (2000 km) than to Beira (300 km).[65] This trend is likely to continue, in light of the fact that South African shipping companies appear to be in desperate trouble. Reportedly, the SA-Europe Container Service (SAECS) is operating at only half its capacity; the state-owned rail and harbor monopoly, by September 1986, had been operating at a loss for twelve months; and six shipping lines have closed down in the last two years.[66]

Amidst South Africa's destabilization of the Maputo Port Transport System, the apartheid regime is "helping in the rehabilitation of Maputo harbour, costing millions of rands, and exporters have been encouraged by the South African Foreign Trade Organization to use it after Richards Bay became inoperative because of the floods and long delays on the main Natal railway line."[67] When asked about this seemingly major contradiction, Figueiredo responds that Mozambique's relationship with South Africa regarding the development of Maputo Port is purely business.

> The strategy adopted is to involve as much as possible the exporters and importers into development facilities in the port. By involving these people, we have greater assurances that those facilities will be used because it's their money involved . . . These South African exporters also know how to play the game. So they went to their government, and in order to have assurances from South Africa that they will not decide to cut even more traffic, they mobilized government money.[68]

Figueiredo further notes, "Unfortunately, we can't cut South Africa from the map."

The reality is that 50 percent of all goods handled at the port of Maputo are of South African origin. A visitor to the port sees many Mozambicans gainfully employed preparing South African oranges for export, as well as large stockpiles of South African coal waiting to be shipped. Sidik Juma Abdula, public relations director for Maputo Port, quickly points out that Mozambicans do not handle this South African coal,[69] which supposedly is a victim of international sanctions.

Since the South African government is investing heavily in the port, it is likely that there will be an increase in South African goods being handled at Maputo. Currently, the port handles only 3.5 million tons annually, although it has the capacity to handle approximately 14 million. Prior to independence in 1975, the port handled 8 to 10 million tons annually.[70]

Since South Africa is the major user of the port, Figueiredo points out that it is not a major recipient of aid from SADCC's international cooperating partners. In addition, SADCC could never have a Maputo Corridor Conference because of South Africa's direct involvement in the development of Maputo Port. "Instead, we will have a Limpopo Conference, only for the

Zimbabwe-to-Maputo line."[71]

Angola

South African and UNITA destabilization of Angola has closed the Benguela Railway to the port of Lobito since 1975. It is not likely that this route will become operative again until UNITA is defeated. Nonetheless, a ten-year plan for the development of the Lobito Corridor was presented at the 1988 SADCC Annual Consultative Conference. Most donors at the conference did express concern about the prospects for rehabilitation of the Corridor, given the current civil war in Angola.

Food, Agriculture, and Natural Resources

> Mysterious problems resulting in delayed delivery of petroleum products and fertilizer have been experienced by at least five SADCC members—Botswana, Lesotho, Malawi, Swaziland and Zimbabwe. Apart from reminding them of South Africa's ability to cripple their economies, these actions may be intended to hamper food production and thus reinforce South Africa's "food power" vis-à-vis its neighbors—a power eroded by Zimbabwe's large 1981 maize surplus.[72]

Regional destabilization has only exacerbated the present decline in the per-capita growth rate in food production experienced by the SADCC states as a result of (1) the drought, (2) rapid population growth, (3) weaknesses in agricultural development, and (4) a hostile external economic environment.[73] Consequently, since 1980, SADCC member states have increased their food dependency on both South Africa and the West. Although Zimbabwe, lauded as the bread basket for the region, is a major exporter of maize to Mozambique, Zambia, Botswana, Malawi, and to South Africa ($20 million in 1986), without appropriate transportation facilities, Zimbabwe will continue to experience difficulties in getting the maize to its SADCC neighbors. During 1987-1988, Zimbabwe was scheduled to deliver food-aid purchases of 150,000 tons to Mozambique, of which 117,000 were to be delivered between May and September. However, only 30,000 tons actually were delivered, due to railway problems.[74]

The continued South African destabilization of the transportation sector thus directly guarantees the continued reliance of the regional nations on the apartheid regime's imported food products. As Joseph Hanlon notes:

> One of South Africa's oft-cited arguments for white rule is that black Africa cannot feed itself. Now, the newly independent Zimbabwe was exporting maize—including to countries like Zambia and Mozambique that had previously bought from South Africa. What was worse, the good rains meant South Africa too had a surplus that it wanted to sell. The South African generated rail crisis curtailed low value maize exports. Again, the South African press was open about the implications, noting that South Africa might be called on to fill the demand Zimbabwe could not meet.[75]

In Angola and Mozambique, destabilization has basically destroyed the agricultural sector, leaving millions in danger of starvation. In Mozambique, the MNR has

> ruined 1,900 health centres and destroyed 720 schools, 900 rural shops, 1,300 lorries, and 44 agriculture enterprises, including two major sugar factories. They have forced five million people, who lived on subsistence agriculture, from the land. Now they depend on imported food.[76]

By 1988, this figure had increased to six million people. The agricultural sector has been further destabilized by the Anglo-American abandonment of its two cashew factories in 1981. Ironically, cashew nuts are Mozambique's biggest export.[77]

During December 1987, the food crisis in Mozambique became worse after Renamo terrorists fired on a Red Cross aircraft delivering food to a refugee center. The Red Cross responded by suspending its flights to fifty refugee centers, thus leaving tens of thousands of refugees without food.[78] By February 1988, Italy had stepped in to partially replace the flights.[79]

According to James Ingram, executive director of the World Food Program (WFP), "The large number of Mozambicans dependent on food aid will, together with other pressing emergency needs in sub-Saharan Africa, severely strain WFP's emergency resources during 1988." In addition, "Mozambicans form the largest refugee group in Africa and the second largest in the world, after the Afgans." [80] It is estimated that currently there are one million Mozambican refugees.

By 1983, President dos Santos estimated that total losses caused by South African aggression against Angola were $10 billion. This figure is even greater now, with whole towns being razed and agriculture and transportation being disrupted, resulting in increased foreign-exchange expenditure on food imports.[81] In 1984 UNITA attacked the northern province of Uije, raiding coffee plantations; in 1985, many of the crops of the peasants near Huambo rotted as a result of the "lack of transport and the absence of consumer goods, which left the peasants with little incentive to sell their crops." [82] Currently, "coffee exports are being impeded by transport problems exacerbated by the war." [83]

The carrot, instead of the stick, has been used in Malawi to destabilize SADCC's overall strategy of agricultural development. After Malawi hosted the November 1981 SADCC Conference,

> South Africa's Agriculture Minister, P.T.C. Du Plessis, visited Malawi and promised R 1.7m for the National Seed Company and for fish breeding research—fisheries having been the SADCC sector that Malawi had been asked to coordinate. He noted that food would be as strategic a weapon in the 1980s as oil was in the 1970s, and offered 15,000 tonnes of wheat at reduced prices.[84]

In 1980, South Africa had provided R 11 million in export credits for a massive grain silo in Lilongwe.

The current food crisis in Malawi, which has been exacerbated by the estimated 600,000 Mozambican refugees, resulted in a recent $5.5 million barter deal between Malawi and South Africa. The agreement, the first of its kind to be established between the two countries, entails the exchange of 20,000 tons of South African maize for 10,000 tons of Malawi peanuts.[85]

The food crisis has resulted in a similar barter deal with Zimbabwe: "Zimbabwe's Grain Marketing Board will provide Malawi with 27,600 tonnes of maize in return for 27,300 tonnes of wheat." [86]

In Botswana, one is indeed hard-pressed to find food that is not from South Africa on the grocery shelves in this landlocked country. Recently the apartheid regime took advantage of the dependency of both Botswana and Lesotho to sell them tainted wheat; the South African Wheat Board had determined that the produce could not be sold in South Africa. The wheat, imported from Canada, contained the fungus *Aspergilus flaxus*, which secretes a toxin known as aflatoxin. According to the WFP, "small amounts are known to cause cirrhosis of the liver as well as tumors of the liver." [87]

Industry and Trade

Perhaps no SADCC sector exhibits the kinds of contradictions in its relationship to South Africa than that of industry and trade. While on the one hand historical constraints to industrial development in the region exist as a result of the imperialist strategies pursued by the South African government, on the other hand, it appears that several nations have consciously chosen to be lured into increased dependence on South Africa through the carrot, which has resulted in a boost to apartheid's regional hegemony. This pattern of increased dependence reinforces the reality that although these nations have committed themselves politically to regional cooperation, the loose SADCC organizational structure allows them to work cooperatively with the apartheid regime when it is advantageous economically. But it was precisely this loose organizational structure that allowed Botswana, Lesotho, and Swaziland, as members of the South African Customs Union (SACU), to join SADCC.[88] While Lesotho and Swaziland can argue that their economies are so weak that they are not in a position to reject any offers of new South African investment, can Botswana, which has perhaps the strongest economy in Africa, make the same argument?

Some Historical Realities

As members of the South African Customs Union (SACU), Botswana, Lesotho, and Swaziland (BLS) have historically been constrained by South Africa from developing viable industrial sectors. Although technically the SACU agreement prevents

South Africa from hindering industrial growth in these nations, in practice this is not the case. In fact, several years ago, "South Africa took steps to prevent the establishment of a fertilizer factor in Swaziland and a motor vehicle assembly plant in Lesotho." [89] Also, South Africa made a concerted effort to lure investors away from BLS by offering attractive subsidy packages to persuade them to invest instead in South African bantustans.

Prior to 1987, South Africa undermined Botswana's attempt to develop its soda ash potential by refusing to support the Sua Pan Soda Ash Project. Once developed, Botswana has the potential to supply the subcontinent for the next century with salt, soda ash, and potash. South Africa continued to insist that unless the two countries come to an agreement about security, South Africa's support for the project would not be forthcoming.[90] There have been numerous other South African attempts to undermine Botswana's efforts to industrialize.[91]

Fundamentally, the polarization effects of SACU have meant that South Africa has developed industrially at the expense of Botswana, Lesotho, and Swaziland. As Gavin Maasdorp notes:

> Industry in the three states seems to have benefited little from the large markets offered by South Africa. The BLS countries have not attracted much industry because of their long distance from major markets, an inability to match South Africa's industrial decentralization incentives, their high labour training costs, and perceptions among industrialists of greater risks.[92]

The intensity of the involvement of Botswana, Lesotho, and Swaziland in the SACU structure is not necessarily by choice, for as Gerald P. Khojane, counselor for the Permanent Mission of Lesotho to the United Nations, commented:

> It is true that Lesotho is the most dependent of the SADCC members on South Africa. And it is true Botswana, Lesotho and Swaziland are members of SACU, which has certain objectives which one might say could conflict with those of SADCC . . . Where there are conflicting interests between SADCC and the Customs Union, we would give preference to SADCC objectives. However, Lesotho would like to be realistic and will weigh the pros

and cons of choosing SADCC objectives vis-`a-vis the Customs Union.[93]

Presently, the reality of the economic situation in BLS makes withdrawal from SACU difficult, particularly for Lesotho and Swaziland. For example, as Table 16 indicates, a large percentage of their annual revenue comes from the SACU revenue-sharing formula, although it actually is designed to benefit South Africa. In fact, it has been suggested that BLS could benefit more from withdrawing from SACU.[94] In addition to being members of SACU, Lesotho and Swaziland remain within the Rand Monetary Area. Thus their currencies are tied to the South African rand, and, in effect, they have no right to discretionary monetary policy.[95]

Under the present circumstances, Botswana, Lesotho, and Swaziland will find their participation in the SADCC industrial sector problematic, mainly as a consequence of their present economic relationship with South Africa. Even if the South African government were not to hinder these nations from developing a modern industrial sector, industries would find it difficult to compete with cheap imported South African products. The inability of Botswana, Lesotho, and Swaziland to effectively implement their designated industrial projects will have serious implications for the proposed regional industrial sector, since these three nations are not planning to assume an insignificant role in project development. As the next section indicates, however, to the extent that South Africa can benefit from specific industrial development, it is allowed to occur in BLS.

While the South African constraints imposed on Zimbabwe are different from those imposed on BLS, the impact on SADCC industrial development may be similar. The pros and cons of Zimbabwe's active participation in regional industrial development will center on the threats of economic leverage likely to emanate from South Africa's attempt to curtail the amount Zimbabwe exports to SADCC member states. As an example of such economic leverage, it was reported that in 1984, Zimbabwe was "forced to take action to limit certain imports from Botswana." [96]

Even though Zimbabwe is the most industrialized SADCC

TABLE 16

CUSTOMS UNION REVENUE AS PERCENTAGE OF TOTAL GOVERNMENT REVENUE, 1981-1987

	81-82	82-83	83-84	84-85	85-86	86-87
Botswana	36.9	33.0	30.5	22.1	—	—
Lesotho	63.7	56.9	64.7	69.7	—	50-70
Swaziland	48.3	66.6	67.1	63.7	50	Over 50

Source: Davids, *Impact of Economic Sanctions,* p. 14; *Facts and Reports.*

member state, its ability to trade openly with other SADCC states is partially hindered by the existing structural linkages and the difficulty of their termination, given South Africa's coercive capabilities. In fact, in 1981, when South Africa threatened to terminate the 1964 Zimbabwe-South African trade agreement by 1982, the Zimbabwean government was fearful of the economic impact such a decision would have on the country. Cancellation of the agreement would have meant that Zimbabwean exporters would no longer be given preferential tariffs and thus would have been priced out of the South African market. In addition, Zimbabwe would have lost about Z$50 million annually in foreign currency and 6,500 permanent jobs in the manufacturing sector.[97] Only if the SADCC states can provide Zimbabwe with the economic advantages that presently exist with the Zimbabwe-South Africa trade agreement, can it be envisaged that the agreement will be terminated. Although in 1986 President Mugabe announced that sanctions would take precedence over the trade agreement,[98] Zimbabwe's inability to implement sanctions against South Africa to date is an indication of its chronic dependence on Pretoria.

In Angola and Mozambique, industrial development has been basically impossible. According to the 1986 *SADCC Macro-Economic Survey:*

The negative impact of destabilization and aggression has been felt most in Mozambique and Angola, where not only have circumstances necessitated reallocation of resources away from industry, but even some of the existing industrial capacities and their supportive structures have been physically destroyed.[99]

Sanctions and Destabilization:
A Boost to Apartheid's Regional Hegemony

When the international community began to impose limited economic sanctions against the apartheid regime in 1985, the fear existed that South Africa would retaliate against its neighbors with increased destabilization. Instead, in an effort to protect the $2.5 billion trade surplus with the SADCC member states, to protect against economic repercussions from the west, and to protect their imperialist regional domination, South Africans began to increase their capital investments in the region. Botswana, Lesotho, and Swaziland became the target of this strategy.

In a recent paper on Lesotho, James Cobbe noted that "those sanctions that close markets to South African exports . . . are by far the most important for Lesotho, and to be blunt, their imposition is easily the most positive development for the Lesotho economy for several years."[100] Similarly, Alan Booth argues that "it would not be out of line to conclude that . . . sanctions have been good to Swaziland."[101]

Since international sanctions were imposed against South Africa, Lesotho also has been used for sanctions evasion:

> There are already small businesses in Lesotho which help South African companies to bypass sanctions on their exports. Semi-finished goods are brought into Lesotho, where some value is added through local labour, and then the goods are sold to Europe and America as if they were products of Lesotho.[102]

According to Cobbe:

> This process of transfer of capacity, or attraction of flight capital . . . is what both Lesotho and Swaziland are trying to encourage . . . In the Lesotho case, at least, the pro-

cess is quite open, and civil servants and high government officials bring it up spontaneously and are not in the least apologetic about it, even when their own opposition to the apartheid situation in South Africa is beyond question.[103]

Swaziland, more than any other country, is being used by the apartheid regime for sanctions "busting." "By October 1987, the government-owned Swaziland Industrial Development Company [SIDCO] was processing 15 new foreign investment projects, most of them South African, amounting to 150 million emalangeni [E] ($75 million). Several more were in the discussion stage." As a result of both South African and Western investment (including a Coca-Cola concentrate plant that pulled out of South Africa, reinvested in Swaziland, but maintained its South African franchising rights), Swaziland's economy has experienced significant growth, there has been a decline in inflation, and an estimated three thousand new jobs have been created.[104]

In Botswana, South African capital responded to international sanctions by finally investing in the Sua Pan Project, providing 52 percent of the $450 million equity required. South African investment includes a consortium of private companies, led by the Anglo-American owned chemical company, African Explosive and Chemical Industries (AECI). Once this project is completed, Botswana will supply the apartheid regime with the 240,000 tons of soda ash it needs each year, mainly for the manufacture of glass.[105] According to Fred Morton:

> The Sua Pan arrangement has provoked a critical reaction from well-informed observers. Jack Parson, noted authority on Botswana's political economy, regards Botswana's method of developing in Sua Pan as "directly investing in apartheid" and "deepen[ing] the cooperative relationship which has developed over the years between . . . Botswana and South African capital." Concern over increased dependency has also been sounded by Botswana's leading independent newspaper, *Mmegi wa Dikgang*. In an editorial, "Walking a Tight Rope," *Mmegi* notes Anglo-American's increased stake in Botswana's mineral development and implies that such deals as Sua Pan increase the "dangers that arise out of our closer ties to South Africa."[106]

In addition to increasing its investment in Botswana, South African capital has responded to sanctions by increasing Botswana's influence within the De Beers Botswana Diamond Mining Company [DEBSWANA], which was created by De Beers (owned by the Anglo-American Corporation) and the Botswana Government.

> Since sanctions, DEBSWANA has been further capitalized by De Beers and invited onto its board of directors. In August 1987, De Beers paid $200 million to DEBSWANA for its 1982-85 stockpile accumulated during the price depression, and gave DEBSWANA 20 million shares of De Beers, representing $225 million and 5 percent of its total capital. In addition, DEBSWANA was given two seats each on the boards of De Beers and its marketing arm, the Central Selling Organization.[107]

This increase in economic relations between South Africa and Botswana is not viewed favorably in the region.

> Perceptions do exist . . . that Botswana's links with South Africa are defeating the efforts of SADCC countries to reduce their dependency on the white juggernaut. Without naming Botswana, but not having to, President Mugabe of Zimbabwe recently bemoaned SADCC's problems in confronting South Africa when some of its members were tied to South Africa "like Siamese Twins." When these remarks were being published, Zimbabwe was announcing that it was suspending its Open General and Import Licenses (OGIL) agreement with Botswana, as of 31 March 1988. The reason given was that Botswana was selling Zimbabwe certain goods that had originated in South Africa.[108]

Investment in Production and Intra-SADCC Trade

In 1987, SADCC's interest in increased investment in the region was outlined at the Annual Conference, with the theme "Investment in Production." To date, SADCC has had limited success in attracting either local or foreign private investment.

With respect to intra-SADCC trade, a September 1987 article quoted President Mugabe as stating, "'Contrary to the wishes and expectations of the architects of the SADCC, the intra-SADCC volume of trade was still very small,' adding that statistics showed that the nine countries constituting SADCC were not producing for each other." In fact, since SADCC was formed, with the exception of Angola and Tanzania, its member states have increased their trade with the apartheid regime.

> Currently, intra-SADCC trade represents about 4 to 5 percent of the total external trade of the SADCC countries . . . Angola exports only about 2.1 percent of its exports to other SADCC countries—Botswana 11.9 percent, Lesotho 0.1 percent, Malawi 9.7 percent, Mozambique 11.6 percent, Tanzania 0.8 percent, Zambia 3.5 percent and Zimbabwe 11.5 percent.[109]

In addition to the above, the readily available trade financing offered by South Africa, but not offered by SADCC member states, is also a constraint to intra-SADCC trade. Furthermore, the SADCC states, unlike South Africa, are not able to provide export credit. This will continue to be a problem for SADCC member states, in that "the international commercial banking system tends to provide credit for commodities well established in world markets, where there is less financial risk."[110]

However, SADCC is in the process of working on an "export pre-financing revolving fund for the region," and studies are underway regarding the "possibility of establishing a regional export credit and guarantee facility, a regional stock market or a development bank."[111] If implemented, these projects should help alleviate the constraints on intra-regional trade caused by shortages of foreign exchange.

In addition to the above, the Industry and Trade sector has developed a list of goods produced by all member states, with a view toward encouraging greater intra-SADCC trade. One of the problems is that the member states are not aware of the fact that they themselves produce many goods imported into Southern Africa.

Although on paper SADCC member states have made a commitment to increased intra-SADCC trade, in practice this does not appear to be the case; in fact, there exists intra-regional competition. For example, in July 1987, Zimbabwe terminated its 28-

year-old system of importing electricity from Zambia. Instead of continuing to rely on Zambian electricity, Zimbabwe went ahead with the development of Phase II of the Hwange Project, thus eliminating its need for Zambian electricity. Clearly, this poses a serious contradiction with respect to SADCC's stated objective of increased regional cooperation.

Another controversial issue relates to the deterioration of trade relations between Zimbabwe and Malawi.

> Since the establishment of the PTA Treaty (Preferential Trade Agreement) in July 1984, Malawi's exports to Zimbabwe have declined drastically from MK 20m in 1981 to MK 10m in 1986 (then $5.46m), while Zimbabwe's exports to Malawi have increased from MK 19m in 1981 to MK 29m in 1986, swooping Malawi's trade balance with Zimbabwe from a surplus to a deficit.[112]

Once Malawi joined the PTA, its Open General Import License (OGIL) agreement with Zimbabwe was terminated because, according to the PTA Treaty charter, "no country may get more favorable trade terms than those accorded to member states." Since efforts at bilateral consultations have not restored the balance, Malawi is considering retaliatory action against Zimbabwe.[113]

In Southern Africa there exists a great deal of controversy over SADCC and the PTA. The Ministry of Trade and Commerce of Zimbabwe is currently completing a study on the issue of SADCC and the PTA, and the Heads of State and Government at the Annual SADCC Summit meetings routinely address this issue. In addition to the duplication said to exist between SADCC and the PTA with respect to goals and objectives, there is criticism that within the PTA, the giants of the organization, Zimbabwe and Kenya, having the most goods to trade, are the major beneficiaries of the trade agreement. Also, the PTA often has served as a hindrance to intra-regional trade (as in the case of Malawi and Zimbabwe), rather than as a conduit. If Botswana were to join the PTA (which it is under pressure from Zimbabwe to do), for example, the OGIL agreement between Zimbabwe and Botswana would automatically be abrogated, as occurred with the agreement between Malawi and Zimbabwe. This, of course, would likely cause a serious alteration in trade between Botswana and Zimbabwe, to the disadvantage of Botswana.

During the latter part of 1987 and early 1988, it looked as if the Zimbabwean government would abrogate the OGIL agreement between itself and Botswana. From the perspective of Zimbabwe, the trade problem between the two countries grew out of the belief that Botswana was involved in South African sanctions busting. Others suggest, however, that the real problem centered around the fact that there was a shift in trade in Botswana's favor.[114] This conflict was no doubt increased by the fact that,

> when Botswana allowed an investor to set up a soap factory in the country, it did not take regional conditions into account. The setting up of a factory was indeed a good idea for Botswana, which had previously wholly depended on supplies from South Africa. But the move resulted in all tallow in the country being diverted to the new factory and not, as previously, being sold to Zimbabwe. Consequently, this affected production of soap in Zimbabwe and resulted in a severe shortage of the commodity.[115]

Fortunately, the two countries were able to work out a new OGIL agreement. Had they not been successful, Botswana would have been forced to increase its trade with South Africa.

The effort by the SADCC states to increase intra-regional trade will not be enhanced by the recent agreement between Lesotho and South Africa for the exchange of trade missions. Three other SADCC countries—Mozambique, Swaziland, and Zimbabwe—also have such missions.

Energy

While proposed project development in the energy sector focuses on electricity, renewable sources of energy, and wood fuel, the potential development of both the oil and the coal subsectors has been of major concern to the SADCC countries. However, the development of three subsectors—electricity, oil, and coal—has been hindered by South Africa's destabilization and is certain to be further undermined by cooperative agreements signed between South Africa and other SADCC member states since 1980.

In the area of electricity production, the gap between the regional capacity for electric-power generation and the projected regional consumption is likely to widen, resulting in even greater dependency on South Africa by 1990 than had been anticipated. In terms of South African regional destabilization, two countries, Angola and Mozambique, have been directly affected.

In Angola, an attack by South Africa in 1983 destroyed both the hydroelectric station and the dam at Lomaum; hydroelectric power is still not being provided by the station at Rucana, along the Namibia border, because of South African occupation of Namibia (the generating station is on the Namibian side of the border). It is not anticipated that a secure supply will be available until Namibia is independent. In the interim, Angola is in the position of having to "freely" export power to multinationals in Namibia.[116] Then in 1986, UNITA forces cut the 159-km-long power line to Luanda on several occasions.[117] The same line was cut also in 1988.

In Mozambique, Renamo has consistently destroyed the transmission line of the Cahora Bassa which connects the dam to the South African grid. Consequently, "since mid-1985 and the sabotage of over 500 pylons by Pretoria's MNR bandits, no power has flowed to South Africa."[118] Between 1977 and mid-1985 electrical power flowed to South Africa from Cahora Bassa and power to Maputo from Cahora Bassa went via a converting station in South Africa.[119] Since the Cahora Bassa hydroelectric system is nonfunctioning, the government of Mozambique is forced to import 24,000 megawatts of electricity from South Africa each month to meet the needs of southern Mozambique at a cost of approximately $900,000.[120]

Ironically, two months following the signing of the Nkomati Accord (nonaggression pact) between South Africa and Mozambique in 1984, an agreement was renegotiated among South Africa, Mozambique, and Portugal to more than double the rate South Africa would be paying for power from the Mozambique dam. Following the signing of the agreement, the South African foreign minister, Pik Botha, stated that the way was paved "for a new era of close economic co-operation . . . It is the first major tangible benefit of the March non-aggression pact signed by Mozambique and South Africa. Under the Cahora Bassa agreement the two countries will 'jointly take immediate steps to protect the transmission lines from attack.'"[121]

Prior to the signing of the nonaggression pact, Mozambique was not certain whether South Africa intended to continue using the Cahora Bassa Dam. If South Africa does not use the dam, Mozambique will need to find another market for its electricity, since it is a significant source of governmental revenue.[122] After Nkomati, however, MNR attacks on the line continued. Less than three weeks after the Accord was signed, MNR cut the line from South Africa to Maputo for the first time; between October 1984 and February 1985, the line was cut at least eight times.[123]

In response to recent talks among South Africa, Mozambique, and Portugal designed to restore the power line between South Africa and Mozambique and possibly increase security (which could mean deploying South African troops), the MNR "threatened to render unviable" any such agreement.[124]

In 1981, the MNR began to attack the power line to Beira, and between 1982 and 1986, more than "$50 million worth of electrical power lines and substations were destroyed."[125] As a result of MNR attacks, Beira has basically had to depend on local generators for electricity since 1983. Efforts to reconnect destroyed lines have been fruitless. Goncalo Antonio Ferrao, Jr., economist for the BCA, noted with much relief that after October 1988, the MNR can destroy all the power lines to Beira, because the city will be self-sufficient in electrical production. By the end of October, Sweden will have delivered generators capable of supplying the entire city with electricity.[126]

Another example of South Africa's destabilization of Mozambique's energy sector occurred following the March 26, 1985, catastrophic cyclone in Maputo. Thirty-one pylons on the power lines were hit. To assist in the emergency, the United States gave Mozambique $250,000 to purchase coal from South Africa for its coal power station. South Africa delayed the shipment for several weeks, and when Pretoria finally agreed, the night before the coal was to be shipped, a railway bridge 8 km from the border was sabotaged.[127]

The SADCC control of the regional electricity subsector has been further undermined by two agreements between South

CHART 2

DESTABILIZATION OF THE ENERGY SECTOR

1980

- SA raided Lobito oil terminal.

1981

- SA destroyed part of the oil pipeline over the Pungue River near Beira.
- SA raided Luanda oil refinery.
- Power line to Beira was cut repeatedly.

1982

- SA attacked Beira, blowing up the depot which contained fuel for Zimbabwe and Malawi.

1983

- UNITA sabotaged Angola's Lomaun dam, cutting power to the cities of Lobito and Benguela.
- UNITA raided Alto Catumbela and destroyed a power station.
- SA bombed Lesotho's water-storage tank.

- SA attacked one of Lesotho's fuel depots.
- SA ended fuel shipments through Maputo.
- Numerous raids were made on the Zimbabwe oil pipeline.
- MNR's sabotage of the power lines leading to Beira resulted in the city being forced to depend on electricity from local generators.

1984

- Four attacks on the Zimbabwe oil pipeline.
- SA raided Cabinda oil pipeline.
- MNR hit the power line between SA and Maputo several times (line to Cahora Bassa).
- MNR continued to attack electrical lines to Beira.

1985

- MNR continued its attacks on the SA-to-Maputo power line (line to Cahora Bassa).
- Zimbabwe oil pipeline attacked.
- MNR continued to attack power lines to Beira.

1986

- Power line to Luanda was cut several times.

- MNR blew up 64 pylons leading from the Revue hydro-electric station to Beira.
- MNR blew up the Zimbabwe pipeline more than 27 times.

1987

- MNR continued to disrupt the Zimbabwe pipeline.
- MNR sabotaged the new Entrelagos power line between Cahora Bassa dam and Zambezia province.

1988

- UNITA cut power line to Luanda.

Sources: *Destructive Engagement* (1986); *Beggar Your Neighbours* (1986); *Washington Post*, December 1, 1986; Economist Intelligence Unit (various documents); *Facts and Reports; Africa Economic Digest; African Business*, September 1987.

Africa and three SADCC member states. The first is the 1984 plan involving South Africa, Swaziland, and Mozambique, to dam the Komati and Lomati rivers. According to the plan, six dams will be built on the two rivers.[128] The second is the Highlands Water Scheme signed by South Africa and Lesotho. Under the treaty, four dams will be built, and Lesotho will be allowed to sell water to agricultural and industrial sectors in South Africa. When the project is completed in 2019, water will run into South African tunnels at the rate of 70 cubic metres per second, and a hydropower installation will generate 700m kilowatt-hours of hydroelectric energy a year. Without the water, it is projected that the industrial heartland of South Africa would be faced with a severe water shortage by the mid-1990's. Reportedly, South Africa needs the water so badly that it engineered the January 1986 coup in order to control the project after the deposed prime minister, Chief Jonathan Leabua, refused to allow South Africa to participate in the project, noting that it should belong entirely to Lesotho.[129]

All the agreements signed between SADCC member states and South Africa, as well as regional destabilization, point to the reality that South Africa has tremendous control over the development of the electricity subsector, especially in Angola, Mozambique, Swaziland, and Lesotho. Nonetheless, the development of the Luphohlo-Ezulwini hydroelectric project in Swaziland has allowed that country to decrease its dependence upon South Africa for power.[130]

The attempt by South Africa to hinder the SADCC states from developing self-sufficiency in oil production has been more significant than in the electricity subsector. In 1980, South Africa raided the Lobito oil terminal, and in 1981, the Luanda oil refinery, causing $12.5 million in damage. The refinery was closed for four months, which prevented the export of $24 million in oil. In 1984, South Africa raided the Cabinda oil pipeline, and on May 21, 1985, there was a failed raid on Gulf Oil installations in Cabinda.[131]

During December 1982, the petroleum refinery at Beira in Mozambique was badly damaged, and there had been earlier acts of sabotage on the Beira-Mutare oil pipeline. Efforts by Mozambique to send oil via other routes only exacerbated the problem, with increased MNR and South African attacks, which created a severe fuel crisis in Zimbabwe, upsetting transport and production in both countries. This inevitably had a negative impact on foreign exchange earnings.[132] According to Barry Munslow and Phil O'Keefe:

> The South African Government tried to use the situation to force Zimbabwe to sign an official three-year contract for petrol and diesel fuel. Prime Minister Mugabe successfully resisted the pressure, but at some cost. Attacks on energy supplies were clearly aimed at exposing the vulnerability of Zimbabwe and were all part of a strategy to destroy SADCC efforts and increase dependence on South Africa.[133]

Prior to 1982, Zimbabwe had experienced delays in the shipment of oil from South Africa, but after the December 1982 raids, Zimbabwe sent the first troops into Mozambique to guard the pipeline. Throughout 1986 and 1987, however, the MNR continued to attack the Zimbabwe pipeline.

South Africa also has destabilized the oil subsector in other regional countries. On February 13, 1983, South African forces raided one of three main fuel storage depots in Lesotho, completely destroying 60,500 gallons.[134] In 1984, South Africa refused to transport to Lesotho a donation of crude oil that had been refined at Maputo. In Malawi, MNR attacks cut off that country's access to oil from Mozambique; and in 1983 Pretoria ended fuel shipments through Maputo.[135]

Botswana's complete dependency on South Africa for oil has been very problematic. For example, in 1980, to protect itself against South Africa's oil leverage, Botswana built tanks to hold three months' supply of oil. However, for over a year, South Africa would not provide fuel for the tanks. Then, between December 1980 and January 1981, South Africa's disruptions in oil deliveries caused fuel shortages, interrupting Christmas travel. By mid-January, transport services were brought to a virtual standstill for several days.[136] Available alternative oil routes currently are not being sought by either Botswana or Swaziland because of destabilization. As Joseph Hanlon notes:

In principle, Botswana and Swaziland could import refined oil directly, because they have direct rail links to Maputo that do not pass through South Africa. But South African raids on oil storage facilities in Lesotho, Mozambique and Angola are a reminder of how far South Africa is prepared to go to maintain its fuel monopoly.[137]

The development of the regional oil subsector is particularly threatening to South Africa. This is to be expected, since South Africa, as a non-oil-producing state, has been able to maintain much control over this subsector by first importing oil, then exporting it to neighboring countries. Consequently, even if an appropriate regional infrastructure were developed to allow Angola to supply the SADCC member states with oil, South Africa would continue to hinder SADCC regional plans for self-sufficiency, through either regional destabilization or threats of economic leverage. In recent discussions between Nigerian and Angolan ministers, however, a plan for providing emergency oil supplies to Botswana and other Frontline States has been drafted, for use in the event of South African oil sanctions.[138]

Finally, prospects for the development of the regional coal subsector depend on the development of a regional surface transport system. But such a system does not seem possible in the near future.

SADCC: What Future?

The factors militating against SADCC are particularly formidable in that they constitute a historical, political and socio-economic reality from which by its very objectives SADCC wishes to disengage . . . In the final analysis it helps to shore up the apparent economic indispensability of the South African hinterland. It reinforces the view that the future of SADCC itself is dependent on what happens in South Africa, and not, as some SADCC protagonists would like to believe, that SADCC will significantly affect the future of that country.[139]

As this chapter has indicated, at the regional level (first order of dependency), SADCC has not had much success in implementing the Lusaka Program of Action. Consequently, the member nations have not experienced any transformation of the structural linkages of dependency on South Africa; in fact, some countries have increased their dependence. In addition, the geopolitics of the region have proven a major hindrance to internal structural transformation; thus minimal development has occurred within the SADCC member states since 1980.

It is obvious that SADCC will not be able to achieve its development objectives until South Africa is liberated. With a liberated South Africa as a member of SADCC, no doubt the member states would be able to move beyond a mere political commitment to regional cooperation and include an economic commitment as well. Until South Africa is liberated, however, the political unity that does exist probably will allow the organization to survive. Although SADCC has been criticized for lacking a commitment to economic cooperation, in some respects it is a miracle that today even a political commitment to cooperation continues to exist. The survival of SADCC can be viewed in this light, given the political, economic, and military leverage Pretoria has used in an effort to "divide and rule" the member states.

NOTES

1. Dan O'Meara, "Destabilization in Southern Africa: Total Strategy in Total Disarray," *Monthly Review*, Vol. 37, No. 1, April 1986, pp. 52-53. See also R. Davies and Dan O'Meara, "Total Strategy in Southern Africa: An Analysis of South African Regional Policy Since 1978," *Journal of Southern African Studies*, Vol. 11, No. 2, 1985.

2. O'Meara, "Destabilization," p. 53.

3. *Ibid.*, p. 54.

4. Carol B. Thompson, *Challenge to Imperialism: The Frontline States in the Liberation of Zimbabwe* (Boulder, Colo.: Westview Press, 1986), p. 266.

5. O'Meara, "Destabilization," pp. 55-56.

6. See Joseph Hanlon, *Apartheid's Second Front: South Africa's War Against Its Neighbours* (New York: Penguin

Books, 1986); Joseph Hanlon, *Beggar Your Neighbours: Apartheid Power in Southern Africa* (Bloomington: Indiana University Press, 1986); *Destructive Engagement: Southern Africa at War*, ed. Phyllis Johnson and David Martin, (Harare, Zimbabwe: Zimbabwe Publishing House, 1986); Lina Magaia, *Dumbanegue: Run For Your Life: Peasant Tales of Tragedy in Mozambique* (Trenton, NJ: Africa World Press, 1988).

7. Carol B. Thompson, "SADCC's Struggle for Economic Liberation," *Africa Report*, July-August 1986, p. 62.

8. Stephen R. Lewis, Jr., "Southern African Interdependence," *Africa Notes* (Washington, D.C.: Georgetown University Center for Strategic and International Studies), March 27, 1986, p. 3.

9. Pedro de Castro Van Dunon, "SADCC Countries Have Chosen to Resist Rather Than Give In to Pretoria," *SADCC Energy*, Vol. 1, February-April 1984, p. 3.

10. "Southern African Transport Routes," Foreign and Commonwealth Office, London, March 1987, p. 1.

11. Interview with Pedro Figueiredo, director, Caminhos de Ferrode Mozambique Sul (CFM Sul, the regional railway system servicing the southern area of Mozambique), Maputo, Mozambique, July 1988.

12. Johnson and Martin, *Destructive Engagement*, p. 67.

13. Interview with Rui Fonseca, executive director of the Beira Corridor Authority (BCA), Beira, Mozambique, July 1988.

14. Hanlon, *Beggar Your Neighbours*, p. 183.

15. Johnson and Martin, *Destructive Engagement*, p. 71.

16. Allister Sparks, "Africa Route Revival Faces Many Problems," *The Washington Post*, December 1, 1986.

17. "Southern Africa," *Africa News*, Vol. 27, No. 12, December 22, 1986, p. 16.

18. Patti Waldmeir, "Costly Stalemate in Mozambique's Guerrilla War," *Financial Times* (London), May 9, 1986.

19. Johnson and Martin, *Destructive Engagement*, pp. 68-69.

20. For a detailed explanation of freight-forwarding agencies, see Hanlon, *Beggar Your Neighbours*, pp. 193-196.

21. "Regional News," *Southern Africa: Political and Economic Monthly*, July 1988, p. 3.

22. Beira Corridor Authority, Minutes of the Beira Port Advisory Committee (B-PAC), May 18, 1988, p. 2.

23. *Ibid.*, Annex, pp. 1-2.

24. *Ibid.*, p. 7.

25. Rui Fonseca, director of the Beira Corridor Authority, believes that the name Beira Corridor Group (BCG) was adopted specifically to confuse people, which is what has happened.

26. Interview, Fonseca.

27. ZBC, "The Nation," Harare, Zimbabwe, June 1988.

28. *Ibid.*

29. "Cross Raps Port Congestion," *Sunday Mail* (Zim.), March 6, 1988.

30. Interview with Hasu Patel, professor of Political and Administrative Studies, University of Zimbabwe, Harare, Zimbabwe, July 1987.

31. Interview with Eddie Cross, managing director, BCG, Harare, Zimbabwe, July 1987.

32. Eddie Cross, "Distasteful Attack on Afrikaans," *Sunday Mail* (Zim), June 26, 1988.

33. "Locus from SA," *Herald* (Zim.), October 27, 1987.

34. Chris Davids, *The Impact of Economic Sanctions Against South Africa on the SADCC States*, CIDA, Ottawa, 1986, p. 19.

35. *Ibid.*

36. Hanlon, *Beggar Your Neighbours*, p. 95.

37. Interview, Figueiredo.

38. "Rail Attacks Seen as SA 'Siege'," *Guardian* (Britain), January 4, 1988.

39. Interview, Figueiredo.

40. Hanlon, *Beggar Your Neighbours*, p. 239.

41. *Ibid.*, p. 240.

42. *Ibid.*

43. Johnson and Martin, *Destructive Engagement*, p. 67.

44. Hanlon, *Beggar Your Neighbours*, p. 240.

45. *Country Profile: Malawi 1986-87*, p. 22.

46. Hanlon, *Beggar Your Neighbours*, p, 238, 240.

47. *Africa Research Bulletin*, May 31, 1986, p. 8189; "Why Banda Supports the MNR," *New African*, November 1986, p. 25.

48. "Why Banda Supports the MNR," p. 25.

49. "Interview with Armando Guebuza, Mozambique Minister of Transport and Communications," *Africa Report*, July-August 1987, pp. 64-66.

50. Interview, Figueiredo.

51. See *Africa Economic Digest*, March 27, 1987, p. 26.

52. Interview, Fonseca.

SADCC and South Africa 235

53. Hanlon, *Beggar Your Neighbours*, p. 252.

54. "Tazara to Expand Traffic," *Daily News* (Tanz.), February 18, 1988.

55. "Zambian President says security alert mounted on Tazara bridges," Radio Report, *Facts and Reports*, Vol. 18, March 3, 1988, p. 26.

56. "Botswana Rail Line is 'Virtually Blocked' by South African Visa Ploy," *African Business*, March 1987, p. 5.

57. Fred Morton, "South African Capital in Southern Africa: Botswana's Sua Pan Project," paper presented at Third Symposium on Post-apartheid South Africa, University of Pittsburgh, March 17-19, 1988, pp. 10-11.

58. "SADCC Ponders Its Economic Nightmare," *Weekly Mail* (SA), July 22, 1988.

59. Hanlon, *Beggar Your Neighbours*, p. 114.

60. Allister Sparks, "S. Africa's Neighbors Forge a Link to the Sea: New Rail Line May Ease Pretoria's Grip," *The Washington Post*, September 1986.

61. Chris Davids, *Impact of Economic Sanctions*, p. 18.

62. "The Role of Transport in Mozambique's Economy," *BCG Bulletin*, November 1987.

63. Interview, Figueiredo.

64. Hanlon, *Beggar Your Neighbours*, p. 38.

65. Chris Davids, *Impact of Economic Sanctions*, p. 18.

66. *African Business*, September 1986, p. 8.

67. "Remano Cuts Maputo-SA Link and Hits Exporters," *South Africa Report* (SA), December 23, 1987.

68. Interview, Figueiredo.

69. Interview with Sidik Juma Abdula, Public Relations director for Maputo Port, Maputo, Mozambique, July 1988.

70. *Ibid.*

71. Interview, Figueiredo.

72. Reginald Green, "Southern African Development Coordination: The Struggle Continues," *Africa Contemporary Record* (New York: African Publishing Co., 1980-81), p. A97.

73. SADCC, *Macro-Economic Survey* (SADCC, 1986), p. 76.

74. "Food Supplies in Crisis," *Africa Economic Digest*, December 11, 1987.

75. Hanlon, *Beggar Your Neighbours*, p. 191.

76. "Mozambique Switch to Self-Help," *Times* (Britain), February 6, 1988.

77. Hanlon, *Beggar Your Neighbours*, p. 135.

78. Paul Vallely, "Red Cross Halts Aid to Mozambique Refugees," *Times* (Britain), January 9, 1988.

79. "Italy Takes Over Mozambique Rescue Flights," *Southscan* (Britain), March 2, 1988.

80. Victor Mallet, "Mozambican Refugees 'Strain on Food Supplies'," *Financial Times* (Britain), February 25, 1988.

81. Johnson and Martin, *Destructive Engagement*, p. 100.

82. Hanlon, *Beggar Your Neighbours*, p. 163.

83. *Africa Economic Digest*, February 5, 1988.

84. Hanlon, *Beggar Your Neighbours*, p. 239.

85. "Barter Deal," *Times* (Britain), December 19, 1987.

86. *Africa Economic Digest*, October 23, 1987.

87. "Tainted Wheat Sold," *Farmer's Weekly* (SA), January 22, 1988.

88. This was pointed out to me by Nelson Moyo, chair, Department of Economics, University of Zimbabwe, August 1988.

89. Gavin Maasdorp. "Reassessing Economic Ties in Southern Africa," *Optima*, Vol. 30, 1981, p.117.

90. Johnson and Martin, *Destructive Engagement*, p. 158.

91. See Hanlon, *Beggar Your Neighbours*, pp. 232-233.

92. Maasdorp, "Reassessing Ties," p. 115.

93. Interview with Gerald P. Khojane, counselor for the Permanent Mission of Lesotho to the United Nations, April 1984, New York.

94. See Hanlon, *Beggar Your Neighbours*, pp. 81-90.

95. Chris Davids, *Impact of Economic Sanctions*, pp. 13-14.

96. *Africa Research Bulletin*, April 15-May 14, 1984, p. 7254.

97. Johnson and Martin, *Destructive Engagement*, pp. 69-70.

98. "Sanctions Take Precedence Over Zim Trade Agreement," *Southern Africa Report*, September 5, 1986.

99. *SADCC Macro-Economic Survey*, p. 107.

100. James Cobbe, "Sanctions Against South Africa: Lesotho's Role." Paper presented at Annual Meeting, African Studies Association, November 20, 1987, p. 6.

101. Alan R. Booth, "South African Sanctions-Breaking in Southern Africa: The Case of Swaziland," paper presented at Annual Meeting, African Studies Association, November 20, 1987, p. 6.

102. *Work for Justice* (Lesotho), September 9, 1987.

103. Cobbe, "Lesotho's Role," p. 12.

104. Booth, "Swaziland," pp. 6-10.

105. Morton, "Sua Pan Project;" *Gazette* (Botswana), March 3, 1988.

106. Morton, "Sua Pan Project," p. 4.

107. *Ibid.*, p. 6.

108. *Ibid.*, p. 10.

109. Makwapatira Mhango, "SADCC Goes into Reverse," *New African*, September 1987, p. 37.

110. United States Agency for International Development (USAID), *Country Development Strategy Statement, FY 1986 Southern Africa*, (USAID, May 1984), p. 11.

111. "SADCC Moves to Cut Investment Barriers," *Herald* (Zim.), February 9, 1988.

112. Mhango, "SADCC Goes into Reverse;"

113. "Malawi Hit by Zimbabwe Trade Policy," *African Business*, November 1987, pp. 47-48; "Trade Row: Will Botswana be the Casualty?" *Southern African Economist*, February-March, 1988, p. 25.

114. Morton, "Sua Pan Project," pp. 9-10; Colleen Lowe Morna, "Temporary Truce on the Trade Front," *South* (Britain), March 1988.

115. Mhango, "SADCC Goes into Reverse," p. 38.

116. Barry Munslow and Phil O'Keefe, "Energy and the Southern African Regional Confrontation," *Third World Quarterly*, Vol. 6, No. 1, 1984, p. 27.

117. Hanlon, *Beggar Your Neighbours*, p. 163.

118. AIM Information Bulletin, "Electricity Prices Explained," No. 143, June 1988, p. 14.

119. Kenneth W. Grundy, "Economic Patterns in the New Southern African Balance," *Southern Africa: The Continuing Crisis*, ed. Gwendolen M. Carter and Patrick O'Meara (Bloomington: Indiana University Press, 1979), p. 298.

120. AIM, "Electricity Prices Explained," p. 4.

121. *Africa Research Bulletin*, April 15-May 14, 1984, p. 7255.

122. Munslow and O'Keefe, "Energy," p. 28.

123. Hanlon, *Beggar Your Neighbours*, pp. 144, 150.

124. "MNR Threatens Cahora Bassa Agreement," radio report, *Facts and Reports*, Vol. 17, December 4, 1987, p. 18.

125. *Africa Report*, September-October 1987, p. 50.

126. Interview with Goncalo Antonio Ferrao, Jr., economist for the BCA, Beira, Mozambique, July 1988.

127. *Africa Report*, September-October 1987, p. 50.

128. *Africa Research Bulletin*, May 15-June 14, 1984, p. 7291.

129. "Lesotho's Water: Down the SA Drain?" *New African*, November 1986, p. 30.

130. EIU, *Country Report: Swaziland 1987-88*, 1987, p. 74.

131. Hanlon, *Beggar Your Neighbours*, pp. 159, 164.

132. Munslow and O'Keefe, "Energy," p. 27.

133. *Ibid.*, pp. 28-29.

134. *Ibid.*, p. 28.

135. Hanlon, *Beggar Your Neighbours*, pp. 114, 135.

136. *Ibid.*, p. 220.

137. *Ibid.*, p. 75.

138. *African Business*, September 1986, p. 51.

139. Ibbo Mandaza, "Perspectives on Economic Cooperation and Autonomous Development in Southern Africa," *SADCC: Prospects for Disengagement and Development in Southern Africa*, ed. Samir Amin, Derrick Chitala, and Ibbo Mandaza (London: Zed Books, 1987), pp. 222-23.

CHAPTER 7
SADCC and the West

Since SADCC was established, the member states have been requesting financial assistance from the advanced capitalist nations to help decrease South Africa's regional economic hegemony. In effect, these nations are being asked by SADCC to help facilitate South Africa's demise as a global semiperiphery within the capitalist world-economy. In order to accomplish this objective, the SADCC member states have been willing to increase their economic dependency on the global center. This, however, has served only to deepen their incorporation into the capitalist world-economy as peripheral nations, making it more difficult to alter their chronic economic dependency on the global center.

Increased economic dependence on the global center is viewed by SADCC as a temporary phase in the process of complete economic liberation. As Paul Repia, former ambassador of Tanzania's Permanent Mission to the United Nations noted:

> We believe that if, in the process of freeing ourselves from South African dependence, we will pass a stage of being dependent to some countries in the West, we want the Western countries to know that that is not the final goal. Our aim is for them to realize that they should also help us to establish structures which will make the countries in Southern Africa economically independent.[1]

In this chapter the Western response to SADCC will be analyzed with a view toward determining whether, in fact, SADCC's increased dependence on the imperialist powers is likely to be a temporary phase, or one that has increased and will continue to increase Western regional hegemony over Southern Africa.

WESTERN HEGEMONY OVER SOUTHERN AFRICA

It is now, however, widely recognized that the SADCC was not solely an initiative of the Frontline States. On the contrary, there was strong encouragement from Western countries who wished to draw the region closer to the West, and by creating a diversion from undiluted confrontation with South Africa, to prevent the Frontline States from giving greater support to the ANC and SWAPO.[2]

In chapter 1, the dynamic of the relationship between the SADCC member states and the West was identified as the second order of dependency (international level), because the SADCC nations determined that decreasing economic dependence on the imperialist powers is of secondary importance during the initial phase of their planned development.

At the international level, the imperialist powers of the West have historically identified as their objective regional hegemony over Southern Africa. These hegemonic aspirations have historically been overseen by the apartheid regime in its capacity as a global semiperiphery. In providing economic, political, and military support to Pretoria, the apartheid regime in turn guaranteed the West that either the carrot or the stick would be used to convince the regional nations that it was in their best interest to cooperate with South Africa. Prior to 1975, South Africa's task as a global semiperiphery was made easy by the fact that Angola and Mozambique were controlled by the Portuguese, and Zimbabwe, by white settlers. Once Angola and Mozambique gained their independence, Pretoria's task became more difficult, and in 1980, when Zimbabwe became independent, South Africa's ability to maintain its position as a strong global semiperiphery was further threatened.

With the support of the global center, the apartheid regime responded to this threat by terrorizing its regional neighbors into submission and acceptance of Pretoria. As Samir Amin notes:

> It remains the case that the regimes in Angola, Mozambique and Zimbabwe, like those in other frontline states (Tanzania and Zambia) remain "rather unreliable" in the eyes of the West. Hence the West has considered it positive and useful—for itself—that South Africa has, since 1974 in Angola and Mozambique and since 1980 in Zimbabwe, carried out destabilizing acts of military aggression there.[3]

While South Africa viewed SADCC as a threat to its regional hegemony, the imperialist powers initially envisaged SADCC as a conduit for strengthening South Africa's declining political and economic power. So, in Phase I of the imperialist powers' response to SADCC, these nations, hoping that the apartheid regime could be saved as their global semiperiphery, attempted to persuade the SADCC states that regional development would not be possible without the involvement of South Africa. To prove their point, the imperialists provided SADCC with limited economic assistance and continued to assure Pretoria of their ongoing support.[4]

Between 1980 and 1986, the West sat back and watched as South Africa wreaked havoc over the region.

> By 1983 Mozambique cried "uncle" and joined the International Monetary Fund (IMF), and the following year signed the Nkomati Accord (a nonaggression pact with South Africa). In a further effort to convince the SADCC nations that regional development would not be possible without the participation of the white minority regime, the U.S. Congress voted to repeal the Clark Amendment.[5]

The Clark Amendment, passed by Congress in 1976, prevented the U.S. government from supplying assistance to any of the factions in Angola's civil war. The U.S. Congress was concerned that Angola might become another Vietnam. In 1981, however, Reagan attempted to have the Clark Amendment repealed. Although he was not successful in 1981, Congress did repeal the Amendment in 1985. By January 1986, the U.S. government began once again supplying the South African-backed UNITA forces in Angola with military assistance. Throughout the period in which the Clark Amendment was in force, South Africa was UNITA's main source of economic and military assistance. Recent information indicates, however, that after the Clark Amendment was passed, the CIA paid Israel to provide military assistance to UNITA. Similarly, it has been said that the CIA has also been paying Israel to provide Renamo with military assistance.[6]

The involvement of the U.S. in regional destabilization must be partially viewed within the context of the Reagan Doctrine. This doctrine aims "to regain for the United States the global strategic initiative by reversing the gains of Third World liberation movements and by positing such reversals as an historic trend." Two of the thirteen countries identified as having been lost to the West are Marxist Angola and Marxist Mozambique.[7] Although Mozambique has been "recaptured," the West has faced a more difficult task in "recapturing" Angola.

It was also during Phase I of the Western response to SADCC that Zimbabwe was forced to show respect for the Lancaster House Agreement, and the IMF; "acting for the global account of imperialism," contributed to the destabilization of the economies of Tanzania and Zambia.[8] As Amin notes:

> The "Soviet presence" in the region, and the presence of the rear bases of the liberation movements of Namibia and South Africa (SWAPO, ANC, PAC), are no more than excuses, and not the real reasons for the West's offensive strategy. For these presences are the result—not the cause—of the refusal by the West to accept regimes in Africa that are other than neo-colonial, and down to the present day, to contemplate the decolonization of Namibia and South Africa.[9]

There is another reason the West refused for so long to contemplate the liberation of Namibia and continues to support apartheid South Africa—the belief in "white supremacy." The "Western powers view themselves, as well as the whites in South Africa, as being part of the superior 'white' race (First World) and blacks as part of the inferior 'darker' race (Third World)."[10]

How else can one explain the fact that between 1980 and 1987, an estimated 700,000 blacks died in Southern Africa as a result of South Africa's regional destabilization; or the refusal of the West to do anything about the genocide taking place against the black majority in South Africa? Would the West have allowed blacks to kill 700,000 whites in Southern Africa? Would the West have allowed a black minority in South Africa to practice genocide against a white majority? Indeed not! The West would long ago have invaded the region. For the West, however, since apartheid kills mostly blacks, not whites, it is not a force that should be destroyed. At best, it needs to be "reformed."

In 1984, however, the West could no longer hide from the world that apartheid was alive and doing well. As a result of political pressure from their constituents, Western leaders in 1985 and 1986 were forced to implement limited economic sanctions against Pretoria. Although the sanctions were limited, the mere fact that the West took any measures to "punish" Pretoria signaled a major defeat for apartheid's survival as the conduit for Western regional hegemony. This left the imperialist powers with no alternative but to increase their direct involvement in Southern Africa. Consequently, by the end of 1986, the West finally began to accept SADCC as a regional entity, though South Africa's destabilization had begun to successfully devastate regional economic, political, and social structures.

By this time the West had proven its point—namely, that SADCC could not be a conduit for regional development without the participation of the racist South African regime. Thus, with the SADCC states refusing to acquiesce to the call for South Africa's participation and the subsequent destabilization that followed, the foundation had been already laid for "Phase II" of the West's attack against SADCC. With the regional security and economic situation worsening, economic assistance to SADCC then became a conduit not for regional development, but for the Western imperialist powers to protect their interest in Southern Africa against South African destabilization.[11]

As a result of what is occurring under Phase II (see below), the West is coming closer to achieving its objective of establishing a neo-colonial Southern Africa.

SADCC: 1980–1986

Phase I of the Western "development scandal"[12] over Southern Africa began at the first SADCC Annual Conference held in Maputo during November 1980. The West responded to SADCC by pledging $650 million. However, less than $20 million was newly committed financial assistance, "since the remainder had already been designated for individual SADCC members and was now being rerouted through the regional body."[13] The pledges received from the 1981 conference also proved a disappointment to SADCC. By 1982, one reason given for the low level of funding was that funds already allocated had not been spent expeditiously; in some cases, not at all.

Of course, at this point, the West was not interested in any organization that would challenge South Africa's regional hegemony, and, as Ed Brown noted in 1982:

> It is one thing to request monies, it is another to spend them. While SADCC is blamed by some for a relatively slow development of projects and therefore, by implication, inadequate outlets for American assistance, it must be recognized that this rationale is a "red herring." If the administration was firmly committed to the SADCC program, the money would be spent.[14]

By 1986, however, the Western response to SADCC had changed:

> One of the achievements for which SADCC has been praised is its ability, within a period of only six years, to win over and attract a greater number of skeptic donor countries and agencies than ever before experienced in Africa. Clearly, as *The Courier* . . . decidedly put it, there 'is indeed no shortage of goodwill for SADCC.'[15]

In fact, at the 1986 Annual Consultative Conference, SADCC signed two historic agreements—one with the Nordic states and one with the EEC. The former

> focuses on the development and implementation of measures to strengthen the productive sector in the SADCC region; to stimulate joint ventures and other forms of commercial investment; to increase intra- and inter-regional trade; to increase cultural cooperation between the regions; and to improve the efficiency and effectiveness of development assistance.[16]

In the latter agreement, the EEC and SADCC "signed a Memorandum of Understanding over the use of resources amounting to U.S. $100 million for regional co-operation under Lomé III."[17]

Although both agreements were significant for SADCC, the donors, with the exception of the Nordic countries, are viewed as supporting their own ideological or commercial interests in any collaborative effort with SADCC.[18] In fact, when talking to SADCC officials about their international cooperating partners, one is always reminded that the Nordic countries must be distinguished from the U.S. and the EEC. Overall, the Nordic countries are viewed as being serious about regional development in Southern Africa and are consequently given credit for much of the SADCC development that has occurred. However, these same officials are aware that the Nordic countries have their own agendas for Southern Africa and that their involvement in the region is not purely altruistic.[19]

At the 1986 SADCC Annual Conference, the U.S., Britain, and West Germany did not even pretend to have increased their acceptance of the regional organization. As Joseph Hanlon reported:

> They opposed sanctions and were generally condescending to SADCC. Timothy Raison, British Minister for Overseas Development, pledged another £10m for SADCC, but he told a press conference that Britain is not giving more, in part because SADCC "would have difficulty spending it." [20]

In another interesting development during 1986, the Reagan administration made a commitment of $500 million to SADCC for project development, in an effort to prevent the U.S. Congress from voting punitive sanctions against South Africa. Since Congress did vote for sanctions (overriding a presidential veto), the United States Agency for International Development (USAID) reportedly informed SADCC that the U.S. contribution for fiscal year 1987 would be "substantially less" than the $30 million allocated for 1986.[21]

Even though by 1986 SADCC's international cooperating partners had pledged significant sums of money to the organization, the bulk of the money had not gone toward project implementation. Instead, it had been used for technical assistance, SADCC research program studies, and conference support. Further, since technical assistance involves a substantial deployment of EEC nationals, it is ensured not only that large chunks of funds return home, but also that they gain access to privileged information and concomitant power, thus enabling EEC influence and considerable control over the decisions and activities of SADCC.[22]

In the following sections, the response by the West to SADCC between 1980 and 1986 will be more closely examined. This will be done within the context of five regional sectors: transport and communications; food, agriculture, and natural resources; industry and trade; energy; and manpower.

Transport and Communications

By 1984, even though SADCC had identified the development of the transport and communications sector as its first priority, the United States identified this sector as its third priority, according to a U. S. position statement prepared for the February 1984 Lusaka Conference: "Transport and Communications is the U.S.'s third priority and clearly SADCC's first, due to the relationships that exist in a region of six landlocked countries between economic growth and transportation and communications links."[23]

Prior to 1983, the United States justified its limited support of the transport and communications sector by arguing that Congressional legislation prevented direct development assistance to Mozambique. This, however, would not have prevented the United States from providing financial assistance to transport and communications projects located in other SADCC member states. Although Mozambique is responsible for coordinating this regional sector, project funding is pledged on a bilateral basis. But even though a 1983 waiver authorizing direct assistance to Mozambique for regional programs was signed by the U. S. Secretary of State, for fiscal year 1985, only $8 million was allocated for "assistance for a regional road maintenance and construction project." [24]

During the latter part of 1985, SADCC regarded the development of the Beira Corridor as its major priority, since it was determined that this Corridor would prospectively be the lifeline to the sea for most of the nations, in the event of South African transport sanctions. A special meeting of SADCC donors was held during April 1986 to raise $200 million for emergency Beira development, to be part of an overall ten-year plan for the Corridor. At the April meeting, $161.3 million was raised, and by the end of 1986 the money needed for the first three years of the project had been pledged. Additional money had been pledged for projects within the overall ten-year plan.

The money for Phase I (the emergency phase) was provided by USAID ($8 million), Zimbabwe ($10 million), and the Netherlands ($35 million). In addition, Austria and Italy made small contributions.[25] The money for Phase II (see Table 17) was donated mainly by the Nordic countries, the EEC, and the African Development Bank (AfDB). Given the reaction of Britain and West Germany to SADCC at the 1986 conference, it is doubtful that they supported the EEC's contribution.

Although the United States has repeatedly criticized SADCC for being too political, it is fundamentally impossible to separate politics from economics in Southern Africa. In fact, the U.S. contributions of $8 million to the Beira emergency plan and $1 million to Phase II reinforced the politics involved in supporting SADCC. This small pledge reflected the reality that the U.S. government was committed neither to ending apartheid nor to enhancing the possibility that the SADCC member states could survive South Africa's continued regional destabilization. As SADCC Executive Secretary Makoni argued:

> But it is nonsensical for USAID . . . to help us re-lay 25 kilometers of railway line and put in 400-ton cranes in Beira, and then tell us the question of defending these infrastructures is none of their business . . . It doesn't make sense to disengage politics from economics in Southern Africa, because what the South Africans are doing is not just political destabilization but economic aggression and destabilization. They are hitting those central targets which are critical to the economic development and security of our member States. For the United States to come and say, "We would like to help you rehabilitate the Beira corridor, but we are not prepared to talk to you about the security and protection of the Beira corridor," doesn't make sense.[26]

TABLE 17

BEIRA CORRIDOR PROJECT FUNDING BY DONORS, PHASE II

(in U.S. $Millions)

Donor	Amount
EEC	43.2
AfDB	32.7
Sweden	26.0
Italy	14.3
Denmark	20.8
Norway	14.0
Finland	14.8
Nordic	6.5
Netherlands	21.2
USAID	1.0
Austria	7.0
Spain	3.0
Belgium	1.0
Portugal	0.5
TOTAL	206.0

Even though the U. S. government indicated that it was not possible to provide assistance to protect the Beira Corridor, ironically, at the 1986 SADCC Annual Conference, the U. S. did indicate that such assistance could be forthcoming if all the states surrounding South Africa would agree to Nkomati-type nonaggression pacts with the apartheid regime. If this were to occur, the SADCC member states were informed, the Reagan administration would "make sure that the inoperative Maputo-Chicualacuala rail line would be reopened, the Beira rail and port system rehabilitated, and its security assured." In addition, the U. S. reportedly offered SADCC "unlimited funds" for project

SADCC and the West   251

development (mainly in the transport sector) on the condition that SADCC establish a dialogue with South Africa in order to facilitate a peaceful transition in that country.[27] No doubt the U.S. was speaking on behalf of South Africa. The SADCC has refused these as well as other suggestions of compromise by the government.

Food, Agriculture, and Natural Resources

The one sector that both friends and foes of SADCC support is food, agriculture, and natural resources. Even this sector, however, is not above politics.

> At the 1984 Lusaka Summit, the EEC enlisted the support of the USA and the Nordic group to make donors' support for agriculture conditional on changes in SADCC member states' agricultural policies, attitudes to small farmers and pricing systems.[28]

While SADCC did admit that the regional agricultural strategy was not designed to address the needs of the small farmer, and therefore plans were made to revise the strategy, throughout SADCC's existence, its international cooperating partners have attempted to impose their development priorities on the organization. As Mulenga Bwalya notes:

> Despite SADCC's claim to "call the tune," in practice, the EEC and other Western donors have twisted the former's arm either directly . . . or subtly by dangling a carrot in front of SADCC. For example, SADCC's major programme on food security and agriculture was adopted at the insistence of the EEC and other donors during the 1981 SADCC at Arusha.[29]

The U. S. continued, through 1986, to play political games with SADCC over this sector. At the 1986 SADCC Annual Conference,

> the U.S. also offered U.S. $30m as part-finance for an agricultural research institute at Matopos in western Zimbabwe, on condition that the results from research

work at the centre would not be shared with Angola, Mozambique or Tanzania. When SADCC rejected this precondition, the U.S. compromised by insisting that only research funded by other donors for the centre would be shared with these countries.[30]

This proposition was reminiscent of the original 1983 U. S. sorghum-millet grant which excluded Tanzania, Angola, and Mozambique from receiving any benefits from the research. "The SADCC Council of Ministers rejected the exclusionary clause; the grant was rewritten and other donors picked up the cost of the three, after more than a year delay." [31]

Not only has the U. S. identified its own priority for SADCC sectoral development, but it also has identified its own sector objectives. As Carol Thompson argues, "The U.S. also joins the World Bank in pushing for privatization of agricultural marketing, when SADCC has made it clear that it rejects the analysis that a 'free market' is a panacea for agricultural development." [32]

In addition, in 1986, when making arrangements to purchase wheat from the U. S., Zimbabwe offered to pay by shipping surplus white maize to Mozambique as part of the U. S. food aid to Mozambique. While the U. S. agreed to the triangular arrangement, Zimbabwe was allowed to send only 7,000 tons of white maize, which represented less than one-tenth of the U. S. yellow maize sent. In commenting on this situation, a USAID official in Harare declared, "The goal of food aid is to make the people of southern Africa change their preference from white maize to yellow maize, in order to create a market for U. S. yellow maize." [33]

Industry and Trade

Of the four major sectors, industry and trade received the smallest percentage of needed project funding from SADCC's international cooperating partners between 1980 and 1986. It appears that the overall policy of the advanced capitalist nations has been not to support this sector. At the February 1984 Lusaka Conference, the U. S. stated:

> The U. S. has no plans at present to participate in the industrial sector. An informal reading of the industry

paper indicates that the projects are not very well thought out. It appears that most of the projects proposed have a national orientation rather than regional.[34]

Canada's financial commitment to SADCC at this time focused on food security and agriculture, energy, transportation, and human resources development; EEC's commitment was to agriculture and transport and communications.[35]

Notwithstanding the small markets of the economies of the SADCC countries and the regional instability due to South African destabilization, lack of interest by the advanced capitalist nations in developing the regional industrial sector was to be expected, given the nature and extent of their investment in the industrial sector of South Africa. If the SADCC states were to develop the regional industrial sector as outlined in the Lusaka Program of Action, South Africa would lose a sizable market for its commodities, and this could have serious implications for its economic leverage over the region. Between 1980 and 1986, the advanced capitalist nations had no interest in altering South Africa's regional economic hegemony.

The exception to the above seemed to be the Nordic countries. In signing the region-to-region cooperation agreement with SADCC, they intend to increase trade and strengthen the productive sectors in the region (i.e., promote joint ventures, investment, and technological transfers in agro-industry, manufacturing). The Nordic Initiative was developed as a concrete step toward the "new international economic order" demanded by the Third World.[36] This is significant in that, fundamentally, the SADCC countries are requesting the advanced capitalist nations to help them establish a new division of labor between themselves and South Africa, specifically, and between themselves and the advanced capitalist nations in general. This, however, seems not to be part of the Western agenda.

Energy

The U. S. position on the development of SADCC's energy sector was made clear at the February 1984 Lusaka Conference when the first major projects were presented. The U. S. delegation noted that "since Angola has the responsibility for coordinating this sector, it would be very difficult for the U. S. to get involved." [37]

The U. S. decided not only not to get involved, but also to participate directly in the destabilization of Angola. In addition to giving military assistance to the South African-backed UNITA rebels, the Reagan administration took further measures to undermine the development of the petroleum sector. In an effort to put further pressure on U. S. oil companies and "resolve the contradiction between military backing for the rebels and U. S. corporate support of the Angolan government through taxes and royalties," in October 1986 Congress passed two amendments to legislation affecting U. S. oil companies that do business in Angola. The first requested the President to "consider using his authority under the Export Administration Act to restrict U. S. business transactions that conflict with U. S. security interests in Angola." The second prohibited the Department of Defense (DOD) from purchasing Angolan petroleum products from U. S. oil companies in Angola (Chevron, Shell, Conoco, Caltex, and Texaco).[38] Angola therefore turned to Europe for new credit lines for further development of this subsector.

The conclusion of a SADCC energy study indicated that the major problems encountered by SADCC in developing this sector are definitely not due to a lack of resources; regional energy resources are quite large and, in some parts of the region, diversified. The ability of these nations to develop the potential of the sector, however, was "linked to options as to the nature and amount of investment to be undertaken to balance energy supply and demand and to provide a better distribution of modern commercial energy in each country." [39]

The development of a regional oil pipeline from Angola to the other SADCC member states would make these nations self-sufficient in oil. Prior to the signing of the 1984 troop-withdrawal accord with South Africa, Angola had made an offer to "supply the region with oil at a mutually agreed price." According to Barry Munslow and Phil O'Keefe, the implication of the offer was that in return, the regional countries would provide Angola with "strong political support in the face of South Africa's continued acts of massive aggression." [40] For both South Africa and the advanced capitalist nations, SADCC self-sufficiency in the supply of oil would considerably decrease their economic and political leverage over the region. Therefore, it would be a conflict of interest to allow this to happen.

Similarly, it would be a conflict of interest for SADCC's cooperating partners to invest in developing the regional infrastructure needed to make Botswana, Mozambique, Swaziland, Zambia, and Zimbabwe major exporters of coal. The deposits of coal are so vast in these countries that they could become competitive with the world's main exporters—the United States, Australia, Poland, the U.S.S.R., South Africa, and Canada.[41]

Manpower

The development of the manpower sector is certainly the least threatening to the global center of all the regional sectors. Although the May 1984 USAID report on Southern Africa reported that SADCC has had difficulty in formulating a regional manpower strategy, the U. S. still identified manpower as its second priority for regional development. Specifically, the report concluded that "the Regional Training Council (RTC), under Swaziland's direction, has approached manpower in an ad hoc and piecemeal manner. In fact, the problem facing SADCC has been a strong reluctance by members to approach manpower from a regional perspective." [42]

In an effort to rectify the problem of "absence of leadership within the RTC," USAID identified its own program of action for the development of this sector. It is a two-pronged approach that consists first of providing assistance to the RTC in an "effort to strengthen its central coordination of manpower planning." The second component consists of strengthening "specifically, agricultural and management training capabilities in the region." [43]

Throughout 1986, manpower remained SADCC's weakest sector. What became obvious was that SADCC's cooperating partners continued to import expatriates into the region to work on SADCC projects, thus increasing employment opportunities for these individuals, rather than training opportunities for indigenous workers.

SADCC: 1987

Phase II of the Western "development scandal" over Southern Africa started with a bang. No doubt the nations felt more comfortable with the SADCC member states after they had imposed sanctions on South Africa:

> A new mood of harmony characterized discussions between Frontline States and donors at the eight annual meeting of . . . SADCC in Gaborone, leading Botswana Vice-President Peter Mmusi, the SADCC chairman, to describe the summit as a "landmark" in SADCC's history.[44]

The U.S. committed $93 million over an eighteen-month period, as "a vote of confidence in the economic future of Southern Africa," according to USAID administrator Peter McPherson. West Germany announced that it would be doubling its assistance program to SADCC states over the next five years, and Britain expressed unprecedented support for the organization. Other donors, including the Nordic countries and the Netherlands, also indicated that they would be increasing their aid to SADCC over the next few years. At the 1987 Annual Conference, representatives from thirty-one countries (including many from the Eastern bloc) and eighteen international organizations were present.[45]

The SADCC was no doubt pleased with this response and perhaps felt that the imperialist powers were now seriously committed to the liberation of the region from South Africa's stranglehold. It did not take the organization long, however, to understand that, at least for the U. S., continued support for the apartheid regime remained at the top of its Southern Africa agenda. The U. S. Congress passed the Pressler Amendment, which attached conditions to the $50 million pledged to SADCC for 1987. Specifically, the amendment barred "assistance to countries in the region that advocate the form of terrorism commonly known as 'necklacing' or allow persons who practice 'necklacing' to operate in their territory." [46]

Clearly furious at the passing of this amendment, at its annual meeting, the SADCC Summit

- registered its strong objection to the specific exclusion of Angola and Mozambique from these programmes, and reaffirmed its opposition to actions which violate the integrity of SADCC;

- expressed its displeasure at the attempt to associate SADCC member states with terrorism.[47]

President Mugabe further noted,

> We in the region regard that vote in Congress as an attempt to blackmail us into supporting apartheid, since it concerns a practice over which we have no control whatsoever. To suggest that we condone it is a mere excuse for the U. S. to continue supporting apartheid instead of assisting the forces of freedom and justice.[48]

As the security situation in the region worsened, the West continued to see increased economic assistance to the SADCC member states as: (1) a way to increase direct Western hegemony over the region; and (2) an excuse for not implementing or enforcing sanctions against South Africa.[49]

With respect to the issue of greater direct Western control over the region, 1987 saw the question of "tied" aid become more serious. Perhaps the SADCC state most directly affected by "tied" aid is Mozambique. It was reported:

- Of 700,000 tons of food pledged by donors, only 30,000 had arrived.

- Certain donors insisted on sending food they wanted to get rid of, rather than what was needed.

- Some insisted that the planes, ships, and lorries they financed could be used only to transport their food.

- Some emergency aid took as long as nine months to arrive, and donors then insisted that it had to go to a particular province, even though that area had become oversupplied and others were in need.

- Donors insisted on high levels of accounting,

which required extra government staff, at a time when the IMF package was demanding cuts in government staff levels.

— Several donors would not give permission for food aid to be sold in areas where the population could afford to buy. This demand ruined the market for local farmers and suppressed future production. It also denied the government the opportunity to raise local cash for reinvestment in the relief effort.[50]

Connected to the issue of "tied" aid is the question of whether agreements between SADCC and its cooperating partners are really designed to promote collective self-reliant development in the region. The Lomé Convention signed in 1986 between the SADCC member states and the EEC is a case in point. Instead of promoting regional collective self-reliance, it seems that the agreement was designed to ensure that Southern Africa would continue to export raw materials to the EEC and import manufactured goods from Europe. In fact, one major criticism of the EEC-SADCC relationship is that

> often what might be considered natural trade within the region is strangled by a combination of the foreign exchange shortages which plague the region and predatory financing by developed economies through the use of credit-mixed arrangements. This is a particular problem with the bilateral aid from European Community Member States, which can serve to undermine the productive base of the SADCC region. During the UK-financed electrification of part of the Zimbabwean railway network, Zimbabwean industrialists complained that a large proportion of the inputs required could have been produced locally.[51]

Furthermore:

> Within the SADCC region, there is a certain perception that in matters relating to regional trade and industrial development and their financing, the CEC may not have focused adequately on SADCC's requirements. This is a

point of particular concern given the increasing use of Lomé resources for Sectoral Import Programmes. Where these import programs bring into the region goods which could be produced from within the region's own resources (such as peasant consumer goods), then they have a detrimental impact on the development of intra-regional trade.[52]

Throughout 1987, Britain continued to oppose sanctions, and Alan Clark, Britain's Minister for Trade, went so far as to publicly urge

> private sector companies to continue to do business with South Africa . . . As South Africa becomes more industrialized, it will continue to present new and exciting opportunities and I hope that British companies will continue to be well represented and to keep winning business from our competitors.[53]

As limited economic sanctions were being imposed against South Africa, the Reagan administration quickly assured South Africa that it would

> regard goods produced in Swaziland and exported through South Africa as exempt from the U. S. sanctions against Pretoria. The exemption encompassed such products of Swaziland as were "transerviced" in South Africa; and it included goods produced in Swaziland by private South African capital.[54]

This provision also pertained to Lesotho. Thus, in response to sanctions, many South African companies merely reinvested their capital in Lesotho, Swaziland, and, to a lesser extent, Botswana.[55]

Swaziland became not only a conduit for sanctions-busting by the apartheid regime, but also a place for U. S. corporations to reinvest capital they had withdrawn from South Africa.

> United States-owned multinationals, which pulled out of South Africa with such an initial flurry of favorable publicity during 1986, were also quietly looking at what Swaziland had to offer. One was Coca-Cola, which

announced with great fanfare in September 1986 that its pullout would involve selling R10 million ($5 million) worth of shares to black South Africans. In November 1986 the corporation announced its intention to build a E15 million ($7.5 million) concentrates plant at Matsapha, which would supply all of southern and central Africa, as well as the Indian Ocean islands. Swaziland's free assess to South Africa, of course, allows Coke to ship its product to the republic, where the corporation had retained its franchising rights.[56]

So far Kodak has followed in Coca-Cola's footsteps, and General Electric has announced its intention of relocating in Swaziland.[57]

Although the imperialist powers continued to send a clear signal of support to the apartheid regime through 1987, for the South African government, the decision by the West to impose sanctions was a vote of no confidence. As a nation under siege, Pretoria reacted to this vote by moving to increase its economic control over the region, even if it angered Western capital. South Africa definitely angered the American Natural Soda Ash Corporation (ANSAC), which had been South Africa's principal supplier of soda ash, when it discovered that Pretoria had signed the Sua Pan agreement with Botswana (see chapter 6). The ANSAC responded to this news by sending letters to the International Finance Corporation and USAID, arguing that local financial and development aid should be withheld from Botswana as a way of putting an end to the project.[58] South Africa ignored ANSAC and continued to pursue the project with Botswana. Prior to international sanctions, however, South Africa had ignored Botswana's request to invest in the project. South Africa intends to be prepared to withstand a total onslaught, even by the West.

SADCC: 1988 AND BEYOND

This part of the chapter is divided into two sections: 1988 Annual Conference, Security Assistance, and Sanctions; and What Future for SADCC?

1988 Annual Conference, Security Assistance, and Sanctions

At the 1988 SADCC Annual Conference held in Arusha, Tanzania, in January, SADCC received $1 billion in new pledges over the next four years. In addition, the international community came "to acknowledge that the UNITA and Renamo movements are part of Pretoria's destabilization war against the region." [59]

While the increased recognition that SADCC is receiving from the West as evidenced by these new pledges is no doubt significant, it only continues the cycle of dependency that SADCC has fallen into. Although the organization is partially to blame for this phenomenon, the West is also responsible for the present regional crisis. How is it possible, for example, that it took SADCC's international cooperating partners eight years to collectively agree "publicly" that UNITA rebels (backed by South Africa and the U.S.) and Renamo terrorists (backed by South Africa) are a menace to regional development, when SADCC, from its inception, has been calling on the international community to address this issue?

In recognition of this "incredible" discovery, some of SADCC's international cooperating partners have begun to supply security assistance to SADCC, so that their projects, particularly in Mozambique, can be protected against Renamo attacks:

— Britain is training Mozambican officers in Zimbabwe and at Sandhurst. A licence has been granted for the export of advanced radio-communication equipment to Mozambique . . . Elsewhere in the region, the UK has ongoing assistance programmes with Swaziland, Lesotho, Zambia, Zimbabwe and Malawi, mainly involving the training and the supplying of non-lethal military items.

— The European Community (EC) effected a breakthrough on the issues in November 1987. It signed the protocol on Lomé funding for Mozambique, containing a clause on non-lethal security items.

— Spain adopts a similar line to that of the EC, aiming at "a formula whereby the financing of development projects likewise includes the necessary security factor for guaranteeing their defence." In the context of a rural development project in Mozambique, Spain will train a rural militia unit.

— Italy spends part of its development funds for Mozambique on non-lethal expenditure of the Mozambican troops that guard Italian-funded projects under implementation, e.g., a barrage. By law, Italy cannot supply military assistance.

— Sweden is presently looking for ways to adopt a similar line to that of the EC . . . Meanwhile, Swedish NGOs (non-government organizations) with co-operation programmes in Mozambique, have been supplying non-lethal items for Mozambique's defence forces.

— Portugal has agreed in principle to provide Mozambique with military assistance, including revamping old garrisons and training. A high-level military fact-finding mission had visited Mozambique.[60]

In addition, an Israeli delegation made a secret visit to Mozambique in February 1988 with a view toward offering military assistance. This gesture was refused outright by Mozambique. Although it has been suggested that Israel is interested in assisting Mozambique in an effort to distance itself from Pretoria and the Renamo terrorists, Israel continues to maintain very close military ties with South Africa.[61] Certainly the possibility exists that Israel's desire to establish close ties with Mozambique is part of a South African-orchestrated strategy to further intervene in Mozambique.

Security assistance represents a new phase in the Western "development scandal" over Southern Africa. It gives the illusion that SADCC's cooperating partners are supportive of the organization's efforts to combat the nightmare of South African regional destabilization. In reality, however, this is just another ploy to cover up continued support for the apartheid regime and to increase direct Western hegemony over Southern Africa, in the wake of South Africa's declining power as a global semiperiphery.

During Phase I of the Western response to SADCC, limited development assistance was provided. Now during Phase II, part of SADCC's development assistance must be used for security purposes. A large percentage of the remaining aid is used to rebuild projects previously destroyed as a result of destabilization. When will significant regional development begin?

If SADCC's cooperating partners really were interested in SADCC's development as a viable regional entity, what would they do? First of all, they would stop playing games with SADCC and do something about the real issue in the region—the apartheid regime and the genocide that is taking place against the black population throughout Southern Africa (including South Africa and Namibia). If necessary, this would include arming these nations so that they would be able to defend themselves against South Africa's destabilization. It is indeed interesting that nonlethal security assistance is being made available to protect "specific" SADCC projects against Renamo attacks. Should not the people of Mozambique be protected first?

Second, instead of continuing to reject sanctions, impose limited sanctions, not enforce sanctions, or participate in sanctions-busting,[62] SADCC's cooperating partners would take the necessary measures to isolate this regime. Preliminary studies do indicate that Pretoria is vulnerable to sanctions.[63]

Further, if SADCC's cooperating partners were interested in SADCC becoming viable, it would force South Africa, Israel, and the United States to stop backing the UNITA rebels in Angola. The overall significance of U. S. support for UNITA was summarized by Peter Mmusi, Vice-President of Botswana, at the 1986 SADCC Annual Conference, when he argued that funding Jonas Savimbi (UNITA's leader) "runs counter to American professions of friendship and cooperation with the independent states of Southern Africa. This now places the United States clearly in league with South Africa in formenting instability in the region."[64] Ironically, amidst the strong support given to the idea of providing security assistance to SADCC projects in Mozambique, the issue of providing security assistance to the Angolan government was not mentioned.

What Future for SADCC?

For many in Southern Africa, SADCC is viewed as a success for the West, but not a success for Southern Africa. As Ibbo Mandaza recently noted, "Even some Africans have complained that SADCC is 'theirs not ours.' This is usually a reference also to the extent to which SADCC has, perhaps, become more an obsession among external forces than among Africans themselves." Mandaza further suggests that "it would be no exaggeration to state that the Western countries in general have tended to view SADCC as their own institution." [65]

Whether SADCC is an indigenous regional creation or a Western-Frontline States creation, the organization has been used by the imperialist powers to deepen their control over Southern Africa. Although when the organization was established its member states were aware of the contradiction inherent in pursuing a strategy that would increase their dependence on the imperialists, these nations did not anticipate that they would end up by mortgaging the region to the West.[66]

Even though SADCC now understands that the member states must work toward regional self-reliance as an alternative to increased dependence, it may be too late to reverse the Western "onslaught." Perhaps the only hope for the region to develop its potential as a self-reliant entity within the capitalist world-economy lies in a majority-ruled South Africa becoming a member. Even with a majority-ruled South Africa as a member of SADCC, the real issue may be, How long will it take SADCC to pay off its mortgage to the West?

NOTES

1. Interview with Ambassador Paul Repia, March 1984.

2. Samir Amin, Derrick Chitala, and Ibbo Mandaza, eds., *SADCC: Prospects for Disengagement and Development in Southern Africa* (London: Zed Books, Ltd., and United Nations University, 1987), p. 8. The view that SADCC is not solely a Frontline initiative is expressed by numerous SADCC critics—see Ibbo Mandaza, "Perspective on Economic

Cooperation and Autonomous Development in Southern Africa," *SADCC Prospects*, pp. 210-300.

3. Samir Amin, "Preface," *SADCC Prospects*, p. 3.

4. Margaret C. Lee, "Implications of SADCC Strategy for Post-Apartheid South Africa." Paper presented at Symposium III: After Apartheid, University of Pittsburgh, March 17-19, 1988, p. 18.

5. *Ibid.*, p. 19.

6. "Itemized Account of Alliance Between Israel and South Africa," *Southscan* (Britain), March 16, 1988.

7. Deborah Barry, Raul Vergara, and Jose Rodolfo Castro, "'Low Intensity Warfare': The Counterinsurgency Strategy for Central America," *Crisis in Central America: Regional Dynamics and U.S. Policy in the 1980s*, ed. Nora Hamilton, et al. (Boulder, Colo.: Westview Press, 1988), pp. 80-81.

8. Samir Amin, "Preface," *SADCC: Prospects*, p. 3.

9. *Ibid.*

10. Lee, "Implications of SADCC Strategy," p. 2. This concept is developed further in Lee, "U.S. Involvement in Southern Africa: A Case of International Racism," *Third World in Perspective*, forthcoming, Spring, 1989.

11. Lee, "Implications of SADCC Strategy," pp. 19-20.

12. The response by the West to SADCC is termed a "development scandal" since it became very clear that support for SADCC was used as an alibi to cover up continued support for South Africa. The West, therefore, had no interest in supporting viable development in the region, although it attempted to make the SADCC member states believe that this was the case. By continuing to support the apartheid regime and regional destabilization, the West showed that South Africa's continued strength as a global semiperiphery was of primary importance, not SADCC's regional development.

13. Richard F. Weisfelder, "The Southern African Development Coordination Conference: A New Factor in the Liberation Process," *South Africa in Southern Africa: The Intensifying Vortex of Violence*, ed. Callaghy Thomas (New York: Praeger, 1983), p. 245.

14. Ed Brown, "Foreign Aid to SADCC: An Analysis of the Reagan Administration's Foreign Policy," *Issue*, Vol. 12, 1982, p. 36.

15. Mulenga C. Bwalya, "Regional Co-operation and Imperialist Penetration: A Critical Perspective of SADCC." Paper presented at Seminar on Southern African Responses to Imperialism, University of Zimbabwe, April 22-24, 1987, p. 16.

16. SADCC, Report *on the NORDIC/SADCC Initiative* (Gaborone, Botswana: SADCC, 1987), pp. 3-4.

17. Bwalya, "Regional Co-operation," p. 17.

18. Amin, et al., "Introduction," *SADCC: Prospects*, p. 17.

19. Interviews with SADCC officials, Harare, Zimbabwe and Maputo, Mozambique, June-July 1988.

20. Joseph Hanlon, "SADCC: On Course With New Aid Pledges," *African Business*, March 1986, p. 15.

21. "SADCC Team on Last Leg of Tour," *Africa Economic Digest*, November 22, 1986, p. 16.

22. Bwalya, "Regional Co-operation," p. 15.

23. "Transportation and Communication," U. S. position statement prepared for the SADCC Lusaka Conference, February 2-3, 1984.

24. Ibid.

25. Interview with Eddie Cross, managing director, Beira Corridor Group (BCG), Harare, Zimbabwe, July 1987.

26. Simbarashe Makoni, "Interview," *Africa Report*, July-August

1986, pp. 40-41.

27. "How the U. S. Tried to Twist SADCC's Arm," *African Business*, April 1986, p. 14.

28. Bwalya, "Regional Co-operation," p. 14.

29. *Ibid.*, p. 15.

30. "How the U.S. Tried to Twist SADCC's Arm," p. 14.

31. Carol B. Thompson, "SADCC's Struggle for Economic Liberation," *Africa Report*, July-August 1986, p. 63.

32. *Ibid.*, p. 62.

33. *Ibid.*

34. "Industry," U. S. position statement prepared for the SADCC Lusaka Conference, February 2-3, 1984.

35. USAID, *Country Development Strategy Statement FY 1986 Southern Africa* (USAID, May 1984), p. 24.

36. Hanlon, "SADCC: On Course," p. 15.

37. "Energy," U. S. position statement prepared for the SADCC Lusaka Conference, February 2-3, 1984.

38. "Angola," *Africa Report*, November-December 1986, pp. 48-49.

39. SADCC, *SADCC Energy*, paper presented at SADCC Conference, Lusaka, February 2-3, 1984.

40. Barry Munslow and Phil O'Keefe, "Energy and the Southern Africa Regional Confrontation," *Third World Quarterly*, Vol. 6, No. 1, 1984, p. 40.

41. *SADCC Energy*, 1984, p. 37.

42. USAID, *Country Development Strategy*, p. 43.

43. *Ibid.*, pp. 43-44.

44. "SADCC Summit Brings Partners Closer Together," *Africa Economic Digest*, February 14, 1987, p. 2.

45. *Ibid.*

46. Robert G. Mugabe, "Struggle for Southern Africa," *Foreign Affairs*, Winter 1987/88, p. 318.

47. Communique of the Summit of the Southern African Development Coordination Conference (SADCC) in Lusaka, Zambia, July 24, 1987, p. 4.

48. Robert Mugabe, "Struggle for Southern Africa," pp. 318-19.

49. See "Mozambique: The Food Factor," *Africa Confidential*, October 1987, p. 7; "Britain Helping Frontline States," *Independent* (Britain), October 14, 1987; "Greek Connection in SA Arms Deal With Tehran," *International Herald Tribune* (U.S.), November 27, 1987.

50. "Mozambique Switch to Self-Help," *Times* (Britain), February 6, 1988.

51. "SADCC-EEC Briefing," *Issue*, No. 1, May-June, 1988, p. 6.

52. *Ibid.*

53. "Clark Calls on Private Sector to Trade With South Africa," *Financial Times* (Britain), November 27, 1987.

54. Alan Booth, "South African Sanctions-Breaking in Southern Africa: The Case of Swaziland," paper presented at African Studies Association Conference, Denver, Colorado, November 20, 1987, p. 7.

55. See Booth, "Case of Swaziland"; James Cobbe, "Sanctions Against South Africa: Lesotho's Role," paper presented at African Studies Association Conference, Denver, Colorado, November 20, 1987; Fred Morton, "South African Capital in Southern Africa: Botswana's Sua Pan Project," paper presented at Third Symposium on Post-Apartheid South Africa, University of Pittsburgh, March 17-19, 1988.

56. Booth, "Case of Swaziland," p. 10.

SADCC and the West

57. See Booth, "Case of Swaziland"; "Discredited Disinvestment," *African Business*, February 1988.

58. Morton, "Sua Pan Project," p. 4.

59. "Donors Boost Front-Line Assistance," *Africa Economic Digest*, February 5, 1988; *AWEPA News Bulletin* (Netherlands), No. 16, February 1988.

60. "Assistance to Enhance Security," *AWEPA News Bulletin* (Netherlands), March 1988.

61. David Fairhall, "Israel and SA 'Joined in Nuclear Arms Pact'," *Guardian* (Britain), January 1, 1988.

62. "Revealed: Dutch Sanctions Trick," *Observer* (Britain), April 17, 1988; "EC States 'Have Failed to Enforce Sanctions'," *Financial Times* (Britain), September 30, 1987; "Paper Claims EC-SA Trade Figures Were 'Illusory'," *Southscan* (Britain), December 10, 1987; "Euratom Admits Uranium Swaps May Blunt S. Africa Bans," *Financial Times* (Britain), February 19, 1988; "USA Fudging on Sanctions, Says Official Report," *Weekly Mail* (SA), February 5, 1988; "West German Industrialists Find Investment Loophole in Bonn's South Africa Rule," *Southscan*, December 19, 1987; "W. German, S. African Business Sets Out to Divert European Sanctions," *Southscan*, April 20, 1988; "W. German Co's Accused of Aiding SA With Submarines," *Windhoek Adv.* (Namibia), March 22, 1988.

63. "S. Africa Under Financial Pressure, Says New Study," *Times* (Britain), February 9, 1988; "West German Report Confirms Sanctions as Effective Weapon," *Southscan*, October 13, 1987; "Sanctions Nip Turns to Bite—Report," *Weekly Mail* (SA), October 30, 1987; "Pretoria's Budget Hit by Boycott," *Anti-Apartheid News* (Britain), April 1988; "The Money Strains on Apartheid," *South* (Britain), April 1988.

64. "How the U.S. Tried to Twist SADCC's Arm," p. 14.

65. Mandaza, "Perspective," *SADCC Prospects*, pp. 220-21.

66. The idea of SADCC's increased dependency on the West being viewed within the context of a mortgage is presented

by Bwalya, "Regional Co-operation," p. 17.

Children dancing in Mozambique, 1987

Photo by Joel Chiziane, Mozambique Information Agency (AIM)

Terrorist activities of the MNR resulted in this carbonized body and the burned buses in Mozambique's Maputo Province, 1987.

Photo by AIM

MNR terrorism in Mozambique's Tete Province left many displaced families in its wake, 1986. Photo by Anders Nilsson (AIM)

Ondjiva, a city in Angola, was destroyed by South African forces in 1985. Photo by Joel Chiziane (AIM)

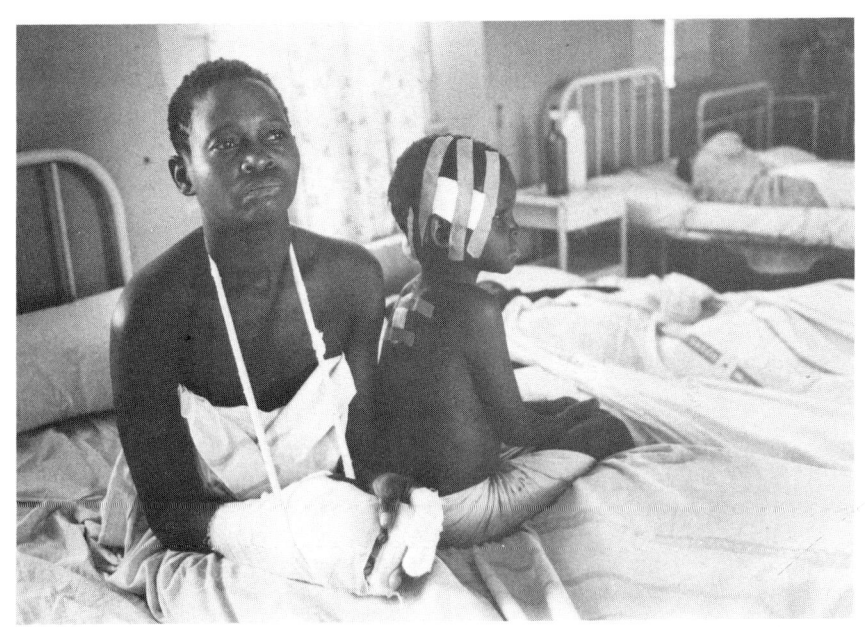

Victims of MNR bandits in Mozambique's Inhambane Province, 1986. Photo by Anders Nilsson (AIM)

Bridge over Zambezi River in Cazombo, Angola, destroyed by South African forces, 1985. Photo by Joel Chiziane (AIM)

Nacala Port, Mozambique, 1984.

Photo by Antonio Muchave (AIM)

Nacala Port, Mozambique, 1984.

Photo by Antonio Muchave (AIM)

Maputo Port, Mozambique, 1984

Photo by AIM

Men working at Beira Port, Mozambique, 1988.

Photo by Anders Nilsson (AIM)

Cahora Bassa Dam, Tete Province, Mozambique, 1983.

Photo by Antonio Muchave (AIM)

Cahora Bassa Dam, Tete Province, Mozambique, 1983.

Photo by Antonio Muchave (AIM)

Photo by Ministry of Information, Zimbabwe

SADCC Annual Summit, Harare, Zimbabwe, July, 1981.

L-R: Former President Samora Machel, Mozambique; President Robert Mugabe, Zimbabwe; President Kenneth Kaunda, Zambia; President José dos Santos, Angola; and Julius Nyerere, former president, Tanzania.

SADCC Annual Summit, Maputo, Mozambique, July, 1988.

L-R: President Ali Hassan, Tanzania; President Quett Masire, Botswana; President Joaquim Chissano, Mozambique; President Kenneth Kaunda, Zambia; President Robert Mugabe, Zimbabwe.

Photo by Joel Chiziane (AIM)

SADCC Annual Consultative Conference, January, 1986.

President Robert Mugabe of Zimbabwe, speaking, and Dr. Simba Makoni, SADCC executive secretary.

Photo by Ministry of Information, Zimbabwe

Photo by Ministry of Information, Zimbabwe

SADCC's international cooperating partners at the SADCC Annual Consultative Conference in Harare, Zimbabwe, January, 1986.

Participants at SADCC Annual Summit, Maputo, Mozambique, July, 1988.
Photo by Joel Chiziane (AIM)

Photo by Ministry of Information, Zimbabwe

SADCC Annual Summit, Luanda, Angola, August, 1986. Former president of Mozambique, Samora Machel and President Robert Mugabe of Zimbabwe.

CHAPTER 8

Conclusion

The need and desire by the independent nations in Southern Africa to transform the production structure in the region from one of great economic dependency on both South Africa and the imperialist powers to one of greater intra-regional interdependency, leading to enhanced regional development, culminated in the official establishment of the Southern African Development Coordination Conference (SADCC) in 1980. Rejecting as conducive to the specific development needs of Southern Africa the approaches to regional cooperation and development previously pursued by developing countries (e.g., the ANDEAN Pact, ECOWAS, EAC, etc.), the SADCC member states developed their own unique approach to regional cooperation and development, outlined in the SADCC organizational document, The Lusaka Declaration, *Southern Africa: Toward Economic Liberation*. Using a political economy theoretical framework, this study described the incorporation of South Africa and the SADCC member states into the capitalist world-economy and the resulting implications for post-independent regional development. Without an understanding of how South Africa and the imperialist powers came to dominate the political and economic structures of the SADCC states, it is impossible to understand the problems these nations confront in their effort to implement the SADCC Program of Action.

In order to analyze the extent to which the SADCC member states have been successful in fostering regional cooperation and development, an extensive investigation of the SADCC Program of Action and SADCC's institutional framework was undertaken. Two chapters devoted to this endeavor reveal the level of complexity involved in the creation of a strategy that attempts to address the specific development needs of all the members. Such a strategy has strengths as well as weaknesses.

The extent to which the member states have been successful in implementing the SADCC Program of Action was examined by looking at the relationship between the SADCC member states and South Africa (regional level) and between the SADCC member states and the West (international level). Overall, the study concludes that because of the geopolitics of the region, the SADCC member states have not had much success in fostering regional cooperation and development.

At the regional level, since SADCC was established, the objective of the apartheid regime has been to make sure that the organization did not become a viable regional entity, since it served to challenge South Africa's economic and political regional hegemony. In order to prove its point, Pretoria, beginning in 1980, intensified its strategy of regional destabilization, wreaking havoc throughout Southern Africa. South Africa has therefore proved to be the greatest impediment to regional cooperation and development in Southern Africa.

The SADCC member states themselves, however, have adopted strategies that have proved to deter cooperation and development at the regional level. Although politically these nations have made a commitment to implementing the SADCC Program of Action, economically, this is not the case. Intra-regional competition is a problem, and therefore often gets in the way of regional cooperation and development. While on the one hand SADCC's loose organizational structure is a conduit for regional cooperation and development, it is also a constraint, since when it is advantageous to do so, member states can decide not to cooperate, with no repercussions. The national orientation of the SADCC Program of Action certainly contributes to this problem.

At the international level, the Western nations have provided economic assistance to the SADCC member states for regional development, but have continued to support the apartheid regime and its policy of regional destabilization. Fundamentally, the Western nations (with the exception of the Nordic countries) have used support for SADCC as an alibi to cover up their continued support for the apartheid regime. To this day, the imperialist nations have refused to deal with the real problem in the region—the apartheid regime.

The SADCC member states recognize the serious contradiction in the fact that, while they requested the imperialist powers' economic assistance to help decrease their economic dependency on the apartheid regime, eight years later they have become more chronically dependent on those nations than in 1980. As the imperialist powers sat back and watched South Africa destroy SADCC infrastructural development, paid for by grants and loans from the West, it became clear that the West had no intention of seeing these nations develop strong economic structures. After all, if such development did occur, it would challenge the Western powers' regional hegemony over Southern Africa.

Although South Africa's regional destabilization has made these nations more vulnerable to increased economic assistance and, consequently, to dominance from the West, many SADCC officials are aware that the SADCC states could have done more to develop intra-regional self-reliance. To this end, at the 1988 Annual Summit held in Maputo, Mozambique, in July, Botswana made a pledge of $3.5 million dollars toward the development of the Limpopo railway (Zimbabwe-Maputo line). This was the first time a member state had made such a commitment to another member. This is the type of self-reliant development that SADCC has been talking about for the past eight years. We hope it will be the beginning of greater regional self-reliance.

Since the apartheid regime is the major hindrance to regional development in Southern Africa, the expectation is that once South Africa is liberated, a SADCC that includes a majority-ruled South Africa will result in enhanced regional cooperation and development. While this probably will be the case, the geopolitics of the region probably will militate against any meaningful structural transformation.

One of the perennial issues in the debate about a majority-ruled South Africa is whether the country will remain a prisoner to the forces of imperialism that currently dominate the region, or whether a socialist form of government will be implemented, leading to an alteration in the historical pattern of regional dependency and underdevelopment. It is likely that the former will occur. With a post-apartheid South Africa as the regional giant, the economic policy adopted by its government will have serious implications for the entire region.

At the regional level, internal class conflicts within the region, and the capitalist orientation of the ruling class, will, in all likelihood, militate against the successful implementation of a socialist strategy in South Africa. Post-independent development in Zimbabwe is a clear example of the forces that can prevent the implementation of socialist development. Although Zimbabwe was for some time lauded as the revolutionary success of "socialism" in Africa, today it is obvious that the ruling class has maintained the economic structures it inherited from colonial rule. In addition, no doubt the white minority that controls the economy has ensured that these structures cannot be altered. The class conflicts likely to arise in post-apartheid South Africa will certainly be more pronounced than in Zimbabwe, and the forces militating against a socialist strategy will be even stronger.

Suppose, on the other hand, that the ruling class in South Africa were inclined to implement a socialist strategy for post-apartheid South Africa. Would the Western countries allow this to happen? Indeed not. In fact, they have made it clear, with the destabilization of Angola and Mozambique, that they will prevent any socialist strategy from gaining ground in the region. Furthermore, unless the post-apartheid regime in South Africa is pro-Western and capitalist, it will reinforce the West's belief that the real struggle in South Africa was against communism, not against white supremacy. Therefore, the alliance between the Western powers and those forces that represent apartheid South Africa will be strengthened, making it difficult for a post-apartheid South Africa to be a conduit for democracy.

This brief discussion of internal class conflicts in Southern Africa once again brings us to the major weakness of this study. Specifically, it does not address the issue of class relationships in Southern Africa and their implications for the SADCC Program of Action. In this present effort, I have consciously chosen not to deal with this issue, since it warrants an entirely separate study. It would be impossible to do justice to it in a broad study of this nature. Now that those who are interested in understanding SADCC as an organization hopefully have a valuable resource in this book, the next task will be a closer examination of the class forces in the region in relationship to SADCC.

APPENDIX A

SADCC Organizational Documents

SOUTHERN AFRICA: TOWARD ECONOMIC LIBERATION

A DECLARATION BY THE GOVERNMENTS OF INDEPENDENT STATES OF SOUTHERN AFRICA MADE AT LUSAKA ON THE 1ST OF APRIL, 1980

We, the undersigned, as the Heads of Government of majority-ruled States in Southern Africa, offer this declaration to our own peoples, to the peoples and Governments of the many countries who are interested in promoting popular welfare, justice and peace in Southern Africa and to the international agencies who share this interest. In it we state our commitment to pursue policies aimed at the economic liberation and integrated development of our national economies and we call on all concerned to assist us in this high endeavour.

Dependence in Context

Southern Africa is dependent on the Republic of South Africa as a focus of transport and communications, an exporter of goods and services and as an importer of goods and cheap labour. This dependence is not a natural phenomenon nor is it simply the result of a free market economy. The nine States and one occupied territory of Southern Africa (Angola, Botswana, Lesotho, Malawi, Mozambique, Namibia, Swaziland, Tanzania, Zambia and Zimbabwe) were, in varying degrees, deliberately incorporated —by metropolitan powers, colonial rulers and large corporations—into the colonial and sub-colonial structures centering in general on the Republic of South Africa. The development of national economies as balanced units, let alone the welfare of the people of Southern Africa, played no part in the economic integration strategy. Not surprisingly, therefore, Southern Africa is fragmented, grossly exploited and subject to economic manipulation by outsiders. Further development must aim at the reduction of economic dependence not only on the Republic of South Africa, but also on any single external State or group of States.

Liberation: Political and Economic

While the struggle for genuine political independence has advanced and continues to advance, it is not yet complete. We, the majority-ruled States of Southern Africa, recognise our responsibilities, both as separate nation States and as a group of neighbouring majority-ruled African countries, to assist in achieving a successful culmination of our struggle.

Our urgent task now is to include economic liberation in our programmes and priorities.

In the interest of the people of our countries, it is necessary to liberate our economies from their dependence on the Republic of South Africa to overcome the imposed economic fragmentation and to coordinate our efforts toward regional and national economic development. This will be as great for Namibia as it is for all the independent States of the region.

Southern Africa is a focal point of conflict. How can it be otherwise when a racist regime holds Namibia under military occupation, grossly exploits the people and the economies of the independent states and is a major barrier to our national development? It is not the quest for liberation, but the entrenched racism, exploitation and oppression which is the cause of conflict in Southern Africa. The power behind this is in large measure economic. Economic liberation is, therefore, as vital as political freedom.

We, the majority-ruled States of Southern Africa, do not envisage the regional economic coordination as exclusive. The initiative toward economic liberation has flowed from our experience of joint action for political liberation. We envisage regional coordination as open to all genuinely independent Southern African States.

In this spirit we call on Governments, international institutions and voluntary agencies to give priority to increasing financial resources to support Southern African efforts toward economic liberation and independent economic development.

This we believe is the route to genuine interdependence and represents the best hope for a just and cooperative future for the region as a whole:

Development Objectives

The development objectives which we will pursue through

coordinated action are:

1. the reduction of economic dependence, particularly, but not only, on the Republic of South Africa;

2. the forging of links to create a genuine and equitable regional integration;

3. the mobilisation of resources to promote the implementation of national, interstate and regional policies;

4. the concerted action to secure international cooperation within the framework of our strategy for economic liberation.

Strategies and Priorities.

We will identify areas in which, working in harmony, we can gear national development to provide goods and services presently coming from the Republic of South Africa and weave a fabric of regional cooperation and development.

Key to this strategy is transport and communications.

The dominance of the Republic of South Africa has been reinforced and strengthened by its transport system. Without the establishment of an adequate regional transport and communications system, other areas of cooperation become impractical. The economic liberation of Namibia, following its attainment of genuine political independence, will require the creation and operation of adequate transport and communication links with its natural partners to replace the artificial ones which currently bind it to the Republic of South Africa.

We will therefore create a Southern African Transport and Communications Commission to coordinate the use of existing systems and the planning and financing of additional regional facilities.

The ports of Mozambique serve four States in the region and with the genuine independence of Zimbabwe can be developed to serve two more. Zambia uses transport facilities in five regional States. The development of Mozambican, Tanzanian and Angolan ports and the coordination of facilities more effectively to meet requirements of the land-locked States are necessarily of regional concern. Transport and Communications will be a major focus of regional action. The coordination of transport facilities to meet the needs of the land-locked States is crucial. With the attain-

Appendix A 279

ment of genuine interdependence in Zimbabwe it is urgent to restore transport routes linking it to the Indian Ocean through Mozambique. Additional areas in which coordinated action will be needed include major new projects such as a possible railway from Botswana through Namibia to the Atlantic Ocean, thereby creating an alternative route to the sea for Botswana, Zambia and Zimbabwe: the coordination of airline schedules so that movement within the region is practicable; the study of existing and proposed micro-wave and ground satellite facilities to identify how they can be interlinked, possibly through the Rift Valley Station. The Commission will be located in Maputo and serviced by a small technical unit. It will coordinate transport and communication links among participating States. The Commission will seek participations of all genuinely independent States in the Southern African region. In addition, in many fields, notably in transport, observer status will be open to Liberation Movements wishing to participate in anticipation of genuine independence. Similarly, in manpower development and research, the involvement of Liberation Movements is essential to amass the knowledge and train the personnel necessary once political liberation is achieved.

Regional coordination must be operational—it must result in concrete programmes and projects. This will require both domestic and external finance. Present estimates, for example, show that in excess of U.S. $1.5 billion will be needed to finance urgent transport and communications projects over the next decade.

We emphasize the importance of additional resources being made available to assist efforts to coordinate regional economic development projects. In the first instance, we intend to use the Regional Transport & Communications Commission to mobilise finance for urgent projects in priority sectors by holding ad hoc pledging sessions with existing bilateral and multilateral funding agencies. As economic cooperation develops, a Southern African Development Fund will be created and research to this end is being initiated.

Its scope would be subsequently broadened and it might prove desirable to create a separate regional development bank. We therefore urge the friends of Southern Africa to pledge financial support to this Fund.

Concerted Actions

Regional cooperation in the field of transport and communications is seen as crucial to economic liberation and has therefore been given the greatest attention. In other sectors, similar programmes of concerted action are envisaged.

For trade and development we recognise that many of us have existing bilateral and multilateral trade and customs arrangements. But even within these constraints we believe that there is room for substantial increases in trade among ourselves. To this end existing payment systems and customs instruments will be studied in order to build up a regional trade system based on bilaterally negotiated annual trade targets and product lists.

A majority of the people of Southern Africa are dependent on farming and animal husbandry. Their future livelihood is threatened by environmental degradation and in particular by desert encroachment as well as recurrent drought cycles. Even today few of the States of the region are self-sufficient in staple foods. Both environmental protection and food security are major challenges both nationally and regionally. We, therefore, urge that the International Centre for Research on Agriculture in the Semi-Arid Tropics (ICRASAT) set up a Southern African Regional Centre in Botswana.

We further urge the development of existing facilities in Botswana for production of foot-and-mouth-disease vaccine to provide for the needs of all of the majority-ruled countries in Southern Africa. The spread of this disease currently threatens Angola, Botswana, Namibia, Zimbabwe, Swaziland and Mozambique. A coordinated approach to its control and elimination is urgently needed.

Likewise, we will undertake concerted projects in order to exploit natural resources, in particular those of common hydrological basins.

It is a matter of urgency to identify ways in which the coordination of research and training as well as the exchange of information can strengthen programmes to protect our environment and increase food production. In the field of food security the possibility of coordination of national reserve policies and the facilitation of interstate exchanges will receive priority attention.

We have decided to give special attention to the sharing of training and research facilities.

We have further decided to stimulate the exchange of information aimed at achieving a concerted policy in the fields of mining, industry, energy and agriculture. In particular, consultations among those States requiring petroleum products and electricity on the one hand and those with petroleum refining capacity and electricity surpluses on the other must be undertaken to achieve regional solutions.

The effort for economic development is an essential condition to free the Southern African States from the exploitative migrant labour system.

External Cooperation

We are committed to a strategy of economic liberation. It is a strategy which we believe both needs and deserves international support. Southern African regional development must be designed and implemented by Southern Africans. It will, however, be achieved more rapidly and will be more effective if development takes place within the context of global cooperation.

International bodies and States outside Southern Africa are therefore invited to cooperate in implementing programmes towards economic liberation and development in the region.

This preliminary identification of aims, strategies and sectors illustrates both the magnitude of the task facing us and some of the broad areas within which outside assistance will be welcomed.

It is envisaged that Southern African Development Coordination meetings of member Southern African States and other invited participants should be held annually. This will provide a mechanism for surveying results, evaluating performance, identifying strengths and weaknesses and agreeing on future plans. Economic liberation and development in Southern Africa cannot be attained either easily or speedily. What is therefore needed is sustained cooperation.

We view this declaration as a statement of commitment and strategy. Under-development, exploitation, crisis and conflict in Southern Africa will be overcome through economic liberation. The welfare of the peoples of Southern Africa and the development of its economies requires coordinated regional action. It is our belief that in the interest of popular welfare, justice and peace, we in Southern Africa have the right to ask and to receive practical international cooperation in our struggle for reconstruction, development and genuine interdependence. However, as with the struggle for political liberation, the fight for economic liberation is neither a mere slogan to prompt external assistance nor a course of action from which we can be deflected by external indifference. The dignity and welfare of the peoples of Southern Africa demand economic liberation and we will struggle toward that goal.

JOSE EDUARDO DOS SANTOS
PRESIDENT OF THE PEOPLE'S
REPUBLIC OF ANGOLA

SERETSE KHAMA
PRESIDENT OF THE
REPUBLIC OF BOTSWANA

SAMORA MOISES MACHEL
PRESIDENT OF THE PEOPLE'S
REPUBLIC OF MOZAMBIQUE

JULIUS K. NYERERE
PRESIDENT OF THE UNITED
REPUBLIC OF TANZANIA

KENNETH D. KAUNDA
PRESIDENT OF THE
REPUBLIC OF ZAMBIA

MABANDLA F. N. DLAMINI
PRIME MINISTER OF THE
KINGDOM OF SWAZILAND

ROBERT GABRIEL MUGABE
PRIME MINISTER
ZIMBABWE

MOOKI V. MOLAPO
MINISTER OF COMMERCE, INDUSTRY,
TOURISM AND LABOUR,
THE KINGDOM OF LESOTHO

DICK TENNYSON MATENJE
MINISTER OF EDUCATION
REPUBLIC OF MALAWI

This Declaration is produced in ten original copies, eight in the English language and two in the Portuguese language. All are equally valid.

Appendix A 283

MEMORANDUM OF UNDERSTANDING ON THE INSTITUTIONS OF THE SOUTHERN AFRICAN DEVELOPMENT COORDINATION CONFERENCE

[Memorandum signed in Harare on the 20th July, 1981 as amended (in Article III, para. 2) in Gaborone on the 22nd July, 1982]

The Heads of State or Government of the member States of the Southern African Development Coordination Conference (hereinafter called SADCC), namely,

> The People's Republic of Angola;
> The Republic of Botswana;
> The Kingdom of Lesotho;
> The Republic of Malawi;
> The People's Republic of Mozambique;
> The Kingdom of Swaziland;
> The United Republic of Tanzania;
> The Republic of Zambia; and
> The Republic of Zimbabwe:

In pursuance of their Declaration—SOUTHERN AFRICA: TOWARD ECONOMIC LIBERATION—signed in Lusaka on 1st April 1980 and, in particular, the following development objectives enunciated in the said Declaration:

(a) Reduction of economic dependence, particularly, but not only, on the Republic of South Africa;

(b) The forging of links to create a genuine and equitable regional integration;

(c) The mobilisation of resources to promote the implementation of national, interstate and regional policies;

(d) Concerted action to secure international co-operation within the framework of a strategy for economic liberation:

HAVE AGREED AS FOLLOWS

ARTICLE I
INSTITUTION

The Institutions of SADCC shall be:

(a) The Summit of Heads of State or Government (hereinafter called "the Summit")

(b) The Council of Ministers (hereinafter called "the Council")

(c) Sectoral Commissions

(d) The Standing Committee of Officials (hereinafter called "the Standing Committee")

(e) The Secretariat.

ARTICLE II
THE SUMMIT

1. The Summit shall consist of the Heads of State or Government of all member States, and shall be the supreme institution of SADCC and be responsible for the general direction and control of the functions of SADCC and the achievement of its objectives.

2. The Summit shall meet at least once a year.

3. The Summit shall decide upon a Chairman, from among its members for an agreed period.

4. The decisions of the Summit shall be taken by consensus.

ARTICLE III
THE COUNCIL

1. Each member State shall appoint one of its Ministers to the Council which shall be responsible for the overall policy of SADCC, its general coordination, the supervision of its institutions and the supervision of the execution of its programmes.

Appendix A

2. The Chairman of the Council of Ministers shall be appointed by the member State holding the Chairmanship of the Summit. The Vice-Chairman shall be elected from among members of the Council and his term of office shall be two years.

3. The Council shall meet at least once a year.

4. The Council shall adopt a work programme for SADCC and designate a member State to coordinate activities in specified areas.

5. The Council shall convene annually consultative meetings with cooperating Governments and Agencies.

6. The Council shall report and be responsible to the Summit.

7. The Council may, at its discretion, appoint Ministerial Committees for programmes in functional areas. The Ministerial Committees shall report to the Council.

8. The decisions of the Council shall be taken by consensus.

ARTICLE IV
SECTORAL COMMISSIONS

1. In addition to the Southern Africa Transport and Communications Commission (SATCC) the Summit may establish other Commissions for programmes in functional areas.

2. Each such Commission shall be governed by a Convention to be adopted by the Council and ratified or acceded to by SADCC member States.

3. Commissions shall report to the Council.

ARTICLE V
STANDING COMMITTEE OF OFFICIALS

1. There shall be a Standing Committee of officials which shall be responsible to the Council.

2. The Chairman and Vice-Chairman of the Standing Committee shall be appointed by the member State holding the Chairmanship and the Vice-Chairmanship respectively, of the Council.

3. The Standing Committee shall meet at least once a year.

4. The Standing Committee shall report to the Council.

5. The Council may appoint sub-Committees of officials for programmes in functional areas and may designate SADCC Member Governments to convene meetings and coordinate the work of such sub-Committees. Every such sub-committee shall report to the Standing Committee.

6. The decisions of the Standing Committee shall be by consensus.

ARTICLE VI
THE SECRETARIAT

1. There shall be established a Secretariat.

2. The administrative head of the Secretariat shall be the Executive Secretary.

3. The Executive Secretary and his Deputy shall be appointed by the Summit on the recommendation of the Council.

4. The Executive Secretary shall be responsible to the Council for the following functions:

    (a) General servicing of and liaison with SADCC institutions.

    (b) Coordination of the execution of the tasks of SADCC.

    (c) Custodianship of SADCC property.

    (d) Such other functions as may from time to time be approved by the Council.

5. The Executive Secretary shall be responsible to, and report to, the Council and shall provide to the Council an Annual

Report on the activities of SADCC.

6. The Secretariat shall have such other staff as may from time to time be appointed by the Council. The Council may authorise the Executive Secretary to appoint staff to specific posts.

7. Staff regulations shall be approved by the Council.

ARTICLE VII
THE BUDGET

1. The operational costs of the Secretariat shall be borne by member States in proportions to be agreed upon by the Council.

2. The Executive Secretary shall prepare and submit a budget to the Council not less than three months before the beginning of the financial year. The Council shall consider and approve estimates of revenue and expenditure before the beginning of the financial year.

3. Financial regulations shall be approved by the Council.

4. The financial year of the Secretariat shall be from July 1 to June 30.

ARTICLE VIII
EXTERNAL AUDIT

The Council shall appoint external auditors and shall fix their fees and remuneration at the beginning of each financial year.

ARTICLE IX
LEGAL CAPACITY

SADCC shall have in the territory of each member State, to the extent consistent with its laws, such legal capacity as may be necessary for the exercise of its functions under this Memorandum of Understanding.

ARTICLE X
IMMUNITIES AND PRIVILEGES

The Executive Secretary and his Deputy, and such other staff of the Secretariat as may be determined by the Council, shall enjoy in the territories of member States, such privileges and immunities as are necessary for the fulfillment of their functions.

ARTICLE XI
INTERNATIONAL CHARACTER OF THE SECRETARIAT

1. In the performance of their duties, the Executive Secretary and staff shall not seek or receive instructions from any member State or from any authority external to SADCC. They shall refrain from any action incompatible with their position as international officials responsible only to SADCC.

2. Each member State shall respect the exclusively international character of the responsibilities of the Executive Secretary and staff and shall not seek to influence them in the discharge of their functions.

ARTICLE XII
QUORUM

The quorum for all meetings of SADCC Institutions, other than the Secretariat, shall be two-thirds of the member States.

ARTICLE XIII
SIGNATURE AND ENTRY INTO FORCE

1. This Memorandum shall enter into force upon signature by all Heads of State of Government.

2. States not listed in the Preamble to this Memorandum may become members of SADCC by acceding to this Memorandum. Instruments of accession shall, subject to paragraph 4 of this Article, be deposited with the Secretariat.

3. Membership of SADCC shall not be subject to any reserva-

tions.

4. Any State intending to become a member of SADCC but not listed in the Preamble to this Memorandum may, at any time after entry into force of this Memorandum, notify the Chairman of the Summit of its desire to become a member. Admission of a new state to SADCC shall be by consensus of the member States and the accession of the new member shall take effect from the date on which its instrument of accession is received by the Secretariat.

ARTICLE XIV
AMENDMENTS

1. The Summit may amend this Memorandum by consensus.

2. Proposals for the amendment of this Memorandum may be made by any member State to the Executive Secretary for preliminary consideration by the Council. Provided, however, that the proposed amendment shall not be submitted to the Council for preliminary consideration until all member States have been duly notified of it and a period of three months has elapsed.

ARTICLE XV
SETTLEMENT OF DISPUTES

Any dispute arising from the interpretation or application of this Memorandum which cannot be settled by negotiation, conciliation or other means, may be referred to the Summit by any party to the dispute for decision. The decision of the Summit shall be final and binding.

ARTICLE XVI
OBLIGATIONS

The obligations assumed by member states under this Memorandum shall, to the extent necessary to fulfill such obligations, survive the termination of membership by any state.

ARTICLE XVII
PROCEDURE

The Institutions of SADCC shall determine their respective rules of procedure.

IN WITNESS whereof the Heads of State or Government aforementioned have duly executed these presents on this 20th day of July, One Thousand Nine Hundred and Eighty One.

DONE AT SALISBURY, REPUBLIC OF ZIMBABWE, in eight original copies in the English language and in three original copies in the Portuguese language, all of which are equally authentic.

_____ _____
PEOPLE'S REPUBLIC OF ANGOLA   REPUBLIC OF BOTSWANA

_____ _____
KINGDOM OF LESOTHO   REPUBLIC OF MALAWI

_____ _____
PEOPLE'S REPUBLIC OF MOZAMBIQUE   KINGDOM OF SWAZILAND

_____ _____
UNITED REPUBLIC OF TANZANIA   REPUBLIC OF ZAMBIA

_____
REPUBLIC OF ZIMBABWE

APPENDIX B

Regional Transport and Communications Sector

FIGURE 7

PORT TRANSPORT SYSTEMS PROJECTS

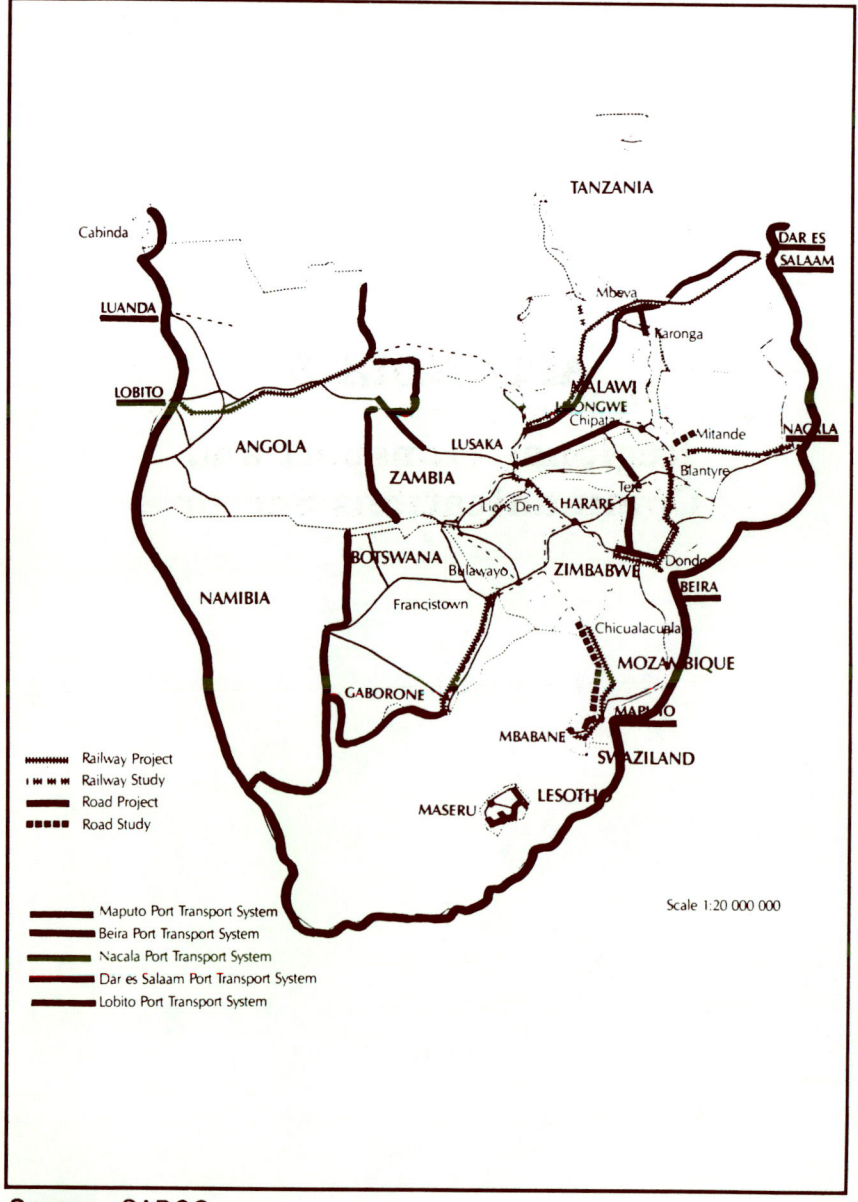

Source: SADCC

Appendix B

FIGURE 8

INTRA-REGIONAL SURFACE TRANSPORT SYSTEMS PROJECTS

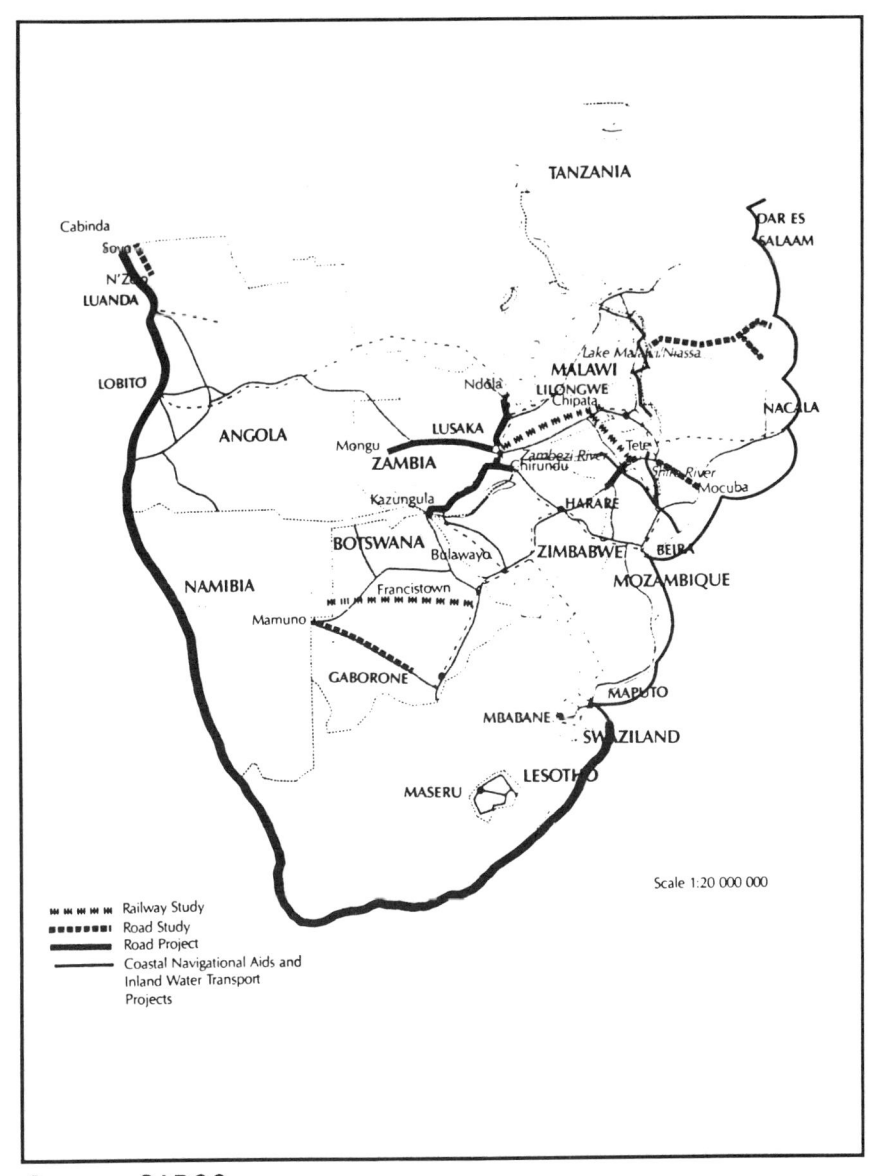

Source: SADCC

FIGURE 9

REGIONAL SURFACE TRANSPORT NETWORKS AND AIRPORTS

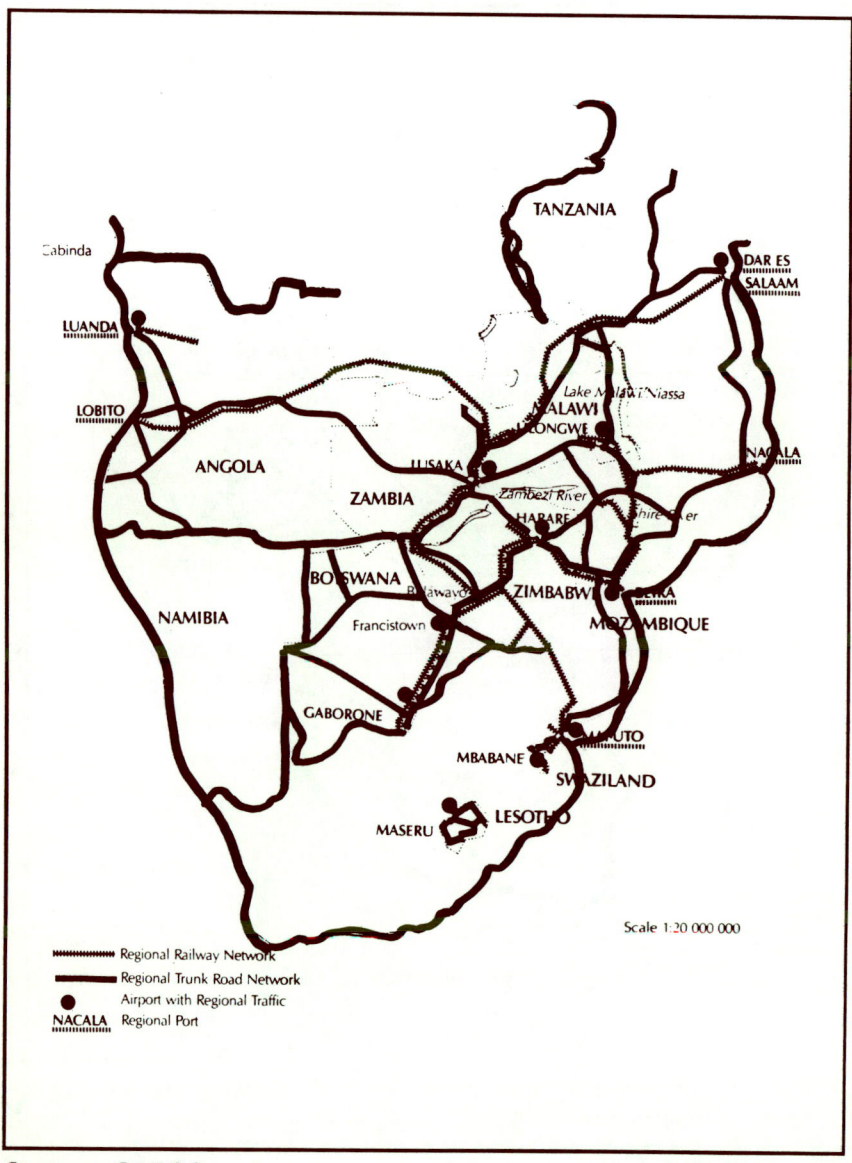

Source: SADCC

Appendix B   295

FIGURE 10

TELECOMMUNICATIONS SYSTEM PROJECTS

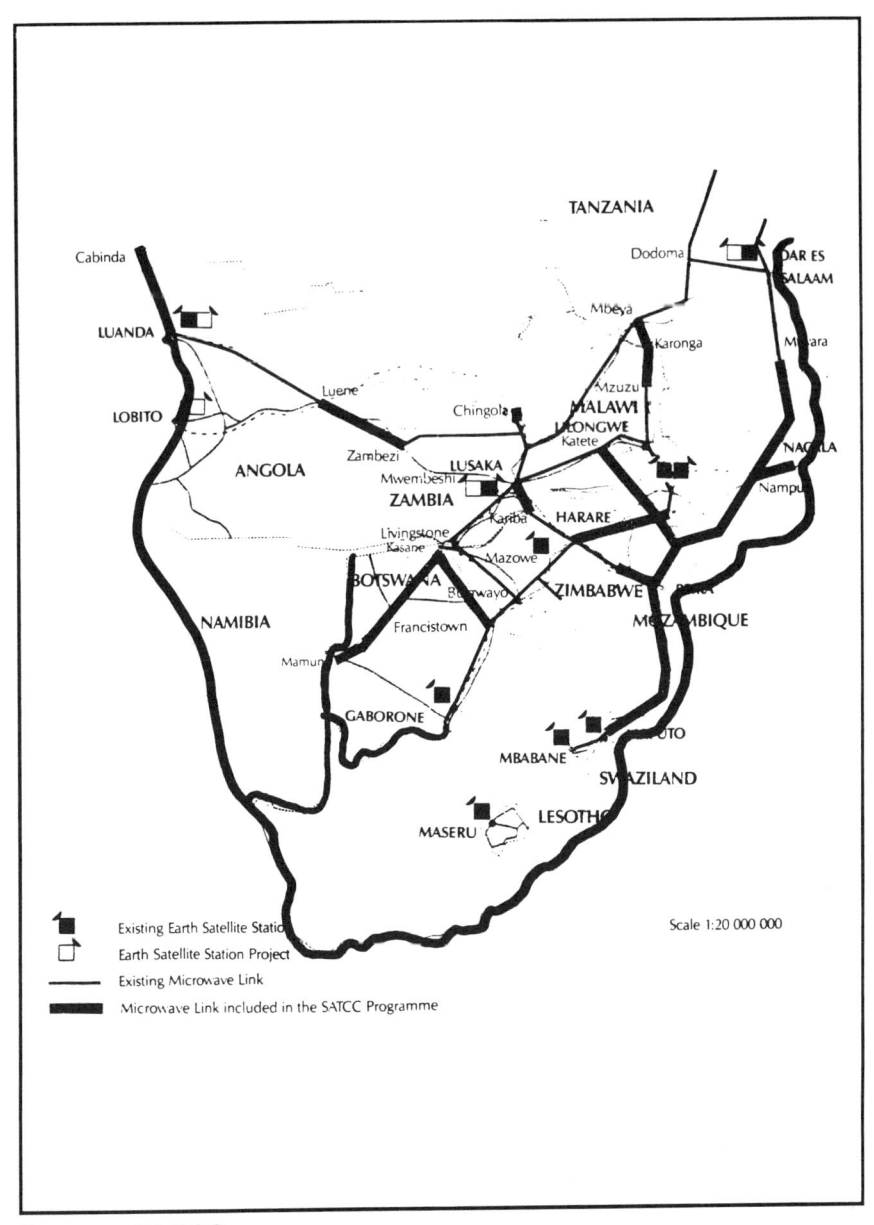

Scale 1:20 000 000

Existing Earth Satellite Station
Earth Satellite Station Project
Existing Microwave Link
Microwave Link included in the SATCC Programme

Source: SADCC

INDEX

A

Abdula, Sidik Juma 209
African Development Bank (AfDB) 249
African Explosive and Chemical Industries (AECI) 218
African Lakes 77
African Reserves (Native Reserves) 30, 45, 46
Afrikaner 29, 32-34, 36, 37, 200
agricultural research 140, 142, 251
Algeria 76
American 74
American Metal Climax (Amax) 74, 78
American Natural Soda Ash Corporation (ANSAC) 260
Amin, Samir 15, 242, 244
ANC (African National Congress) 101, 186, 242, 244
ANDEAN Pact 8, 9, 271
Anglo-American Corporation (AAC) 28, 74-76, 78, 211, 218, 219
Anglo-Boer War 29, 37
Angola 1-4, 39-43, 49, 68, 76, 77, 79, 86-88, 99, 100, 106, 111, 112, 128, 133, 151, 154, 155, 184, 185, 187, 188, 210-212, 216, 217, 220, 223, 228, 230, 242-244, 252, 254, 257, 263, 274, 276, 278, 280, 283
Angola Diamond Company 42
Angolan Civil War 100
animal disease control 140, 143
apartheid 1, 3-6, 12, 19, 32, 38, 101, 103, 146, 172, 183-188, 191, 200, 203-208, 211, 213, 217, 218, 220, 242-245, 249, 250, 256, 257, 259, 260, 262, 263, 272-274
Arrighi, Giovanni 15
Arusha 4, 7, 170, 251, 261
assimilados 40
Association of Southeast Asian Nations (ASEAN) 10
Austria 77, 249

B

Baffoe, Frank 33, 34
Banda, Kamuzu 53, 202, 204
Bantu Self-government Act (1959) 32
Bantustans 32, 186, 214
Barlow Rand 75, 78
Basutoland (see also Lesotho) 33, 36, 37
Bechuanaland (see also Botswana) 33-37
Beira 134, 137, 188-191, 197-199, 200-205, 207, 208, 224, 228, 248-250
Belgian Société Générale 77
Belgium 76

Benguela Railway 42, 188, 205, 210
Bethlehem Steel 42
Boers (see also Afrikaner) 28, 29, 33, 37
Booth, Alan 217
Botha, P.W. 185, 186, 223
Botha, Pik 202
Botswana (see also Bechuanaland) 1, 3, 7, 12, 33-35, 66, 67, 74, 79, 87, 96-98, 105, 110, 111, 127, 133, 134, 137, 138, 142, 152, 154, 155, 166, 172, 184, 198, 206, 207, 210, 213-215, 217-222, 229, 230, 255, 256, 259, 260, 263, 273, 276, 279, 280, 283
Brazil 8, 68
Britain (see also United Kingdom) 15, 25, 27, 31, 32, 34, 37, 39, 44, 47, 48, 54, 247, 249, 256, 259, 261
British South Africa Company (BSA) 45, 46, 50
British Tate and Lyle 75
Bulgarian 77
Bwalya, Mulenga 251

C

Cabinda 228
Cahora Bassa Dam 42, 76, 223, 224
Caledon 36
Caltex 254
Canada 15, 79, 86, 134, 213, 255

Cape Colony 25, 27-29, 34-36
Cape of Good Hope 25, 26
Cape Town 190
capitalist world-economy 15, 17, 25, 29, 31-33, 37-39, 43, 45, 48, 52, 53, 65, 241, 271
Caribbean Community and Common Market (CARICOM) 9
Carnation Seafoods of California 77
Central African Federation (CAF) 33, 43, 51
Central American Common Market (CACM) 8
Central Selling Organization (CSO) 74, 219
Chevron 254
Chicualacuala 250
China 69
CIA (Central Intelligence Agency) 243
civil aviation 133, 137, 139
Clark Amendment 243
Cobbe, James 217
Coca-Cola 75, 218, 259, 260
Commonwealth Development Corporation (CDC) 75
Companhia de Diamantes de Angola (Diamang) 77
Conoco 254
Constellation of Southern African States (CONSAS) 185
Courtaulds 75
Creusot-Loire 77
Cross, Eddie 95, 198-200
Crown land 50

Index

Cuba 2, 186
Cuban forces 2

D

Dar es Salaam 134, 137, 202, 204, 205
David Whitehead 78
De Beers 74, 75, 78, 219
Delta 78
Denmark 86
Department of Defense (U.S.) 254
dependencia 9
destabilization 1, 5, 6, 12, 13, 69, 100, 106, 127, 129, 139, 144, 146, 155, 185, 186, 188-191, 199, 201, 207, 208, 210, 211, 217, 222-224, 228-230, 243-245, 249, 253, 254, 261-263, 272-274
Dhliwayo, K.J. M. 141, 174, 175, 177
Diamond Manufacturing (Pty) 74
displaced persons 100, 112, 113
dos Santos, José Eduardo 112, 212
drought 38, 97, 98, 100, 102, 104, 105, 111, 114, 115, 144, 210, 280
Durban 191, 201-203, 207, 208
Dutch 25, 26
Dutch East India Company 26
Dwanga Sugar Corporation 77

E

East African Community (EAC) 9
East Germany 68, 76
East London 190
Eastern bloc 168, 256
Economic Community of West African States (ECOWAS) 9
EEC (European Economic Community) 7, 67, 112, 206, 246-249, 251, 258
Elf Aquitaine 76
energy 5, 6, 76, 78, 127, 129, 144, 151, 152, 154-156, 176, 179, 184, 187, 222, 224, 228, 229, 248, 253, 254, 281
ESCOM (SA Electricity Supply Commision) 76
Europe 7, 15, 26, 28, 31, 34, 37-40, 43, 50, 52, 54, 57, 67, 77, 206, 208, 217, 254, 258, 261
Export Administration Act 254

F

Federal Republic of Germany (see also Germany) 15, 31, 32, 34, 48, 54, 69, 70, 79, 86, 134, 247, 249, 256
Ferrao, Goncalo Antonio 224
Figueiredo, Pedro 189, 201, 208, 209
Finapetroles de Angola 76
Finland 145
fisheries 112, 140, 142, 144, 178, 212
Fonseca, Rui 189, 190, 197-

199, 205
food security 140-142, 146, 166, 167, 171, 172, 174, 175, 177, 251, 253, 280
food, agriculture, and natural resources 6, 127, 129, 140, 187, 210, 248, 251
foreign investment 5, 10, 41, 42, 73, 76, 77, 78, 99, 148, 151, 218
forestry 140, 144, 178
France 15, 31, 32, 68-70
Frank, Andre Gunder 15
freight-forwarding 191, 208
FRELIMO 43, 100
Frontline States 3, 4, 204, 230, 241, 242, 256, 264

G

Gaborone 3, 127, 137, 166, 256, 283
Gallaher 77
Gencor 75
General Agreement on Tariffs and Trade (GATT) 197
General Electric 260
genocide 244, 263
Germany (see also Federal Republic of) 15, 31, 32, 34, 53, 54, 68-70, 76, 134, 247, 249, 256
Goba 201
Great Trek 29
Gulf 42, 76, 228

H

Hanlon, Joseph 211, 229, 247
Harare 154, 252, 283

High Commission Territories 33, 34
Highlands Water Scheme 75, 228
Hippo Valley 78
Homoine 2
Hull, Blyth Ltd. 77
Hunyani 78
Hwange 221
hydroelectric power 5, 12, 75, 76, 152, 154, 223, 228

I

IMF (International Monetary Fund) 88, 95, 111-116, 243, 244, 258
imperialism 15, 27, 30, 41, 43, 77, 128, 129, 139, 151, 183, 184, 187, 213, 217, 241-245, 256, 260, 264, 271-273
Indonesia 70
industry and trade 6, 127, 146, 147, 176, 187, 213, 220, 248, 252
Iran 70
ISCOR (SA Iron and Steel Corporation) 29
Israel 243, 262, 263
Italy 70, 79, 86, 211, 249, 262

J

Japan 15, 69, 70
Johannesburg 41, 138, 205, 207

K

Katanga 50

Index

Kaunda, Kenneth 3, 51, 191, 205
Kenya 54, 221
Khama, Sir Seretse 7
Khoikhoi 26
Kodak 260
Komati 228

L

Lancaster House Agreement 244
Land Act (1913) 30
Land Apportionment Act (1930) 45
Land Tenure Act (1969) 49
land utilization 140, 143, 178
Latin American Free Trade Association (LAFTA) 8
Leabua, Chief Jonathan 186, 228
League of Nations 53, 54
Legassick, Martin 26, 29
Lesotho (see also Basutoland) 1, 12, 33, 36, 67, 74, 75, 79, 87, 97, 98, 105, 111, 133, 137, 138, 143, 152, 154, 155, 172, 184, 186, 206, 207, 210, 213-215, 217, 220, 222, 228, 229, 230, 259, 261, 276, 283
Lilongwe 77, 137, 204, 212
Limpopo 134, 189, 207, 208, 209, 273
livestock production 140, 143
Lobengula 45
Lobito 134, 137, 188, 205, 210, 228
Lomati 228

Lomaum 223
Lomé 246, 258, 259, 261
Lonrho 75-78
Lourenço Marques (see also Maputo) 41
Luanda 223, 228
Lusaka 4, 127, 145, 168, 205, 230, 248, 251-253, 271, 276, 283
Lusaka Accord 3

M

Mabor 77
Mabrodian MV (Belgian) 74
Machel, Samora 191, 204
Magubane, Bernard 28, 30, 31
Mahler, Vincent 73
Makgetla, Neva 31, 47, 48
Makoni, Simba 127, 147, 179, 249
Malawi 1, 44, 46, 52, 53, 69, 77, 86, 88, 102, 103, 106, 110, 114, 133, 134, 137, 144, 154, 155, 170, 184, 198, 201-204, 210, 212, 220, 221, 229, 261, 276, 283
Mandaza, Ibbo 173, 264
Manica 202
manpower 6, 34, 37, 53, 127, 129, 156, 157, 176, 178, 179, 248, 255, 279
Maphanyane, Emang Motlhabane 148
Maputo 2, 113, 134, 137, 188, 189, 190, 200, 201, 206-209, 210, 223, 224, 229,

230, 245, 250, 273
Maseru 137, 207
Masire, Quett 97
Matola 201
Matolo, Mugama 137
Mazula, Aguiar 113
Mbeki, Moeletsi 128
McPherson, Peter 256
meteorology 133, 138, 178
Mhlume (Swaziland) Sugar Co. 75
migrant labor 30, 32, 35, 41, 42, 46, 51-53, 98, 101, 158
mining 6, 27-30, 35-37, 45-48, 51, 53, 73, 74-78, 103, 104, 127, 129, 140, 154, 178, 219, 281
Minter, William 39, 42
Mitsui 75
Mittleman, James 41
Mmusi, Peter 256, 263
MNR (see also Renamo) 2, 69, 101, 106, 146, 189, 191, 201, 202, 207, 208, 211, 223, 224, 229
Mondi 75
Morgan Guaranty & Trust Company 28
Morton, Fred 218
Morupule Colliery 74
Moshoeshoe, Chief 36
Moyo, Nelson 179
Mozambique 1-4, 7, 12, 38-43, 46, 49, 68, 69, 76, 79, 86-88, 99, 100-102, 106, 112-114, 128, 133, 134, 138, 146, 154, 155, 166, 184, 185, 187-189, 191, 197-201, 203, 204, 207-211, 216, 217, 220, 222-224, 228-230, 242-244, 248, 252, 255, 257, 261-263, 273, 274, 276, 278-280, 283
Mozambique National Resistance (see MNR)
MPLA (Movement for the Popular Liberation of Angola) 43
Mugabe, Robert 50, 186, 191, 216, 219, 229, 257
Mumbengegwi, Clever 171
Munslow, Barry 229, 254
Murray and Roberts 77
Mutare 208, 228

N

Nacala 77, 134, 137, 188, 201-204
Namibia (see also South West Africa) 1-4, 134, 186, 223, 244, 263, 276-280
Natal 29, 209
National Party 32
National Railways of Zimbabwe (NRZ) 200
Native Authorities Ordinance 55
NATO 43
Naziism 3
Ndebele 45
Ndlela, Daniel 171
necklacing 256
Netherlands 27, 68, 69, 79, 86, 88, 249, 256
Ng'wanakilala, Nkwabi 128, 129, 157, 158

Index

Nigerian government 75
Nkomati Accord 3, 223, 224, 243, 250
Nolutshungu, Sam 48
Non-governmental Organizations (NGOs) 114
Nordic 15, 114, 145, 246, 247, 249, 251, 253, 256, 272
Norman, Denis 144, 198-200
Northern Rhodesia (see also Zambia) 44, 50, 51
Norway 76, 86, 145
Nyasaland (see also Malawi) 43, 44, 46, 52, 53
Nyerere, Julius 55

O

O'Keefe, Phil 229, 254
Old Mutual 78
Open General Import License (OGIL) 219, 221, 222
Oppenheimer, Ernest 28
Optichem Ltd. 77
Orange Free State 29, 36

P

Patel, Hasu 199
Peace Accord for Namibia 2
Peak Timbers 75
Petrofina 76
Plate Glass 78
political economy 9, 14, 15, 17, 25, 65, 95, 218, 271
Portugal (Portuguese) 4, 33, 38-43, 48, 49, 68, 76, 77, 100, 134, 187, 223, 224, 242, 262, 282, 290

Portuguese Coup 49
postal services 133, 138, 178
Preferential Trade Area of Eastern and Southern Africa (PTA) 179, 221
Pressler Amendment 256
Pretoria 98, 185, 191, 204, 216, 223, 224, 229, 231, 242, 243, 245, 259-263, 272

R

Reagan administration 247, 250, 254, 259
Reagan Doctrine 243
Reagan, Ronald 185, 243, 247, 250, 254, 259
Red Cross 112, 211
refugees 102, 114, 211, 212
Regional Training Council (RTC) 255
regional cooperation 6, 9, 11, 14, 66, 127, 152, 170, 172, 173, 183-185, 213, 221, 231, 271-273, 278, 280
regional integration 4, 6-8, 10, 11, 127, 171, 278, 283
Renamo (see also MNR) 2, 113, 189, 200, 202, 204, 211, 223, 243, 261-263
Repia, Paul 241
Rhodes, Cecil 44, 45
Rhodesia (see also Zimbabwe) 4, 42, 43-45, 47-52, 187, 191
Richards Bay 201, 209
Roan Selection Trust International 78

Royal Swaziland Sugar
   Corporation 75
Rucana 223

S

SA-Europe Container Service
   (SAECS) 208
SADCC (Southern African
   Development Coordination
   Conference)
   *Annual Consultative
   Conference* 5, 13, 74, 137,
   147, 163, 165, 167, 168,
   170, 202, 210, 219, 245-
   247, 250, 251, 256, 260,
   261, 263
   Council of Ministers 163,
   165, 167, 176, 180, 252
   *International Cooperating
   Partners* 13, 168, 172,
   175, 177-179, 198-200,
   209, 247, 251, 252, 255,
   258, 261-263
   Investment in Production
   74, 147, 148, 151, 219
   Lusaka Declaration 4, 127,
   168, 271
   *Memorandum of
   Understanding* 163, 246
   Program of Action 4, 14,
   129, 138, 139, 145, 147,
   157, 163, 165, 166, 170-
   173, 175, 176, 178-180,
   183, 187, 230, 253, 255,
   271, 272, 274
   Project Cycle 163, 166, 168
   Secretariat 6, 12, 13, 67,
   127, 163, 166, 173, 176,
   178, 179

Sector Coordinators 141
*Standing Committee of
   Officials* 163, 165, 167,
   175
Summit 129, 163, 165,
   166, 206, 221, 251, 256,
   273
San 26
Sanctions 47, 48, 172, 186,
   191, 205, 209, 216-219,
   222, 230, 245, 247, 249,
   256, 257, 259-261, 263
Sanlam 75, 77
Saul, John 39, 42
Security Assistance 260-263
Seidman, Ann 31, 47, 48
Selebi-Phikwe 74
Sena Sugar Estates 42
Shaft Sinkers (Pty) 76
Shell 254
Shipping and Forwarding
   Agents Association of
   Zimbabwe 197
Simwela, E.P.A. 147
Singapore 70
soil and water conservation
   140, 143
Sonangol 76
Sotho 26
South Africa 1-6, 12, 17, 19,
   25-28, 30-35, 37, 38, 41-
   43, 45, 48, 49, 51, 52, 65,
   67-70, 74-79, 98-103,
   111, 113, 114, 127, 138,
   139, 144-146, 148, 151,
   154, 155, 157, 171, 172,
   183-191, 199-220, 222-
   224, 228-231, 241-247,
   249-251, 253-257, 259-

Index

264, 271-274, 276-278, 283
South African Co-operative Citrus Exchange 76
South African Customs Union (SACU) 12, 34, 67, 213-215
South African Department of Defense 185
South African Foreign Trade Organization 209
South African Industrial Development Corporation (IDC) 77
South African Mutual Life Insurance 77
South African Railways 201
South African Reserve Bank 28
South African Transport System 138, 188
South African Wheat Board 213
South West Africa (see also Namibia) 34, 86
Southern Africa Transport and Communications Commision (SATCC) 133, 137, 138, 166, 285
Southern African Centre for Cooperation in Agricultural Research (SACCAR) 142
Soviet Union (U.S.S.R.) 76, 168, 186, 255
Spain 68, 261, 262
Standard Bank 77
Sua Pan Soda Ash Project 214, 218, 260
SWAPO (South West Africa People's Organization) 186, 242, 244
Swaziland 1, 12, 33, 37, 38, 67, 68, 74, 75, 79, 87, 96-99, 105, 111, 133, 134, 138, 154-156, 172, 175, 176, 184, 200, 201, 210, 213-215, 217, 218, 222, 228-230, 255, 259-261, 276, 280, 283
Swaziland Industrial Development Company (SIDCO) 218
Swaziland Sugar Milling Company 75
Sweden 79, 86, 88, 95, 145, 224, 262

T

TA Holdings 78
Tanganyika (see also Tanzania) 33, 53-55
Tanganyika African National Union 55
Taninga 2
Tanzania 1, 3, 4, 70, 78, 86, 95, 104, 105, 110, 116, 133, 154, 155, 170, 176, 184, 204-206, 220, 242, 244, 252, 261
TAZARA (Tanzania-Zambia Railway) 137, 205, 206
telecommunications 133, 137, 138, 203
Texaco 76, 254
Tibiyo Taka Ngwane Fund 75
total strategy 185, 186
tourism 6, 76, 127, 129, 191, 199

transnationals 10, 31, 32, 48
transport and communications 6, 127, 129, 133, 148, 176, 184, 187, 197, 198, 248, 276, 278-280
Transvaal 27, 29, 34, 37, 201
Tswana 35

U

U. S. Congress 256
U. S. Secretary of State 248
U.S. State Department 113
Uije 212
ultracolonialism 39
Uniao 77
Unilateral Declaration of Independence (UDI) 47-49, 70
Unilever 77
Uniply (Barlow Rand) 75
UNITA (National Union for the Total Independence of Angola) 2, 100, 111, 210, 212, 223, 243, 254, 261, 263
United Kingdom (see also Britain) 48, 67-70, 75, 79, 86
United National Independence Party (Zambia) 51
United Nations 53, 100, 101, 214, 241
United Nations Children's Fund (UNICEF) 106
United Nations Security Council Resolution 435
United States (U.S.) 2, 15, 28, 31, 32, 42, 43, 48, 51, 68-70, 76, 79, 86, 111-113, 134, 145, 200, 224, 243, 246-249, 251, 252, 255, 256, 259, 261, 263, 279
USAID (United States Agency for International Development) 247, 249, 252, 255, 256, 260
Utete, Munhamu 45-47

V

Vietnam 243
Vuvuland Irrigated Farms Scheme 75

W

Wallerstein, Immanuel 15
Western nations 42, 48, 73, 115, 128, 129, 145, 168, 178, 185, 218, 241, 242, 244-246, 251, 253, 256, 257, 260, 262-264, 272-274
white supremacy 244, 274
wildlife 140, 142, 144, 178
Witwatersrand 27
Witwatersrand Native Labor Association (WNLA) 41
World Bank 97, 113, 115, 252
World Food Program (WFP) 211
WWII 47, 54, 55

X

Xhosa 26

Y

Yugoslav 77

Z

Zambia (see also Northern Rhodesia) 1, 3, 4, 44, 51, 69, 77, 78, 86, 88, 102, 103, 106, 110, 115, 133, 154, 155, 184, 191, 198, 201, 202, 205, 206, 210, 211, 220, 221, 242, 244, 255, 261
Zambia Consolidated Copper Mines (ZCCM) 205
Zambia Copper Investment (ZCI) 78
Zambian Industrial and Mining Corporation (ZIMCO) 78
ZAMCO 76
Zimbabwe (see also Rhodesia) 1, 3, 4, 44, 49, 69, 70, 77, 78, 86, 88, 95, 102, 104, 106, 110, 115, 116, 133, 134, 138, 140, 142, 144, 146, 154, 155, 174, 175, 179, 184, 186, 188-191, 197-201, 205-208, 210-212, 215, 216, 219, 220-222, 229, 242, 244, 249, 251, 252, 255, 261, 273, 274
Zimbabwe African National Union (ZANU) 49
Zimbabwe Alloys 78
Zimbabwe Reserve Bank 175
Zulu 26